BEYOND PRISON WALLS

BEYOND PRISON WALLS

THE JERIS BRAGAN STORY

By Jeris E. Bragan

REVIEW AND HERALD® PUBLISHING ASSOCIATION
HAGERSTOWN, MD 21740

The author assumes full responsibility for the accuracy of all facts and
quotations as cited in this book.

Unless otherwise indicated, all Scripture passages are from the *Holy Bible,
New International Version*. Copyright © 1973, 1978, 1984, International Bible
Society. Used by permission of Zondervan Bible Publishers.

Verses marked TLB are taken from *The Living Bible*, copyright © 1971 by
Tyndale House Publishers, Wheaton, Ill. Used by permission.

This book was
Edited by Richard W. Coffen
Designed by Helcio Deslandes
Typeset: 9.5/11 Palatino

PRINTED IN U.S.A.

98 97 96 95 94 93   10 9 8 7 6 5 4 3 2 1

R&H Cataloging Service
Bragan, Jeris E
    Beyond prison walls.

    1. Bragan, Jeris E.   2. Tennessee. State
Prison, Nashville.   3. Prisons—Tennessee.
I. Title.
        365.4092[B]

ISBN 0-8280-0716-0

Contents

DEDICATION

This book would never have been written had it not been for the unwavering commitment of two of the finest lawyers I've ever met:

Tom Bloom

Fred Steltemeier

My life has been blessed by their prayers, friendship, and encouragement during the many bleak years when it appeared nothing would come of their efforts on my behalf. They have been my "advocates," both from a legal and Christian perspective.

FOREWORD

Shortly before Thanksgiving Day in 1989, I met Jeris Bragan for the first time in a cramped interview room at "The Walls," the old state penitentiary in Nashville, Tennessee. I had been appointed to represent Mr. Bragan in a habeas corpus petition that he had filed on his own behalf in the United States District Court for the Middle District of Tennessee.

I found the petition compelling as I read it, partly because the writer obviously was an intelligent, articulate man. But as a legal matter I knew his petition had merit because of the number of coincidences, oversights, mistakes, and surprises that had led to his conviction in 1977. These things could not have been dreamed up by even the most pathological of liars!

A cynic by nature, I still expected to meet a pathological liar. Instead, I met a soft-spoken, determined man who simply wanted someone to look at the evidence in the trial record, make an independent assessment of his claims, and use the best efforts to present his case.

I was impressed with Jeris' simplicity, and I suspect that he was surprised by my honesty. I confessed that I had never done a habeas corpus before, that I would have answers for few of his questions without researching the law first. But I did promise to put forth my very best efforts in representing him. As it turned out, I knew just enough to be dangerous, and I was naive enough not to be intimidated or despairing when I probably should have been.

Jeris' story is extraordinary because of its happy ending. But the way in which prosecutors secured his wrongful conviction is not unique. Today there are many people languishing in prison who, like Bragan, are innocent. Others may very well be guilty, but their guilt or innocence was never fairly determined by a jury because prosecutors or courts stacked the deck—intentionally or unintentionally—against them.

As an attorney, I hope the reader will not simply enjoy this book because it's a moving, dramatic story, or because of the strength and inspiration of its author. Rather, I hope the reader will come away with the clear understanding that what happened to Jeris Bragan could happen to anyone—to you, your son, or your daughter. It could happen because of negligence, laziness, mistake, or malevolence on the part of the police, a prosecutor, a judge, or perhaps, even your attorney.

Quite simply, a fair trial is not a given in the criminal justice system. Such a basic right requires the skill and care of an attorney. But even the most skilled attorney will be unable to secure a fair trial when prosecutors or police are intent upon conviction at any cost. Constant oversight and review—whether on appeal from a conviction, in later state court proceedings, or in federal court by way of habeas corpus—is essential for safeguarding the integrity of the system that is only as perfect or flawless as the persons involved.

The criminal justice process requires constant monitoring by every citizen. Each time a criminal defendant is on trial, the criminal justice system

9

is on trial as well. Feel free to speculate about the guilt or innocence of an arrested suspect when you hear about a crime being committed. Many times there is no question. But also, more importantly, look to and be critical of the workings of the system itself, whether it be the investigation of the crime, the arrest, the interrogation, or the trial. If we ignore misconduct in the judicial process because of outrage about a crime or our conviction that a person is guilty, that same misconduct may very well come back to haunt us in our own backyard.

I was—and am—convinced of Jeris' innocence. But I hope that I would have worked just as hard and believed the case to be just as important if I had not.

On May 22, 1992, two and a half years after meeting Jeris for the first time, I watched him push a cart containing his personal possessions through the gates of the prison. For me it was a very happy, unbelievable day. It validated all the time and money I had spent to obtain my education and law degree.

Tom Bloom
Court Appointed Counsel

PART ONE

MURDER, SHE WROTE

1

Slamming Doors

THE NIGHTMARE began as it always did. Although I knew it was just a dream (the same nocturnal bogeyman had tormented me for more than a year), that realization did nothing to diminish overpowering feelings of dread.

I could see a body, draped in surgical sheets, stretched out on something that resembled a morgue table in the middle of an enormous, white room. Only the face was showing, but it appeared frozen, expressionless, lifeless. The unblinking eyes stared straight up at the ceiling.

It was my face.

Despite the appearance, I knew the body was alive. Thanks to the irrational logic of dreams, I was inside the body and detached from it at one and the same time, experiencing both fear and panic from within while observing the phenomenon from a distance.

Surrounding the body on all sides was a baffling array of complex technology. Control panels beeped and lights blinked. Everything shone of stainless steel. The body wasn't directly connected to the equipment but was securely held in place by invisible vicelike grips. No matter how much effort it put forth, this impotent twin of mine was completely powerless. It couldn't even flick an eyelash.

I watched helplessly, transfixed by the futile struggle against paralysis going on before my eyes. That was me suffocating on the table, but I couldn't do anything to free myself. Some indefinable quality in what I saw filled my imagination with terror.

I could feel my pulse pounding in my ears.

I couldn't watch anymore.

I had to wake up.

I began thrashing against the invisible cords.

I screamed something.

A word.

It always was the same word.

But I never heard it.

Startled, I opened my eyes.

It was Monday morning, November 22, 1976. Something had burst through the fog of that terrorizing dream. Cold sweat trickled off my face and dripped onto the pillow. Then I recognized the sound of my business partner's Pinto rumbling through the parking lot below the bedroom window. Slowly I sucked in a lungful of air and then let it out even more slowly, repeating the exercise several times until my pulse slowed and the panicky feelings subsided.

Fully awake, I glanced at my wife Darleen, who slept on. For once that miserable dream and my thrashing around hadn't awakened her. I was relieved, because I always felt embarrassed and irritated by the senseless, irrational fear that invariably lingered long after the dream ended. I rolled over in bed, fumbled with a pack of cigarettes, and lit the first of what would probably be 60 Pall Malls before the day's end. The acrid smoke burned my lungs. I doubled over in a violent coughing spasm as both lungs convulsed, loudly protesting the smoky abuse I inflicted on them.

I've gotta quit these things! I thought.

I didn't know it as I lay in bed that morning, waiting for my nerves to settle down, but cigarettes would be the least of my problems before the day ended.

But I didn't have a clue.

Given the wreckage of my life at the time, admittedly hidden well beneath a veneer of personal and professional success, I should have seen disaster coming in some form. But personal tragedy is like the proverbial tornado that strikes in the dead of night: nobody expects it. We get up each day and go through the ordinary motions and routines of daily life, operating under the illusion that we're independent, self-sufficient captains of our lives. We assume that everything will go on as it always has—no matter how dysfunctional or bizarre—without interruption. For the most part, we're quite unaware of just how little real control we have or of how suddenly and drastically the trajectory of our lives can be altered forever either by external forces beyond our control or in combination with our own poor choices.

I had a lot to learn about choices!

◆ ◆ ◆

Everything had seemed so simple just 18 months earlier. During a relatively minor personal crisis at age 29, after nearly a decade of struggling with religious doubts and alienation from my church community, I experienced the kind of adult conversion that filled my soul with a profound sense of peace and well-being. I decided to abandon my career as a private investigator and return to college to finish the theological education I'd left behind in the mid-sixties.

God was in His heaven, and all was well with my world at last—for a few days!

The first shoe had dropped when my wife of 10 years announced that she was in love with somebody else and wanted a divorce. To make matters even worse, her boyfriend began interfering with my visitation with Tracie, my 7-year-old daughter. I hadn't recognized the signs at the time, but I dropped into a deep depression that would haunt me for the next few years. In order to get away from the constant conflicts, I moved from Takoma Park, Maryland, to Chattanooga, Tennessee.

◆ ◆ ◆

Darleen, my 23-year-old wife, peered at me through sleep and drug-dazed eyes. "What time is it?" she muttered.

"Ten o'clock."

She groaned in protest, pulled the pillow over her head, and retreated into sleep.

SLAMMING DOORS

I lay there, smoking in silence and staring at the ceiling as I thought of all the other November 22s that had come and gone since that awful day in Dallas. I was almost 18 the day John F. Kennedy was killed. Vaguely I wondered if there was some connecting link between that grotesque event and the disillusionment with God, religion, and politics that began its insidious invasion in my life a couple of years later. By the end of the sixties, the heroes who had inspired me during my formative years were either dead or debunked. And if God wasn't dead, He at least seemed largely irrelevant to the chaos of daily life—especially *my* daily life! But I didn't want to explore the thought any further.

Instead, I wanted a drink.

My mouth tasted like the bottom of a bird cage from too much drinking the night before, and the night before that, and . . . An old fear pressed in, hovering around the hedges of my consciousness: Was I turning into an alcoholic? *No way!* I muttered to myself in disgust. *I can hold my liquor any day of the week—or night, for that matter.*

Denial is a powerful weapon for a soul in flight!

I rolled over in bed, propped my head up on my right hand, and studied my sleeping wife. Naked, she slept stretched out on her stomach, breathing heavily from all the Benadryl sloshing through her system. She had kinky dishwater blonde hair, almond-shaped blue eyes, and full lips, which she could turn into a dazzling smile at will. At five feet three inches and 110 pounds, she had a tight, wiry body that could explode with phenomenal strength when she was angry—which was more often than I cared to think about. Come to think of it, there were a lot of things I didn't want to think about these days.

But I dismissed that thought too.

We had been married for just 11 months. But it felt much longer—more like 11 chaotic, tumultuous, exhausting centuries! Somewhere I'd read a line that described my marriage with brutal clarity: "Marry in haste, repent at leisure." I'd certainly married in haste, on the rebound after the breakup of my first marriage, and I had already repented of that haste. But there wasn't anything leisurely about my regret.

◆ ◆ ◆

Although I was just 30 years old and in good health, I felt fatigued most of the time. Just before I got married Dr. Kutzner had examined me. "You've got hypoglycemia," he said after giving me a five-hour glucose tolerance test. "That means low blood sugar."

"What can I do about it?"

He grinned as he ticked off all my favorite vices: "Quit smoking. Quit drinking. Quit eating sweets. Get more exercise. Eat something with protein in it between meals. Oh, and try to cut out some stress."

Wonderful!

Three days later I married Darleen. It was December 15, 1975. John Lanham, a Presbyterian pastor, performed the wedding at my home. Even though the apartment wasn't hot, cold sweat dripped down my face throughout the ceremony. I wanted to bolt from the apartment, get away

15

from something I couldn't define. Instead, I repeated the vows.

My stress level tripled overnight.

✦ ✦ ✦

Now in November I knew that a divorce was inevitable. But I loved her, and the thought of a second divorce in as many years was depressing. On the other hand, I couldn't take much more of the stress and conflict that came with the package of living with her. It seemed like my mind and body were locked in a fierce race to see which would collapse first. Thinking about all the problems, plus my inability to do anything satisfactory about them, added a few more pounds to feelings of guilt and incompetence that were overloaded already. Lines from the apostle Paul crossed my mind: "What I want to do I do not, but what I hate I do" (Rom. 7:15, NIV). At some level I understood his dilemma. What I didn't understand was the sluggish inertia that had taken over my life.

On the surface most people saw me as a decisive person—to the point of being brash. But I knew it was just a good act designed to hide all the fear and uncertainty I felt about myself as a person. Several years would pass before I'd begin to understand that my personal identity—who I am—was too closely connected with what I did for work, the material things I possessed, and the opinions of other people about me. That kind of thinking is both bad theology and bad psychology. It profoundly hurts the person who believes it.

✦ ✦ ✦

"Quit staring at me like that," Darleen snapped.

Jarred by the hostile interruption, I looked at her more closely and realized she was glaring at me.

"Like what?" I asked.

"You know like what! Like you're peering into my brain and looking for something."

I bit off a sarcastic retort, flicking its tail on the end of my tongue. But I couldn't disguise the bite in my voice. "Why, Darleen, do you have anything more to hide?"

The ice melted from her face, replaced with something I couldn't quite define—fear, despair? I wasn't sure. Had I been wiser, I might have recognized something more predatory.

She grabbed me and burrowed her face in my neck before I could say anything. Her body trembled as the tears came. Always the tears! Even though I had become expert in predicting those inevitable tears—I knew she could turn them on and off like a faucet—I also knew those tears held me prisoner. "Please, let's not fight today," she whispered.

I sighed and stroked her back. "I don't want to fight either."

The tears evaporated as suddenly as they came. Her mercurial mood swings left me dizzy and baffled. She sat up in bed. "I'm so excited we're going to have Tracie here for Thanksgiving! I can hardly wait to see her," she said.

Tracie was my only child. Later that evening, at 7:05, I had reservations for Darleen and me to fly from Chattanooga, Tennessee, to Takoma Park,

16

Maryland, where Tracie lived with her mother. I looked forward to seeing her perform in a Thanksgiving play at her school on Tuesday. She would come back to Chattanooga with us after the program to spend the holidays.

"I hope it'll be a good week. Incidentally, how do you feel this morning?" I asked, changing the subject.

Darleen turned away abruptly, scrambled out of bed, and headed for the bathroom. "I'm still pretty sore," she admitted.

My hands shook with unexpected anger as I fired up another cigarette. "Good!" I muttered.

"I heard that, which you probably intended. You do love to stick the knife in and twist it, don't you?"

I looked up to see her standing in the doorway. Her clenched fists were pressed on her hips. Her face was contorted with smoldering rage. "I told you once I was sorry about . . . about . . . not being fair to you . . ."

"Not being *fair?*" I interrupted. "No, no, no, Darleen. 'Fair' isn't exactly the word I'd use. What we're talking about here is your jumping in and out of bed with any male who's polite enough to ask you—although I suspect even courtesy isn't absolutely essential."

"I told you once that I was sorry for running around on you. It happened and I can't undo it. I got drunk. What do you want from me anyway? I said I was sorry!" she shouted.

Sorry! That word, which she used repetitiously like some magical incantation, was supposed to cancel out everything that had happened. I was sick of that meaningless word. At the same time I felt guilty for what struck me as my unforgiving, judgmental attitude. At the bottom of my soul I believed love meant an uncompromising commitment to another person's welfare, fulfillment, happiness, and growth—unconditional love. Those words, though easy to say, aren't so easy to put into practice. But I believed I *should* do just that—no matter what the circumstances.

Darleen's problems weren't new to me. Two months before our marriage she'd gotten drunk with a photographer who worked for me part-time and allowed him to take what by any definition were pornographic photos of her engaged in a variety of sexual acts. When she told me about it several days later, I confronted him, demanded the negatives, and fired him when he refused. I had no idea at the time how those pictures would come to haunt me two years later.

She wasn't engaged to me at the time, and I eventually shrugged off the whole thing as "one of those things" when people have had too much to drink. Besides, I'd married her when I knew she had lied to me about her first husband. So who was I to complain now?

◆ ◆ ◆

In early November I had come home after two days on business in Atlanta to find her sullen and withdrawn. Since that wasn't an entirely new experience, I attributed her moodiness to depression or irritability associated with her period. I'd never heard of premenstrual syndrome, but I knew what it meant. It wasn't until she complained about a large, painful lump on

17

her labia and we met with a surgeon that I got my first clue as to what the real problem was.

"One of the lubrication glands has gotten infected," the doctor explained. "We'll have to open it up surgically, pack the wound with gauze and let it drain. She'll be good as new in a couple of weeks."

"What caused the gland to get infected?" I asked.

"Gonorrhea."

"Gonorrhea!" I almost choked as I spat the word out. I could feel my face turning beet-red.

"Yes, gonorrhea. I assume you've taken care of that, haven't you? If not, I can arrange for you to get a shot."

I looked at Darleen. She sat silently in her chair, staring at some object on the wall above the doctor's head. I wasn't surprised that she had been quite willing to let the doctor think I'd infected her. After all, cleaning up her messes with family members, friends, employees, and the church had become my primary role in life!

In confusion, the surgeon looked back and forth.

My throat felt tight. "Doctor, I've never had . . ." I bit the words off. "I've already taken care of the problem," I said between clenched teeth.

The doctor started to speak, hesitated as he looked at me for a long moment, then abruptly turned his attention to the surgical forms Darleen had to sign.

She might be an irresponsible tramp, but she was *my* tramp. I'd married her for better or worse. Moreover, I'd been programmed from early childhood to believe that a man was supposed to be independent and self-reliant, to solve every problem on his own, to be responsible for everything, to protect the reputation of his wife and family, no matter what the problem. I thought that was the way to behave in a loving way. It never even occurred to me to ask another person for help with personal problems. Many years would pass before I realized just how sexist and totally dysfunctional that idea really was.

Real love has to be tough enough to say a hard No! I could have saved myself a lot of grief if I had known that truth and acted on it before it was too late.

Darleen underwent surgery on Tuesday, November 16, and came home two days later. But late Friday night a rash broke out all over her body. She was hysterical from the itching by the time I got her to the emergency room at midnight. Furious over what she thought was an unnecessary delay in treatment, she created an ugly scene when she engaged two of the nurses in a shouting match. After two hours of this, they pumped enough Benadryl into her to knock out an elephant. It barely slowed her down. She didn't fall asleep until well after sunrise Saturday morning.

The weekend had gone downhill from there!

◆ ◆ ◆

I finished knotting the tie around my neck and got ready to head for the office. Except for dropping her fists to her side, Darleen hadn't moved from the door.

"I told you before we got married that I had . . . some . . . some problems," she reminded me. "I can't help myself. . . . I just lose control. . . . Nobody can stand me for long. I don't know why you didn't leave me months ago."

Her shoulders slumped and she locked her arms tight across her chest. All defense and defiance were gone. "I should've killed myself a long time ago," she whispered. Her voice took on a childish, sing-song quality that scared me.

More than once, when depressed, she'd threatened to kill herself in some violent manner—usually by driving our car at high speed into a bridge abutment.

My anger evaporated, replaced by real fear. At one level I wanted to leave quickly, to escape forever the lunacy that had taken over my life. But at a deeper level I knew that I loved her beyond reason or words. All thought of escape vanished. I reached for her, hugged her tight, unaware that the die had been finally cast for what was to come in a matter of hours.

◆ ◆ ◆

I knew that George was waiting for me, so I left for the office.

George Urice, 50, had been an unofficial partner in my detective agency for eight months. Nobody would have guessed he was a private detective. With iron-gray hair and a slightly owlish appearance from squinting through thick glasses, he looked more like an absentminded professor of biochemistry. George had managed the Knoxville branch of the Pinkerton's Detective Agency before coming to work for me. He had a quick, analytical mind. Although he didn't own stock in the company, I paid him the same salary and perks I paid myself.

Holding a cup of steaming coffee between both hands, he was sitting in the kitchen of our office when I walked in at 11:30 that Monday morning. Dressed in a yellow sweater, polo shirt, and gray slacks, he looked more ready for a round of golf than work. It really wasn't a workday. After several grueling weeks of out-of-town investigations, we both wanted the week off. His elderly mother was flying in from New York the next day for a visit, and I planned to spend the week with Tracie. But first we had to work out the details on a complicated bill for the Pittsburgh and Lake Erie Railroad for services we had performed earlier in the month.

George peered over the top of his black-frame glasses and looked at me closely. "You look like hell!" he said. It was a statement of fact.

"Well, I guess it would be awful to look good and still feel this bad," I replied as I dropped into the chair across from him.

He poured a cup of coffee for me. "Here's a little pick-me-up for you," he suggested, holding up a bottle of brandy. I nodded and he poured a liberal shot into the black coffee.

He raised the cup and offered a sardonic toast, "Here's to me, a black-jack Mormon, and to you, a backslidden Seventh-day Adventist, and we're both drinking at 11:00 in the morning." We both laughed at the old joke, perhaps more from embarrassment than real humor. We drank our coffee in

19

silence, each wondering how to approach the subject we both needed to talk about.

"How's Darleen this morning?" he asked, breaking the silence.

"She's better, I think. We had a rough weekend. I had to take her to the E.R. Friday night. I think she had a bad reaction to the medication the doctor gave her. She got into quite a shouting match with the staff."

"I can imagine," George said dryly.

George and Darleen had gotten along together quite well when he first came to work for me. She liked him initially because he bore a faint resemblance to her Grandfather Chase, then in the early stages of Alzheimer's disease. Plus, George was a gracious and courtly gentleman who made her feel important. He knew about the recent death of her adopted father and the bitter alienation from her mother. "I've got a couple of daughters, but I can always use one more like you," he'd told her once.

There hadn't been any obvious conflict between them at first, but each had grown to dislike the other quite intensely in recent weeks. What had percolated just beneath the surface around the office erupted several times over trivial things pertaining to investigative strategies during recent trips to Pittsburgh and Washington, D.C. I had tried to pass it off as normal personality clashes when three people work too closely together for several days at a time. But she complained that he was a sexist "pig" who treated her like a little girl. And he complained that she pulled rank on him in the office because she was married to me, bossing him around like a rookie detective. Either she had to go, or he was leaving. George was far too polite and sophisticated to issue an ultimatum, but I knew that was the bottom line.

I wanted George to become a full partner in the agency, but I had to live with Darleen. Irritated with both of them, I felt caught in the middle.

"Listen, George, I know things have been a bit stressful around here. It seems to me things might work out better if we hire another secretary after the first of the year."

George peered at me over the top of his glasses. "Is Darleen happy with that?"

I shrugged. "Actually, I haven't talked to her about it yet. I wanted to run it by you to see if you'd feel more comfortable staying on if I, well, sort of made some changes along these lines."

He nodded and the tension between us began to ease. "That would work a little better for me," he admitted, "but I wonder if that won't create additional problems for you at home."

I shrugged again. "Frankly, I don't know how things could get any worse."

"I know how that goes. As you know, I've been divorced three times myself. I just got lucky when I married Wilma. But however you decide to deal with the problem, you'd better be careful with Darleen. She's . . . ah . . . a bit unstable, I think."

I bristled defensively and started to reply when I heard the front door open. Darleen had arrived.

20

"Well, we've got a $6,000 check coming," I said in moving away from an uncomfortable topic, "so let's put our heads together on this bill right after lunch."

We left the office shortly after noon to put my 1976 Oldsmobile, a blue 98 with a white vinyl top, in the shop for repairs. George followed me and then drove us in his car to the Peddler Steak House for lunch. He'd already agreed to drop us off at the airport on his way home that evening.

Always the consummate gentleman, George entertained us at lunch with comical stories from his years of dealing with Japanese business executives when he worked as the national personnel director for a well-known Japanese company.

"Mark my word," he said philosophically over martinis. "Those people are gonna run the big-three automakers out of business in this country." I thought his prediction was a bit silly at the time.

As a result of little sleep during the weekend, plus too many drinks at dinner, I felt bone-weary as we drove back to the office.

"Hey, look at the fresh graves! Isn't that where they buried the Gold Dust twins?" George commented as we drove past the cemetery.

Ray Moss, president of the Golden Gallon convenience stores, and his colleague Bob Kelly had been killed in a crash while flying their private plane over Georgia the previous week. George, the sophisticated and urbane New Yorker, had despised both men, largely because they treated him with typically Southern bemusement toward Yankees. Their ribbing was all in good fun, but George was not amused. Until recently my firm had done all their lie detector tests and internal theft investigations. We had terminated our business relationship when it became increasingly obvious to us that they made hiring and firing decisions exclusively on the basis of unreliable lie detector tests. George was delighted that he didn't have to deal with them any longer.

"Good riddance to that pair of useless rednecks," he chuckled.

Darleen was sitting behind me in George's brown Pinto station wagon. She leaned forward and grabbed the back of my seat. I dropped my hand behind and gripped her knee as a signal to keep quiet. I knew she was about to unload on George. Ray and Bob had always been particularly gracious toward her. She liked them and felt bad because we had been out of town and unable to attend their funerals. George was totally unaware of the fury unleashed behind him.

"Their deaths must be hard on the families," I said, trying to neutralize the subject.

"I suppose so," George admitted. "But they're well rid of 'em. And rich too," he added with a laugh.

I heard the sharp intake of breath from behind me just as we pulled into the parking lot of our offices at 2:30 p.m.

"Listen, George," I said hurriedly, "I'm beat and need to get a few hours' rest before flying out tonight. Could you and Darleen finish up the details on that Pittsburgh bill? Let Darleen type it out and get it in the mail tonight. Christmas is coming, and I suspect we all could use a nice bonus," I added as a thinly disguised bribe.

George slapped the wheel. "Now you're talking," he said happily.

Darleen grabbed my arm as soon as George went upstairs to his office. "I can't stand that old windbag!" she hissed. "He's half drunk, and now you're leaving me alone with him to listen to his garbage all afternoon."

"Darleen, *please*! Let's just get this done with a minimum of fuss and bother, and then we'll take a week off. OK?"

"OK—for now. But you've gotta do something about him. I can't stand being around him anymore."

I left and went home, slamming the door to our house harder than necessary. But another door, unseen and unheard, also slammed behind me as well.

I tossed my jacket onto the living room chair. Too tired to climb the stairs, I slumped down on the sofa and dropped into a deep sleep.

2

Murder, She Wrote

"JERRY, WAKE up! *Wake up!*"

I struggled to sit up on the sofa, but Darleen hovered over me. Her fingers, like sharp talons, dug into my shoulders as she shook me. Irritably, I pushed her away and tried to sort through the cobwebs of her shouting.

"Will you *please* wake up!"

I looked at my watch. Five o'clock. Morning? Evening? I didn't know.

She grabbed my shoulders again and shook me harder. This time I slapped her hands away.

"Are you deaf?" she hissed, thrusting her face close to mine. "George is *dead!*"

"What are you talking about?" I heard what she said, but the words simply didn't register. At some level of consciousness I knew my blood sugar was low because I felt shaky, mildly sick to my stomach, and the clutter through my brain wouldn't clear up enough for me to think.

"Listen to me," she insisted. "I think George is dead." Tears brimmed up in her eyes. Then the words poured out again, an incoherent spraying of words I'd come to know all too well. She grabbed my face in both hands, twisting it back and forth as though that would straighten out whatever was bothering her.

"He got drunk after you left, Jerry. . . . I pushed him away, and he fell down the stairs. . . . I couldn't help it. . . . It was an accident. . . . There's blood all over the place, . . . and I can't clean it up."

That got me wide awake. I swung my feet onto the floor, stood up abruptly, grabbed my coat, and stumbled toward the front door. But she grabbed my arm and yanked on it. "No, not that way," she insisted. "Go out the back door. He's blocking the front door of the office."

The late fall chill slapped me in the face as I ran the 40 yards from the back of our home to the sliding glass door at the rear of my office. We lived at 111 Pacific Road, a two-story town house in a complex of apartments and other town houses located in Hixson, Tennessee, just 10 miles north of Chattanooga. My company, The Searchers Detective Agency, occupied 116 Pacific Road. Even though the sliding door was unlocked, I struggled to force it open. I stumbled on the ledge, nearly falling as I finally forced the door open.

The lights were on in the kitchen, where George and I had talked earlier in the day. Curiously, everything seemed unusually bright, and my mind whirled in slow motion as I glanced around.

Even though I understood what Darleen had said, I also knew her capacity for melodrama and exaggeration. I didn't know what to expect inside, so I entered the reception area cautiously. The room was dark and gloomy, heavily shadowed. I stopped short halfway into the room and froze in place.

I heard a husky voice. "Oh, dear God!"

It was my own.

George lay on his back on the landing at the foot of the stairs. His eyes were closed except for small slits. He seemed to be squinting at some sightless object deep within himself. I noticed at once a bloody wound over his eye and on his upper lip over his left incisor. His face, usually tanned, was a pasty gray-blue, and his arms were twisted awkwardly beneath him, with his right elbow jutting out at a 45-degree angle from his rib cage.

I ripped off my coat and tossed it onto the desk. After dropping down on one knee beside him, I pressed my fingers into his neck and felt for a pulse. Nothing. No sign of breathing. I'd seen dead bodies before, and at some level I knew he was beyond resuscitation. But I couldn't accept that fact. My mind raced, trying to think of something useful to do. When I reached for his arm to check his wrist for a pulse, I discovered that his hands were handcuffed behind his back. Stunned, I sat back on my heels, trying to focus on the scene around me.

"Is he gonna be all right?"

Startled, I turned to see Darleen standing behind me. Her hands were clasped tightly in front of her. Her face was pinched with worry, and she was dressed in a polka-dot pants suit, reminding me of a frightened-looking clown.

"No, he isn't going to be all right; he's dead!" I snapped.

Without thinking, I slipped my arms under his shoulders and lifted the body into an upright sitting position, holding him in place with my left elbow pressed against the back of his neck and my left thigh anchored against his back. His head bumped against the wall, smearing it with his blood. I pulled the key ring off my belt, found a handcuff key, and took the cuffs off before laying the body out flat again.

In the dim light I didn't notice the bloodstains on my sleeve and pant leg. Neither did I notice the marks on his wrists from the handcuffs.

The police would not miss either of them.

My hands were covered with drying, sticky blood. I went to the bathroom and washed it off. I looked at the familiar stranger in the mirror as I slowly dried my shaking hands. I stood six feet two inches and weighed 220 pounds. My long blond hair was fashionably styled for the seventies, over the ears and collar. I had deep blue eyes and a ruddy complexion. The confident facade disappeared. The face looking back at me from the mirror looked old, gray, and tired. "What are you doing here?" it seemed to ask in a mocking voice. *What am I doing here?* The question rattled around inside my mind like a bouncing BB in a tin can. I'd come to Chattanooga to finish my degree in theology, but here I was in a darkened office, the body of my partner lying nearby, blood on my hands, and a hand-wringing wife I loved who would expect me to "fix" it. I felt split down the middle.

"What are you doing here?" the gray face asked again. It was a time to think, but I had no answer.

24

✦ ✦ ✦

Darleen was sitting hunched over in her chair at the secretarial desk when I returned. I paced back and forth, trying to collect my thoughts. I could hear people talking and the blaring of a TV next door. I reached for the telephone. My hands were shaking.

"Who are you calling?" Darleen asked.

I hesitated. "The police . . . rescue squad."

"Don't call the police!"

"I've gotta call them. But first tell me what happened here," I whispered as I replaced the phone.

"After you left, I worked on the billing . . ."

"I don't care what happened several hours ago. Tell me about *this*!" I snapped, pointing behind me toward George.

"Let me explain, and I will!"

Whatever fear had possessed her earlier was gone. She was back in control of her emotions.

"As I started to say, I worked on the bills while George sat here drinking and talking. The more he drank, the more he complained about the way you were running the agency and how he'd run things different."

I took a deep breath, struggling to control my rising anger and impatience. She knew my fuse was burning hot.

"All right, all right," she said agreeably. "Anyway, about 4:00 I went upstairs to your office to put the files back in your desk. George was drunk as a skunk by then. He came up behind me and grabbed me from behind . . ."

"What do you mean 'grabbed' you?" I interrupted. Drunk or sober, that was totally out of character for George.

"I mean, he grabbed my breasts and crotch," she said evenly. "I pushed him away, hard. He was so blitzed that he stumbled, fell backward, and hit the back of his head against the chair in front of your desk."

"Wait a minute. I thought you were behind my desk."

She pursed her lips and squeezed her eyes tight to control her own anger. "Are you gonna cross-examine me or let me talk?"

I held my tongue and gestured for her to talk.

"I was standing in front of your desk, not behind it, when he grabbed me. I thought he was going to do something else . . . maybe hit me . . . so I got the handcuffs out of your desk drawer and cuffed him before he could get back up."

"He just lay there and let you do that?"

"No, he didn't just lie there. He was a little groggy at first, I guess from hitting his head. He yelled at me to take them off, but I told him I wasn't taking them off until you came over. He got up, and I was leading him downstairs when he tripped, . . . and . . . I was just . . . it was an accident . . . not my fault, Jerry. . . . I couldn't stop him. . . ."

I ignored the tears streaming down her face again. "If he was *that* drunk and hit his head *that* hard on the chair, how did he manage to get up by himself?" I asked softly.

"He didn't . . . get up just by himself," she cried. "I helped him get up. Why are you *doing* this to me? I didn't *do* anything, I promise you I didn't."

I noticed a fiberglass nightstick lying on the carpet near the door. "What's this doing here?"

"How should I know?" she complained. "One of the guards probably left it there when he picked up his check. What difference does it make anyway?"

Absentmindedly I rolled the heavy black stick back and forth in my hand, looking at the weapon and then at the body. Something was badly out of focus, but my brain was too muddled to figure out what was wrong. I walked away from her and looked around the office. Several steps up from the bottom of the stairs I noticed a tooth. It was on the fifth stair. I bent closer to look at it and then glanced back at George. It looked like the incisor. I could see a thick drop of blood on the edge of the stair just above.

I stepped over the tooth and climbed the stairs to my office. One of the two chairs in front of my desk was out of place and lying on its back. There weren't any files on my desk. A plastic tumbler was sitting on George's desk. It was half full. I sniffed it. Scotch. I noticed a long scuff mark along the wall at the top of the stairs. A few feet down the stairs a small piece of plaster had broken out of the wall and dropped onto the carpeted treads.

"What are we going to do?" Darleen whispered when I returned to where she sat.

We? Ah, yes, *we.* I didn't know what to do. My head throbbed. I couldn't think. I needed something to eat to get my blood sugar stabilized so I could figure this out. I rubbed my face hard with both hands, trying to focus my thoughts. Accident, she said. An accident?

"Please don't let them arrest me, baby. *Please!*"

I looked at my young wife sitting hunched over in her chair as though she had a bad stomachache. She trembled. Her eyes begged for understanding. "Please, don't let them arrest me. Help me!" she begged.

She knew I couldn't do it. In that one flickering microsecond in time, the decision was made. It was a defining moment, one that would transform my life forever. I made it without hesitation or thought. Fallout from that moment in time would haunt me for years to come in ways I didn't even begin to imagine that night.

"All right, you go back to the house and pack our bags while I straighten this mess up."

She nodded, confident of my ability to resolve this latest crisis. Then she did something that made my skin crawl. She knelt beside George's body, patted his hand like a mother would a sleeping child. I wondered, if only for a second, whether or not she was mildly insane. I loved her and felt revolted by her at the same time. But my *duty* as a man and her husband was clear: A man is supposed to take charge, protect his family—no matter what. Covering for her had become an obsession. Whether it was to protect her or protect my own illusions wasn't clear at that moment. What was obvious? Something I didn't want to confront: a dim awareness that she didn't love me at all, that I was just a means to an end. But I banished the thought from my mind.

Once she was gone, I carried the overturned chair in my office downstairs and laid it on its back. I broke the legs off so it would look as though George had stumbled and tripped over the chair while lugging it downstairs. After laying it near the body, I dumped the handcuffs and nightstick in a brown paper bag and left through the back door.

"I'm going to throw this stuff into the lake," I told Darleen as we drove south toward Chickamauga Dam off Highway 153. "When we get back, we'll go to the office as though nothing had happened. I'll tell the police you left the office with me about 5:30. We've got reservations for a flight to D.C. around 7;00, and we went back to the office to get George to drive us to the airport. Can you keep all of that straight when the police question you?"

"Sure, but why will the police question us? Can't you just call the rescue squad as though there'd been an accident?"

My anger erupted again. "Every unattended death is investigated by the police. I'll call the rescue squad, but you can bet your sweet life they'll call the cops as soon as they arrive."

She whimpered quietly. "I'm so sorry, Jerry. I don't know why you love me after all the problems I've caused you. But it really wasn't my fault. It was an accident."

She kept saying the words over and over, but I wasn't listening anymore. I could be confrontational with her on irrelevant details, but not with what mattered most. I patted her knee and tried to concentrate on what I knew was coming in the next couple of hours.

◆ ◆ ◆

I parked near the boat-loading dock at the dam. Although it was cold, my face felt clammy with sweat. I squeezed my fingers tighter around the paper bag to control my shaking hands. After looking around to make sure we were alone, I heaved the bag containing the handcuffs and nightstick as far out into the lake as I could.

If only intuitively, I sensed that tossing the bag into the lake was a profoundly symbolic gesture: I'd just thrown away my life with the bag.

It was time to go home and begin the charade.

But first I stopped at Denny's restaurant to buy a pack of cigarettes.

◆ ◆ ◆

I took a deep breath as I pulled into the parking place in front of our home at 111 Pacific Road. "Are you ready?" I asked Darleen.

"Yes." Her voice seemed to be coming from far away.

As I stepped out of the car, lines from a poem I'd memorized in college stabbed at my consciousness: "Oh, what a tangled web we weave When first we practice to deceive!" I shivered but not from the cold. I forced myself to stand up straight, pulled my shoulders back, and walked stoically toward the office door. The keys slipped through my fumbling fingers. I bent over, angrily snatched up the keys, and shoved the key into the lock. The door opened three or four inches before bumping into George's lifeless head. I handed the keys to Darleen behind me and shivered again as I saw the sleeve of George's yellow sweater on his right arm through the crack. My stomach lurched.

"George! Are you there, George!" My voice sounded hoarse and raspy.

I felt like an amateur actor reciting a badly written script, resigned to the inevitability of the bad lines and driven—compelled—to go "on with the show" whether it made any sense to do so or not. Something from deep within screamed at me, *Stop! Don't do it! Get away from here!* But, as I did with any uncomfortable feeling, I dismissed it.

"What's wrong?" Darleen asked.

I almost laughed. She should have been an actress. "Give me your keys." I snatched them out of her outstretched hand, ran to her car, and opened the trunk. Even though I jogged several miles a day, I was breathing hard from running just a few feet.

I heard Darleen's nasal voice. "George? George, are you there? What's wrong? Talk to me, George!"

Yeah, "Talk to me, George," I thought bitterly as I grabbed the tire iron and ran toward the back of the building. My plan was to make it look as though George had accidentally fallen down the stairs. The back door was never used because it stuck in the tracks, so it was logical to knock out the glass and enter that way. I swung hard, but the tire tool bounced off the pane. The second time I swung it, the glass shattered. I reached through the jagged opening, jerked the door open, and stepped inside.

George's body lay where I had left it. Nothing had been disturbed. But it looked like a larger pool of blood had collected around his head from where the wounds had continued to drain. From outside the door I heard Darleen's voice, but I couldn't hear her words.

I pulled the door open a couple of inches. "Come around through the back," I said.

"What? What's wrong, Jerry? What's wrong with George?"

I wanted to scream at her: "Quit the act! You know what's wrong with him!"

But I didn't scream anything. "Just come around back," I said again, closing the door.

Standing over the body, I gripped his shirt at the front and pulled him up into a sitting position. His head lolled forward. A noise startled me. It sounded like he had gasped for breath.

"C'mon, George, don't you die on me," I muttered.

Quickly I stepped around, reached under his arms, and turned the body so I could stretch him out flat. Again, I knelt by his right side and checked his pulse. Nothing. I pulled the eyelid back over each eye. Both pupils were fixed and dilated. My frantic hope flickered and died. The sound had just been air escaping from his lungs.

I glanced up and saw Darleen standing in the foyer between the office and the kitchen. Her fists were clenched and pressing together under her chin. She stared at George. For the first time she looked afraid.

3

No Turning Back

I TOOK a deep breath and reached for the phone.

Darleen grabbed my arm. "What are you going to do?"

"I've gotta call the rescue squad," I said, shaking her hand loose. But then my mind went blank. What was the number? I couldn't remember something as elementary as 911. I stabbed the "O," told the operator I had a medical emergency, and asked her to connect me with the fire department.

Moments later I heard sirens in the distance. I knew I had passed the point of no return.

✦ ✦ ✦

EMT Dewayne Pitts and his partner arrived. I told them my story and what I'd done to check George's condition. After a cursory examination, the EMT called the police department.

Officer Eldon Lansford, a young uniformed officer, arrived first. I spoke with him briefly before he talked to the EMTs. Then he turned back to me. "What happened to the chair?" he asked, pointing. It was the chair from my office. After breaking off the front legs, I'd dropped it in the secretarial office near the foot of the stairs.

"I believe that chair came out of my office," I said. "It looks to me like George fell over it while bringing it downstairs."

"Fell over it?"

"Yeah. I tossed it back here when I found him like that."

Lansford nodded without comment and wrote a few notes in a small pad he was carrying.

I went back to the kitchen to check on Darleen. She was huddled over in her chair and rocking back and forth.

"I feel sick," she whispered.

From the next room I could hear Officer Lansford calling over his radio for assistance.

"You'd better pull yourself together," I whispered through clenched teeth. "This place is about to fill up with detectives asking a *lot* of hard questions."

She sat up straight. Her face was chalky white. "I'll be all right, but I feel faint."

"I'll see if Pitts has anything. Just breathe slowly, in and out," I said.

One of the EMTs gave me an ammonium carbonate capsule. I broke it under her nose and squeezed it. She gasped and slapped my hand away. "That's enough!"

I glanced at my watch when I heard the front door open. It was 6:45 p.m. For the first time I thought of Tracie and my flight to Washington, D.C.

29

Another door slammed shut.

◆ ◆ ◆

I stepped back into the office and saw a tall, burly detective with blond hair stepping over George's body. He introduced himself as Carl Booth. He looked young, but I guessed he was in his early- to mid-30s.

"What happened here?" he asked as he glanced around.

Briefly I told him that Darleen and I had left the office about 5:30 p.m. to go home and pack for a trip to Washington.

"What time was your flight?"

"We were supposed to leave at 7:05."

He looked at his watch. "What time did you get here?"

Again my mind went blank. "It was . . . I don't know, maybe half an hour ago. This has sort of taken the starch out of me," I mumbled, pointing toward George.

"I imagine so," he replied. He sounded genuinely sympathetic.

He bent over and looked at the broken chair. "How did this happen?" he asked.

"I really don't know, but I suppose George fell over it while bringing it downstairs. It wasn't here when I left earlier."

The telephone rang. After my recorded message, I heard Wilma's voice. "Is anybody there? George? Jerry?" She knew we sometimes monitored our calls. "Somebody give me a call."

Booth listened to the call. I could feel him looking at me. "Who's that?" he asked.

"That's his wife," I replied, pointing toward George.

"What are you going to tell her?"

Flustered by the raging conflict within, I hesitated before answering. "I can't talk to her now . . . tell her what's happened here over the telephone. If it's all right with you, I'm going to call their Mormon bishop, Phil Smartt, and ask him to talk to her."

Booth shrugged. "Do whatever you want. But let me ask you something about this chair first. Did you say his body was on the chair?"

"No. You asked me how it happened. It wasn't like this when I left, so I'm guessing, you know, from where I found his body, that he must have tripped and fallen over it."

"So his body was on top of the chair, did you say?"

"No, that isn't what I said. His body was sprawled at the bottom of the stairs, there on the floor at the bottom," I said, pointing toward the floor. "The chair was . . . I think it was lying . . ."

I hesitated. Momentarily confused by his insistent questions, I stopped and looked toward the area where I'd found his body earlier. "I think I told Officer Lansford either the chair was lying by his feet or it had rolled over here on the carpet."

"Did you move the chair from the body?" Booth asked.

"Yeah, I . . . it was in my way, so I tossed it over there," I said, pointing toward the chair. "I think that leg lying loose over there fell off after I moved it."

Booth wrote something in his notebook before speaking again. "So you moved the chair from under the body?"

"No. It wasn't under the body, just nearby."

He turned away and knelt beside the chair while I called Bishop Smartt. It was approximately 7:00 p.m. when I reached him at his office. "I'm sorry to tell you this, Phil, but George is dead," I said.

"What happened?"

"It looks like he slipped on the stairs and fell."

"Are the police there?"

"Yes."

"I'll be right over."

"I'd appreciate that. But I was hoping you might talk to Wilma first. She just called and left a message on the answering machine. I don't want to tell her about this on the phone. Could you give her a call or go see her?"

"I'll talk to her when I find out what's happened," he snapped. "I'm coming over there."

The line went dead.

Startled by the hostility in his voice, I slowly put the phone handset back in its cradle. When I turned back toward the office, Detective Booth was watching me from where he had knelt beside the chair. "Has anybody checked the upstairs?" he asked.

"No, I don't think so."

He reached under his coat and took out a snub-nosed pistol before climbing the stairs.

"There's nobody up here," he said moments later. He sounded disappointed. I went upstairs and answered more questions about the layout of the office.

By 7:15 p.m. detectives were swarming over the office. From having seen him on TV, I recognized Inspector Bill Dixon, a seasoned veteran on the major crime squad. Another plainclothesman introduced himself as Detective Rose. Police photographer Jack Gilliland was busy taking photographs. Tag Bailey, from the crime lab, was trying to lift latent prints from the chair leg. Napoleon Dawson, a tall, burly Black detective, was the last to arrive.

◆ ◆ ◆

Phil Smartt walked in through the back door around 7:20. His acne-scarred face was twisted in anger. He glanced around the kitchen after a perfunctory greeting. His eyes zeroed in on several empty liquor bottles sitting on the kitchen sink. "What's this?" he asked.

"George and I had a few drinks today . . ."

"George doesn't drink alcohol," Smartt interrupted. It was a flat statement. The self-righteous tone and thinly disguised hostility set my teeth on edge.

"George drinks. Often, even too much sometimes," I snapped back. "I imagine he was drunk when he fell down the stairs."

"I don't believe that for one minute," Phil replied. He turned away and sat down in a chair near the door, where he could see what was going on in the other room. Occasionally, he glared at Darleen and me, but said nothing.

The phone rang. It was Wilma again. "Bishop, will you talk to her?" I asked.

"No. Not now. I'll talk to her after I hear what the coroner has to say." He bristled with hostility and refused to look me in the eye.

Angrily I got up and pushed through the crowd of detectives. "Wilma, this is Jerry," I said as I turned the answering machine off.

"Where's George? He was supposed to be home a long time ago. Is everything all right?" I could hear the impatience in her voice.

"Everything's OK," I said. "I can't talk to you right now. I'll call you back in a few minutes." I hung up before she could ask anything else.

"You should have talked to her, Phil," I said.

He looked directly at me. His jaw was clamped shut and he didn't reply.

"I called the bishop, but an insurance man showed up," I muttered under my breath to Darleen.

◆ ◆ ◆

Suddenly, a bitter taste of bile surged up in my throat as I realized what probably motivated his feelings about me. Earlier in the summer, Bill Alt, an attorney who owned half the outstanding stock in my company, had helped us obtain a $30,000 line of credit with Commerce Union Bank. I'd told Bill and the bank loan officer that George and I would take out enough keyman insurance on our lives to cover anticipated indebtedness. George had suggested his bishop, Phil Smartt, as the best insurance agent for us. Although Smartt was pastor of the Chattanooga Mormon Stake (church), Mormon clergy are required to be self-supporting. He owned his own insurance agency. I'd met him a few months earlier while attending a concert with George. He seemed cordial, although a bit pushy about religion and insurance—in about equal measure. Nevertheless, we asked him to give us estimates on the cost for a $50,000, $75,000, and $100,000 keyman life insurance policy. He had the figures a day later and met with us to discuss it.

George had pressed for the larger amount because the cost wasn't significantly more and because we both could later convert the company policy to a personal policy with our wives as beneficiaries. At the time he had only a single $5,000 policy for himself with Wilma as beneficiary.

"It might cover the cost of my funeral," he had joked.

Before agreeing to the policy, Bishop Smartt had reminded us that—for a nominal fee, of course—the policy could have a double-indemnity policy for accidental death. We had spent more than 50,000 miles on the road during the previous six months, so that seemed prudent.

◆ ◆ ◆

I glanced over at Bishop Smartt again. He stared back, his jaw tight. I could almost hear the wheels spinning, and I felt terribly fatigued.

That's when Deputy Police Chief James M. "Pete" Davis arrived. I'd seen him several times on television. He was chief of the major crime squad, dealing with murder, rape, kidnapping, and arson. In his late 50s, his hair was thinning and turning gray. His face, lined from squinting cynically at too many criminals, looked like something chiseled out of stone. I could see the outline of a pistol under the wrinkled, tan raincoat he wore. I wondered if he'd remember me as the investigator who had helped win an acquittal in the Gallagher arson trial the previous November. I turned my back to the sink as Davis walked through the kitchen. I drank another glass of ice water to steady my nerves.

✦ ✦ ✦

I had just opened Searchers Detective Agency in September of 1975. In October a few days after meeting with Bill Alt of Scruggs, Seal, and Alt to introduce myself, Bill had called late on a Thursday afternoon. "I've got a dicey arson case that needs a miracle. We're going to trial next Tuesday and it doesn't look good for my client," he admitted.

According to Alt, his client was an Irishman named Patrick Gallagher from New York City. In April of 1975 he had been arrested and charged with the arson of his International House of Pancakes franchise on Labor Day of 1974. Jerry Summers, one of Chattanooga's best trial lawyers, would actually be handling the criminal trial. Bill represented Pat's business interests, but I could tell from Bill's concern that there also was a strong bond of personal friendship between the two men.

"The cops caught one of the arsonists at the scene," Bill continued. "His name is Dennis Dobson. He's a kid Pat employed as a bartender at a bar he owns near Eastgate Shopping Center. Pat thinks he got mad because he sent him over to work at the IHOP. I understand that the D.A. has made a deal with Dobson, offering him an 11-29 [11 months and 29 days, usually served in the county jail] suspended in exchange for his testimony against Pat. But we haven't been able to locate the kid or find out anything about his testimony."

I hadn't much time and little information to go on. But I got lucky when I interviewed Dobson's father, who told me his son had been arrested in Georgia. Dennis faced several drug-related charges plus some counts of armed robbery. The sheriff agreed to let me interview Dobson in the jail. The rest had been easy. I convinced the kid that I was an insurance investigator looking to "nail Gallagher's butt to the wall." He was happy to talk into my tape recorder. He admitted the deal with the state, exhibited considerable hostility toward Pat, and told me, in effect, that he'd say anything to avoid going to jail for what he'd done.

Frankly, I felt a little sorry for Dobson by the time I turned off the tape recorder. He was a typical young drug addict whose life had veered out of control. Before I left, I gave him $5 so he could buy some cigarettes.

Jerry Summers put on a brilliant defense. In addition to showing that Gallagher didn't profit by the arson, he used a transcript of my taped interview and destroyed Dobson's credibility on cross-examination. An angry jury quickly returned a not guilty verdict. Not surprisingly, Dobson tried to cover himself by claiming that the $5 I'd left him for cigarettes was a bribe I'd paid to get him to say what he did on tape.

One of the detectives had cornered me outside the courtroom after the jury rendered its verdict. "I hope you enjoyed yourself," he hissed. "I can't prove you paid that kid off, but you did it and you can bet your _____ life we're not gonna forget this! We know how to deal with someone like you down here."

This wasn't the first controversial case I'd worked on as a private investigator. But that kind of personal animosity was a totally new experience for me. During a trial it's not unusual for lawyers on either side of a case to erupt in anger toward the other side, especially when things aren't going well. But I'd never seen the anger get that personal once a trial was over.

Bill Alt warned me later that the state was looking for some angle on which to indict me. "Gary Gerbitz just got elected as the district attorney general *last year*," he explained. "He's won every case that's gone to trial since he took office. He plans to keep winning, and he and his staff have no qualms whatsoever about making up evidence as they go along if that's what it takes to get a conviction. Consider this a warning: They'll indict you in a New York second if they can find an angle, so don't give them any free shots at you."

I thought Bill was being a bit melodramatic. I'd soon learn to my own peril that he had a real gift for understatement!

◆ ◆ ◆

"Look at those marks on his wrists!" I heard one of the detectives saying in the next room. "Here, shine that flashlight right here. Yeah. Looks just like handcuff marks. I'll tell you what I think: Somebody cuffed the poor _____ and then beat him to death."

"Lansford, gimme your handcuffs for a second." I recognized Chief Davis' voice. Seconds later I heard the ratchet sound of handcuffs locking.

"Let's roll him over a second and take a look at his back," another voice said.

"That's it! Look at that! See that indentation on his back."

"Looks like an old surgical scar to me."

"Nah. That's where the cuffs dug into his back while he laid on 'em."

"Any cuffs around here?"

"They got guard uniforms and web gear in that closet," I heard Dawson say.

"Jack, c'mere. I want you to take some pictures of this," Davis said.

I felt icy-cold. How could I have missed something that obvious? I looked at Darleen. She had recovered from any feelings of shock and wasn't paying attention to what was going on in the next room.

I glanced at Phil Smartt. He looked hard at me. A faint, grim smile played around the corner of his mouth.

Inspector Bill Dixon stepped into the kitchen. He was a slender detective in his late-40s or early-50s. There was something faintly cadaverous about his appearance. He made me think of an undertaker. His facial features had been carved into a perpetual scowl long ago. His voice was harsh and accusing. His abrasiveness was accentuated by a brutal massacre of basic English.

34

"C'mere. I wanna ask ya something," he said, crooking his finger at me to follow.

I followed him through the larger office and to the foot of the stairs. He pointed at George's glasses, neatly folded and lying in the corner at the bottom of the stairs. "Didja fold them glasses up?" he asked.

"No. I didn't even notice them."

He squinted his eyes and looked at me skeptically. "Didja take any handcuffs offa that there body?"

"I certainly didn't!" Somewhere deep inside I heard an old child's chant: "Liar, liar, pants on fire!"

"That's mighty odd, you know. Here ya'll claim ya discovered the body. Somebody has put cuffs on 'im and beat 'im up. But ya don't know nothing about that, huh?"

"No, I don't."

"All right, you can go." He dismissed me with a wave.

I stepped around Detective Dawson, who was looking in our uniform supply closet. Two pair of handcuffs were lying on the floor beside him. One set was lying loose. The other was still in a leather case. Just as I passed he pulled out a nightstick. He stood up and stepped over closer to the bathroom door and looked at the stick under the light. He turned it back and forth in his bare hands.

"I think this stick may have blood on it!" he said to somebody.

"Well, bag it up and we'll send it to the lab," another voice said. "Take them handcuffs, too. You never know what might turn up."

I shook my head in amazement as Dawson laid the stick on top of the towel I'd used to wipe my hands. *What they'll turn up is his own silly fingerprints and blood from the towel*, I thought.

Davis and Dixon came out into the kitchen. "How'dja get that blood on your sleeve?" Dixon demanded.

I looked down at the sleeve. I hadn't noticed the bloodstain before. I glanced at Bishop Smartt. He seemed to be enjoying himself for the first time. Another tight, thin smile cracked his lips.

"Looks like ya got some on your pants, too," Dixon continued. He pointed at an area on my left thigh. "How'd that happen?"

"I guess I must have gotten that on me when I moved his body," I said. "I didn't realize I had any on me."

"You didn't notice that, huh?" Davis asked softly. I thought he would have done a wonderful Lieutenant Colombo impression. "You wouldn't mind if we took a picture of that would you, just so we have a picture of it?" Davis asked.

"Sure, I guess so." I could hardly say no!

Dixon stood beside me and took the sleeve in his own hand, twisting it around so Jack Gilliland could take the picture.

"I understand you live near here?" Davis said conversationally as the flash bulbs popped.

"Yeah, we live a few doors down, at 111."

"Would you mind just showing us around your place? You know, Jerry,

35

just look around a bit. You wouldn't mind that, would you?"

"No, I guess that's all right. But I do need to get something to eat. I've got hypoglycemia—low blood sugar—and I'm not feeling very good right now."

"Sure, sure," Davis said agreeably. "In just a few minutes. The detectives want to ask you a few more questions first, so maybe Mrs. Bragan could show us around while you do that. OK, Jerry? Fine. Would you come with us, Mrs. Bragan?"

Even though I felt sick, like a rat trapped in a maze, I almost laughed at the smooth way Davis operated. *He's a slick piece of work*, I thought. But I knew there was nothing in the house that was incriminating, so why not let him look around. Within a few months, however, I'd discover just how "slick" he was—and I wouldn't be laughing!

I saw Bishop Smartt outside talking to the Deputy Coroner, Bobby Hudson, as Darleen left with Davis, Dixon, and Booth. Dawson called me into the living room area.

"I want to ask you about that chair," he said. "Booth says you told him your partner's body was on the chair when you came in. Could you show me how it was?"

"I didn't tell him anything of the kind," I said irritably. "In fact, I told him two or three times that the . . . He asked me what I thought happened," I began again. "I said it looked to me like he'd tripped and fallen *over* the chair. His body was sprawled at the foot of the stairs . . ."

Dawson was courteous but persistent. "I thought I heard you say the chair was under him when you came in?"

My mind went blank again. What had I told the uniformed cop, Lansford? Or Booth? Or Dixon? I had a blinding headache. I kept my fists stuffed in my pockets so Dawson wouldn't see them shaking. But I couldn't hide the cold sweat beading up on my forehead.

"No, I don't think I said that," I insisted. "He must have misunderstood me. I said I thought he fell *over* the chair. . . . I mean tripped and fell over it. Maybe that's where . . ."

"You saying he just misunderstood you or something?"

"I dunno what I said . . ."

"You don't know what you said now?" Dawson pressed harder.

"No, I know what I said. I just don't know what he misunderstood . . . maybe . . . you know, there's a lot of confusion here with everybody talking and . . ."

"OK. Could the body have been *on* the chair?"

"No. . . . Maybe . . ." I took a deep breath and tried to collect my thoughts.

Chief Davis and Inspector Dixon returned then. "Jerry, I think you'd better come down to our office and give a formal statement, if you don't mind," Davis said.

"OK, but do you mind if I get something to eat first? I'm really feeling bad right now."

"No, not now. We'll get you a sandwich downtown."

36

NO TURNING BACK

"All right. We'll follow you downtown in our car."

"No, you and Mrs. Bragan come with me. We'll drive you back."

I felt the walls closing in as I looked at Darleen. She smiled agreeably. I wanted to slap that silly grin off her face. She didn't realize we were only moments away from being arrested.

4

Midnight Interrogation

IT WAS 10:15 p.m. I glanced around my office before following Chief Davis out the door. I didn't expect to see it again. Curiously, I hoped they did arrest me. At least I wouldn't have to make any more decisions.

Darleen and I rode in the backseat of Chief Davis' car. As we turned off Highway 153 onto Amnicola Highway, just blocks away from the police department, I suddenly realized I still had a handcuff key on my key ring. While Davis chatted, I fumbled with the key ring and slipped the handcuff key off, dropping it so that it slid down between the seat and the door casing.

Davis left us waiting in an office while he met with Dixon and several other detectives in another room. Detective Dawson remained with us. He had several boxes of items taken from my office, and he was tagging them for identification.

Davis appeared at the door a few minutes later. "I know you must be tired, Mrs. Bragan, so we'll interview you first. Follow me, please."

It was 10:47 p.m.

I pulled the pack of cigarettes out of my pocket. It was empty. I'd chain-smoked one cigarette after another since I'd gotten the pack at Denny's. I knew I shouldn't smoke any more of them because I needed a clear head for what was coming. But the addiction to smoking was stronger than good sense. Moreover, I felt sick to my stomach and was afraid of throwing up.

"Is there any place . . . . a machine . . . where I can get a pack of cigarettes?" I asked Dawson. "And I need to get a candy bar or something to eat. My blood sugar is dropping through the floor."

"I'll get you something just as soon as I finish here," he replied.

I wiped my forehead with the back of my hand to get the sweat off and forced myself to sit down. *Maintain!* I told myself. I figured I'd be arrested in a matter of minutes, but at least I could retain my composure.

I glanced at my watch when Darleen returned. It was 10:55 p.m. Dawson left the room.

I hugged her close. "Be careful what you say. This room is probably wired for sound," I whispered. She nodded in understanding.

"Are you all right?" I asked in a normal voice.

"I'm fine. They asked me a lot of questions. That's all. But they obviously think somebody killed George," she said.

I shook my head in warning.

Moments later Inspector Dixon came for me.

Chief Davis sat behind his desk. A tape recorder sat on the desk in front of him. Inspector Dixon directed me to a straight-backed metal chair in front of the desk, and he sat to my left.

"It's been a long evening, Jerry," Chief Davis said, "but we'll have this wrapped up in a few more minutes."

"That's fine," I said, "but I need to get something to eat . . . and a cigarette. I'm pretty upset. Dawson said there was a machine where I could get . . ."

"Yes, we'll get you a cigarette here in a minute. Let's just get this out of the way. It's all right with you if we record this, isn't it?"

"Sure."

"Good." He turned on the tape recorder. "This will be a statement of Mr. Jeris E. Bragan." He spelled my first and last name. "A white male, 30, date of birth 1/11/46. He lives at 111 Pacific Road." His voice droned on as he dictated phone numbers, place of employment. Then he gave me the Miranda warning and asked me to sign the form. "His employee is George Urice, white male, 50. I believe he lives around Boyington, Georgia."

"That's right," I said.

Davis continued. "Present for this interview will be Chief Davis and Inspector Dixon. This interview is being taken at the detective office, 3300 Amnicola Highway, and it will be in regard to a homicide that happened at 116 Pacific Road. The victim was Mr. George Urice. I believe the call came in about 6:45 p.m., this date."

Davis then began the interrogation: "Jerry, about what time did you first see George today?"

"I'd be just approximating the time, but I saw him the first time this morning when I went into the office about 10:30 or 11:00. I overslept. I was supposed to have a dental appointment this morning, and I went in sometime between 10:30 and 11:00."

"And he was in the office at that time, Jerry?"

"He'd just arrived."

"And you and he were in the office alone at this time?"

"Yes, we were."

"How long did you all stay there this first time, Jerry?"

"We were there until approximately 12:30 or so. We were discussing various cases, and we had some coffee with some brandy that he'd given me. My wife came in about 12:30. I think we left the office about 12:30, and went over to the Peddler Steak House . . ."

A detective I hadn't seen earlier came into the office and handed me half a dozen cigarettes and a candy bar.

"Thank you. You're a gentleman and a scholar," I said. I lit one of the cigarettes and began eating the candy bar before continuing. "We went to the Peddler Steak House over on . . . what is it, Hixson Pike, I guess."

"Hixson or Brainerd?"

"Hixson Pike, right. There's one down in Brainerd. This was on Hixson Pike right near the United Bank. We had, I don't know, two or three drinks, something like that. I've got the charge slip here in my pocket. We were there until about 2:00 or 2:30. We came back to the office. I had, I don't know, one or two drinks. George had quite a few drinks, I think. I didn't even look at the bottle of Usher's there, but I think he polished off that bottle of Usher's Scotch."

MIDNIGHT INTERROGATION

I knew I was babbling, answering questions that weren't being asked, but I couldn't stop. Davis didn't interrupt. He just sat there and studied me through hooded eyes.

"If you'd ask me some questions as we go along here, it'd be helpful," I said.

"Well, you came back, and all of you went to the office—you, your wife, and George—and this was about . . ."

"I would estimate we got back about 2:30, quarter to three, because when we left I think we were the last people in the place."

"Well, Jerry, then you sat around and talked?"

"Yeah, we sat around and talked. His mother was supposedly coming tomorrow, and I was going up to Washington tonight to pick up my daughter. And we talked about getting together over the holidays and planning someplace to, you know, go out to dinner while his mother was here. We talked about the cases. Our biggest case most recently was this thing up in Pittsburgh. We were feeling pretty pleased about that and sort of congratulating ourselves and this sort of thing and basically after today planning to, you know, turn off the phones for the next week. Enjoy the visit with my daughter, and he was going to enjoy the visit with his mother."

I realized I was babbling again and forced myself to stop.

"Were you just going to Washington and back?"

"Yeah, I was flying up tonight. She has a . . . she's in the first grade, and she has a play that she's going to be in tomorrow morning at 10:30. She still doesn't know I'm not going to be there."

"What were you going on, what flight was it?"

"Delta, I can't remember the flight number. I think it was 705 . . . 720 . . . something like that. It was leaving for Washington and connecting with another flight in Atlanta. I had confirmed reservations tomorrow afternoon, I think 1:45, 1:50, something like that to come back."

"Jerry, you all stayed over there and talked to him for . . ."

"Oh, several . . . several hours, two, three hours, I guess."

"And about what time did you leave?"

"I've been asked that a dozen times tonight. I really wasn't paying that much attention to the time. It could have been 5:15, 5:30. It was somewhere after 5:00."

"And you and your wife left."

"Yes."

"And you left George there by himself?"

"Yes."

"Where did you go, Jerry?"

"We went over to our house. She was going to pack a few things. I was out of cigarettes. She did pack a few things. We did something around the house then, I don't remember now. And we went up to a restaurant there in Northgate to get a pack of cigarettes. I wasn't drunk by any stretch of the imagination, but with low blood sugar and about two or three drinks I needed to get out and get some fresh air. And we came back. I think we

41

went into our house, but I'm not absolutely sure. And at any rate, some time around . . . I can't pin the time down as I told you there [at the scene]."

I heard Dixon grunt something. Out of the corner of my eye I saw him twist his mouth into a grimace of irritation.

"I called the rescue squad within a minute and a half or a couple of minutes of being in there and realized, you know, that he was probably dead." I knew I should stop talking, but I couldn't. "And, well, to backtrack, I first went to the door. Darleen was with me. I tried to open the door. I didn't push it hard. I don't know, maybe I could have gotten, you know, gotten through, pushed him out of the way or something, I don't know. But I realized that something was wrong, he was lying there."

Davis interrupted my monologue. "Could you see him, Jerry, when you unlocked the door, or any part of him?"

"I saw blood on the floor, and I think I saw the top of his head or something like that. I'm not sure."

I struggled to remember what I'd seen when I did unlock the door, but it was a blur.

"Did you say anything to your wife? She was standing right there with you, I believe you said."

"I said something. I think I asked her for the keys to her car, and I went back to the car and I got the jack handle out of the car and went across to the back of the house and knocked the window out, unlocked the door, and went inside. He was lying there."

I remembered Dawson and Booth questioning me about the chair and the location of George's body. What had I told them? I couldn't remember. No matter how hard I tried to concentrate, everything was turning fuzzy on me. "And I . . . well, I told you over there at the office, I can't tell you now whether he was lying on top of the chair, face down, face up, what, I don't remember. I pulled the chair away, and I pulled . . . I think there was a leg or something lying there, pulled that away, and I pulled him out flat. He was sort of in a crumpled kind of position."

"Right at the door?"

"Pardon?"

"Up against the door?"

"Up against the door."

"That's at the foot of the steps now?"

"Yes."

"From the steps, I believe [the steps] come right down and right to the front door?"

"Yeah, give about three feet, something like that," I replied.

"Two or three feet."

I rushed on. "I earned my way through college working in an emergency room of a small hospital up in Maryland, so it didn't take any genius to figure that he was in real bad shape or probably dead. I couldn't feel any pulse or anything. And I didn't know the number for the fire department or the emergency or rescue squad, whatever it is called down here, so I phoned the operator, and she put me through."

42

MIDNIGHT INTERROGATION

Chief Davis' voice was friendly and conversational, but I knew he was zeroing in on me. "Did you check the back door, Jerry, before you struck it with the tire tool, to see if it was locked? You said you reached through and unlocked it, though, didn't you?"

"I'm quite sure I reached through and unlocked it. I don't think I checked."

"Before you hit it?"

"It never even occurred to me to check the door to see whether it was locked or unlocked. I'm quite sure the door was locked, though."

"Jerry, you did move him before the police got there?"

"Yes, I did."

"Moved him around, and I believe that . . . I didn't see it, but they said you had some blood . . ."

Now you're talking to me like an idiot, I thought. *You and I both know you saw it, because you asked me to pose for photographs. Why don't we just end this little charade and get the arrest over with?*

But the game continued.

"I had blood under my left arm and on this . . ."

"On the shirt?"

"Yes."

"Could I . . . you don't mind me seeing it? I didn't see it, Jerry."

I stood up. "Here and on the back."

"And you were moving him around?"

"Pardon?"

"Did you . . ."

"I got down underneath him and I pulled him."

"Turn around just a minute," Davis said. "Any on the other sleeve?"

"No, there isn't. I took my coat off, obviously to move him."

"You took your coat off after you went in?"

"Yes. In fact, I think it was the first thing I did before I even walked over. I threw my coat over onto the typing table or onto my wife's desk or something like that."

Davis turned to Inspector Dixon. "Dixon, is there anything you want to ask him?"

Before Dixon could say anything, Davis continued: "Well, being a detective, in the detective business, Jerry, and I assume that you must be a pretty good detective, is there any way . . ."

"I handle civil stuff."

"Can you explain, or . . . I just can't understand the three of you being together all day, you leave, leave there, leave George there, and you are gone 45 minutes to an hour, well, give or take 10 or 15 minutes, both doors locked, and the man lying there in the shape he's in when you get back?"

Chief, you've got Lieutenant Colombo down pat! I thought.

"That I can't explain. As I told you, I keep hearing the word 'homicide' mentioned. I tell you right now I didn't do anything like that. And so far as I know, George doesn't have an enemy in the world. As a matter of fact, even though there's 20 years difference in our ages, George is probably the

43

best friend I have. And you mentioned at the beginning of this thing, and I'd like to correct that . . . that he was an employee. He was only technically an employee. For the past three months, we've functioned as partners and acted as partners. And sometime in the next month or so he was going to come into the company on an equity basis."

"I didn't know . . ."

"I thought I'd told you."

"You hadn't talked to me."

"I talked to some other detective who asked me about it."

"Jerry, you said you heard someone say that it could be a homicide. What did it appear to be to you?"

"What it appeared to me was scrambled eggs for brains when I saw him there. I've investigated murder cases, never quite like you gentlemen do. It's always been for the defense. I've never walked into a room and seen anything like that, and quite frankly it scared me. That's why your officers keep asking me to pin down times. Good gracious, I'm not even sure of my own name right now! You said at the beginning of this conversation that, you know, everybody is considered a suspect."

"Yes, sir."

"The only thing I can tell you is that George was just about the best friend I have, and George's wife is probably the closest thing to a mother my wife has."

"Did she . . . has she been up today?"

"Pardon?"

"Has she been up today?"

"Has *who* been up today?"

"His wife, George's?"

"Up to the office?"

"Uh-huh."

"No, no, she works. I think 9:00 to 5:00, something like that."

"Jerry, is there anything that any employee or anybody you can think of . . ."

"I've been racking my brains. I can't even remember who I've talked to tonight. We have several cases pending. The only immediate thing that would make anybody mad is . . . in fact, I think I told you of this or somebody, we got this case going up in Pittsburgh, but somebody come all the way down here to commit murder . . . Our work is . . . it's civil. We have no domestic cases pending, have no criminal cases of any sort pending. We've worked on some things in the past and may have made a few people mad, but most people don't sit around and hold a grudge. If they are going to do something, they go out and do it."

"Well, Jerry wa— . . . nobody had been there all day, just the three of you?"

"Well, so far as I know, I believe George . . . I'm quite sure George had just gotten there when he came in late today too."

"Did you all go anywhere other than to the steak house?"

"No, sir."

"You didn't take your car to . . ."

"Oh, oh, I'm sorry. Yes, we took the car to Oldsmobile Park. I'm sorry. We took the car to Oldsmobile Park before we went to Peddler's. I'd forgotten all about that."

Davis smiled. My face felt hot, flushed in embarrassment. I thought about the poem again: *"Oh, what a tangled web we weave, When first we practice to deceive!"*

"Did George follow you down and bring you back?"

"Well, he followed . . . he followed my wife and me down to Oldsmobile Park, and then he picked us up there, and we went from there directly over to Peddler Steak House."

"Your wife is still with you?"

"Pardon?"

"Your wife is still with you?"

"Yes, my wife, she's . . . just so you understand, she's a bit more than a wife and a bit more than a secretary. She always goes with us when we go out of town and on cases. She's my wife and sort of George's little girl, so that's the way it's been just about ever since he came to work with us."

Why did I say that? I wanted to throw up!

"Anything else you want to ask him?" Davis asked Inspector Dixon.

"Didja see any handcuffs or anythin' in the room when ya moved George?" Dixon asked.

"No, I didn't see anything like that."

"All right, ya'll do have handcuffs and things there in the building, don'tja?"

"We've got web gear and handcuffs and this sort of thing, but the security, you know, . . . what we have there I honestly couldn't tell you."

"That's what I was goin' to ask ya. Would ya know if there's a pair of your handcuffs missin'?"

"Well, I suppose we could do an audit of our bookkeeping and figure out what's out on issue and what we've gotten back. I have virtually nothing to do with the security end. George and Stan pretty well run that."

I realized I was speaking of George in the present tense, as though he were alive. I wanted him to *be* alive, to walk in and laugh: "Ha! The joke's on you!" But I knew he wasn't alive. He'd never walk into any room, ever again, and this was no joke!

"Whenever ya went in there with George, after you've had time to think an' everythin' on it, can ya recall at all how his body was positioned? Was he on his face or face up or was he in a cramped position or . . ."

I froze again.

"I've racked . . . I've racked my brain since you asked me that question and, you know, I could tell you one thing or another, but I'd be talking off the top of my head."

"You said that ya turned 'im over, I think, when I first got there, that's the reason that gave me the impression he was face down. When I first asked ya up at the house, you said ya turned 'im over. Do ya recall that?"

"I got my arms . . . It seems to me vaguely that he was lying in a slumped position there, but I'm talking off the top of my head right now. I just don't recall. I got my arms under his armpits; I pulled him back; I checked him over."

"That's not what you told me. You might have told me you pulled him back instead of turned 'im over then?"

"I think so."

"He was probably already on his back, isn't that correct?"

"That could be, I don't . . . I just don't know."

I remembered the deputy coroner at the scene. By now they would have checked his body carefully. They already knew from lividity what position he was in at the time of death and after. But I drew a blank every time I tried to recapture the picture in my mind from just a few hours earlier.

Inspector Dixon continued. "Do ya know . . . of course, in movin' 'im ya got some blood on your hands?"

"Yes, I did."

"You stated to me later that you . . . after we'd seen the blood on the towel and the soap in the bathroom, that you'd washed your hands."

"Yes, I did."

"Do ya know how ya got the blood on the backside of your sleeve from 'im? I mean, I could understand on your hands . . ."

"I think when I was leaning over him . . . You mean how I got it on me? I don't know."

"Do ya know what'd cause the splatter of blood on the front side, on the left side of your shirt?"

"Splatter?"

"There's two little splatters on your shirt."

"Unless I got it off his hair. . . . It seems to me that I recall he had a lot of blood on his hair. I could have gotten it off his hair. I don't know."

"Well, from this, ya *did* move 'im from the head side. Ya never did get over the body at all, you . . ."

"Pardon?"

"Ya didn't straddle the body or anythin'. Ya moved 'im from the head position, and . . ."

"I got my arms underneath his armpits. I pulled him back away from the door so that he was out straight. It seems to me when I walked in there, one or both of his feet were cocked up on one of the stairs or something, you know, this sort of . . ."

"Was his glasses and all layin' right over in the corner just like they was when I arrived? Ya know they was folded neatly layin' over in the corner."

"I don't remember his glasses being there."

"Did 'e wear 'is glasses all the time, or did 'e . . ."

"All the time."

"He wears 'em all the time?"

"He's blind in one eye and can't see out of the other without his glasses."

"But ya didn't notice 'is glasses layin' in the corner there by the door an' the wall?"

46

"I could have; I just don't know. I don't recall seeing them there, no."

"Not even folded like he'd taken 'em off and folded 'em up to put in a case, ya know what I mean? Did it appear like he'd fell down those steps?"

"Well, obviously that . . . yeah, that was my initial impression until I started hearing somebody saying something about handcuffs or something like that out there at the office. I thought he'd fallen down the stairs. He'd had a lot to drink. George doesn't get . . . when he'd had a lot to drink, he doesn't get rowdy or ugly or anything like that, but he'd get a little bit wobbly on his feet. Some . . . somebody killing him, that's off in left field. I mean, no offense to you gentlemen, but . . ."

Dixon didn't like my characterization of their theory. "All right," he interrupted. "Let me ask ya this: Since we said the homicide an' all, an' he was against the door in the manner that he was, if anybody left that apartment and for the back door to be locked, they had to go out the front door, didn't they?"

"I would think so."

"There's no way to lock that back door from the outside?"

"Not that I know of. I assume you checked that."

A nasty tone crept into his voice. "I think you saw me and Detective Rose tryin' that up there while you was standing in the kitchen. We was tryin' to . . ."

"There's no way to lock that back door that I know of."

"There's no way to lock it from the outside. There's no way ya can leave an' lock it?"

"Not that I know of."

Now we've got a locked door murder mystery, I thought. But Dixon seemed to like the theory.

"In other words," he continued, "for it to be locked it had to be locked from the *inside* and for the front door to be locked, he left outta the front door?"

"Right. Locking . . . I'm sure you checked the doors. Locking the front door, all you gotta do is push the handle in and turn it."

"Yeah, I checked that. But his body was across the front door."

"Yes, it was."

"Nobody could've left that way, could they?"

"I really have no idea. I don't think anybody did, but . . ." I wanted to end the charade right then and there.

Dixon pounced: "Ya don't think anybody did, but what?"

The moment passed.

"But you folks obviously think so," I finished.

"I 'obviously think so' what?"

He wanted to hear me say it for some reason. Anger crept into my voice. "That somebody murdered him and left. This is not just a . . . you're not just taking a, you know, crime scene statement. You've asked me to come down here. You're taking a formal statement. You've advised me of my rights."

"We do that to everybody."

I knew that was a bald-faced lie, but it seemed minor compared to my own. I didn't press the point. "Well, OK. I'm not familiar with the procedures down here."

"I explained that to you."

I felt light-headed and my stomach churned dangerously. "Listen, I'm not hostile toward anybody, but I feel sick. I feel like I'm going to throw up any minute. I haven't had anything to eat since 2:00. And I don't know whether I'm coming or going right now. Have you ever walked into a room where you saw your best friend lying like that?"

"No, I've never seen my best friend . . . I've walked into a room where there have been bodies."

"I'm sure you have."

Davis interrupted. "Anything else, Inspector?" he asked.

"No, that's all I can think of, Chief."

Davis turned off the tape recorder. "Are you feeling all right, Jerry? If you're feeling sick or something, there's a bathroom right down . . ."

"No, I'm all right," I said. I squeezed my face in both hands.

"Why don't you go ahead and wait out there with Mrs. Bragan for a minute. We'll be finished here soon."

Dawson had left Darleen alone in the office. I slumped into a chair without speaking to her. Moments later I heard a detective out in the hall telling somebody that Chief Davis was on a conference call with the district attorney general. I glanced at my watch again. It was 11:30. I weighed in my mind the wisdom of insisting on a call to my attorney.

Just then Detective Dawson returned. "If you folks are ready to go, I'll be driving you home," he said. "But the Chief said he wanted you to give me your shirt and pants so we can check 'em out."

"You want me to give them to you here? What am I supposed to . . ."

"No, no. You can give them to me when you get home."

◆ ◆ ◆

Twenty minutes later I climbed the stairs to my bedroom. Another shock was waiting for me when I saw the suitcase lying on the bed: *six packs of cigarettes*. Now I knew why the detectives kept pressing me about getting the cigarettes at Denny's.

I changed clothes and put the bloodstained shirt and pants in a paper bag before giving them to Detective Dawson. As soon as the door closed behind him, I rushed into the kitchen and poured a tall shot of vodka over ice. I tossed it back, letting the fiery liquid warm my throat and stomach.

"Whew, I'm glad that's over!" Darleen said moments after we heard the sound of Dawson's car starting.

I turned and looked at her. "Did any of the detectives go upstairs?" I demanded.

"Yeah. They all trooped through the bedrooms and looked through the closets. Why? What's wrong?"

"Darleen, you don't know what's going on if you think *this* is over," I said. "It's just begun."

"But they let us go, and . . ."

"Get your coat. We're going for a ride."

MIDNIGHT INTERROGATION

"It's midnight. I'm tired and wanna go to bed," she whined.

I grabbed her shoulders and squeezed hard. "Just get your coat and come with me!" I whispered through clenched teeth.

I had the car started and the heater turned on when she climbed in. "What's the matter with you anyway? We need to get some sleep. Why can't we talk in . . ."

"Listen to me, Darleen, they could have bugged the house for all I know while we were gone. They let us go tonight because they're not worried about somebody like me taking off. What they're gonna do for the next couple of days is this: They're going to build an airtight case, and then they'll be back with a warrant for my arrest. You can bet your sweet life I'm their prime suspect. *Numero uno!*"

"They can't prove a thing," she scoffed.

"You've been watching too much TV. For crying out loud, Darleen, why didn't you tell me you'd packed my cigarettes in the suitcase?"

"Cigarettes? What are you talking about?"

"I told them I was out of cigarettes and picked up a pack at Denny's. You can bet that every one of those cops saw those packs of cigarettes."

"What difference do those cigarettes make? Besides, you did get a pack from Denny's."

"A lot of good that will do me. I don't know that anybody saw me go in."

I glanced in the rearview mirror and saw a patrol car pull in behind us. He'd been waiting at the service station at the end of our street.

"Well, somebody's keeping an eye on me now," I said.

"What's going on?" Darleen asked, looking behind us.

"A cop is following us."

"Is he gonna stop us?" I could hear the alarm in her voice.

"I doubt it. I imagine Chief Davis has him keeping a close eye on our movements for tonight."

She turned back in her seat. "What for?"

I shrugged. "Who knows? Maybe he figures I'll lead him to something or other. He's already zeroed in on me as the suspect, so he's in no hurry. He can arrest me any time he wants." I laughed. "I'll bet he likes to fish."

"Fish? What on earth are you talking about?"

"Patience, Darleen. Patience. A good fisherman knows where the fish are. If you dangle the bait and wait long enough, it's just a question of time before a fish strikes, and then you reel 'em in at your leisure."

"What are you going to do?"

Weariness closed in on me. My bones ached. I glanced at my watch. It was 1:00 in the morning. "For now I'm gonna turn around here at Brainerd Road and go home."

The patrol car slowed and dropped back when I turned my signal light on. Only a few cars were on the highway, so I could see him easily, even though he followed us home at a distance. As I turned the corner toward our apartment, I saw him turn off his headlights and drive into the parking lot of the convenience store on the corner.

49

"They'll be back in the morning," I said.

Suddenly, I had to turn hard to the right to avoid colliding with another car roaring past me. I recognized Wilma, driving George's Pinto. Bishop Smartt was behind her. He stopped when I rolled down my window and waved at him.

"Is Wilma all right?" I asked.

"She's pretty upset right now," he admitted, "but we'll take care of her."

She was more than upset. I would learn later that the good bishop had told her of George's death. Before that fully registered, he also said he believed I'd murdered him to collect on the insurance policy.

◆ ◆ ◆

Darleen took a tranquilizer and went to bed. She didn't say anything more to me. An invisible wall had crept up between us as the evening had passed.

It would get a lot higher before it came crashing down on top of me.

5

No Genie in the Bottle

I STRUGGLED to focus on the alarm clock: 8:00. My head throbbed from a brutal headache. Another hangover. But I didn't understand why my heart was pounding. Darleen rolled onto her stomach and pulled the pillow over her head. She mumbled something.

"What did you say?"

She pushed the pillow away. "I said somebody's banging on the door."

The cobwebs took flight. Everything from the previous night tumbled head over heels into my consciousness. It wasn't just another bad dream. George really was dead. I scrambled out of bed and pulled the curtains back. Chief Davis' car was parked in front of my home.

Another thumping on the door, louder this time, followed by three quick jabs on the doorbell.

Darleen threw her pillow across the room. "Who *is* that?" she snapped.

"Lieutenant Columbo is back," I said as I hurriedly pulled on some clothes.

Darleen knew whom I was talking about. She grabbed the other pillow, digging her fingers deep into the fabric, and clutched it close to her chest. "Oh, dear!" she whispered. "I didn't think they'd bother us anymore."

"This isn't just another family argument where you can kiss and make up when you're over being mad," I muttered. "They believe George was murdered, and they also think yours truly did it."

"What do you think Davis wants now?"

I shrugged. "Who knows?" I left the room before she said anything else.

Chief Davis was wearing the same tan trench coat he had had on Monday evening. He smiled amiably when I opened the door. "Good morning, Jerry. You look wore out. Did I wake you up?"

"Yes, I didn't get to bed until quite late."

He nodded. "I don't suppose you did." He peered over my shoulder. "Is Mrs. Bragan up yet?"

"No, she had a rough night, and I'm not gonna wake her up unless it's absolutely necessary."

He looked directly at me through crinkled eyes and let a long silence hang in the air before speaking again. I thought about a crocodile when he finally smiled and said, "Well, I don't suppose I need to talk to her now. Plenty of time for that later."

He started to turn away, then stopped. "Since you're already up and I'm here anyway, why don't we walk over to the office and talk some more. You don't mind talking to me some more about this murder do you, Jerry?"

"I don't mind talking to you, but I've already said I don't believe George was murdered," I said, closing the door behind me. Across the parking lot I noticed two men I didn't recognize going door to door. I knew they were detectives from the bulge under their coats.

51

"Yup, you surely did say that," Davis agreed as we walked across the grass toward my office. "But this whole thing is mighty peculiar to me, Jerry. I just don't understand how this thing could of happened the way you said it did."

I ignored his comment, unlocked the door, and stepped inside. The property manager hadn't replaced the broken glass in the sliding door, so a draft of cold air blew through the downstairs office. The pungent smell of blood and death hung over the place. I noticed the fingerprint powder scattered on the carpets. Otherwise, everything appeared to be just as I'd left it the night before—except for the bloodstains on the door, walls, and carpet. Those had turned dull brown.

Davis' voice brought me back to the present. "Do *you* understand it?"

Confused, I just looked at him. "Understand what?"

"I said, I just don't understand how this thing could of happened the way you said it did."

"Chief, I didn't say how it happened. I wasn't here, so I don't know *how* it happened. I just told you what I saw when I arrived last night."

He sighed heavily as he wandered toward the middle of the room. "So you did," he admitted. For several minutes he studied the bloodstains on the carpet before speaking. He looked up at me and smiled through hooded eyes. "I guess I'll just have to figure this one out all by myself, won't I, Jerry?"

"I can't think of anything else to tell you, Chief."

He opened the door to leave, then turned. The Columbo routine was over. His face was hard, his voice threatening: "Jerry, you'll be sure and call me if you think of anything you'd like to talk about."

The door closed behind him before I could reply. My fingers trembled as I lit another cigarette and sucked in deeply to steady my nerves. I knew he'd have a warrant for my arrest the next time we met. I looked at the cigarette. *No reason to quit now,* I thought. My ankles were sunk deep in quicksand. My life was over for all practical purposes, and I felt powerless to do anything about it.

I wandered from room to room, picking up little pieces of paper that detectives had placed on furniture or dropped on the floor to mark items they wanted photographed, fingerprinted, or seized for evidence. George's pocket tape recorder was missing from his desk, along with all the tapes he'd used for dictation. Also the trash cans were empty in both offices. Each one had been full the day before. I couldn't remember what had been thrown away.

Nothing else appeared to be missing, so I sat down behind my desk and studied the office. The chairs were in disarray. Both the top of my desk and the contents within it were scattered about from a hasty and clumsy search. A heavy silence permeated the room.

What had happened here?

What was I supposed to do?

Why had this happened?

52

NO GENIE IN THE BOTTLE

I didn't have any answers.

◆ ◆ ◆

The days slowly turned into weeks without any further contact from the police department. But I knew they were busy. Shortly before Christmas I received a telephone call from a policeman who had worked for me part-time a year earlier. He didn't waste time with preliminaries: "I probably shouldn't even be talking to you. I'd get fired if they ever found out. But you need to know it's just a matter of time before Davis charges you with murder."

"I didn't have anything to do with George's death, and they don't have any evidence to connect me with it," I insisted stubbornly.

A derisive laugh burst over the line. "Jerry, you better wake up and smell the coffee. Those people don't need any *evidence*. I'm telling you, they'll make up any evidence they need, and you can be sure it will be solid enough for a jury to convict."

"How can they get the D.A. to go along with that?"

My question was answered with a snort of disgust. "Buddy, these people work together, *together*! Do you understand what I'm saying? Gary Gerbitz and Stan Lanzo will simply refine anything Davis offers."

"So how am I supposed to defend myself?"

"You can't. There isn't a lawyer in town who can help you if these people decide to take you down. The best thing for you to do is get outta Chattanooga and hope they don't want to bother coming after you."

"I'm not going anywhere—at least not until this is resolved one way or the other."

"It's your life," he muttered. "I can't talk to you anymore after today. But let me give you a good piece of free advice: When they bust you, don't talk to nobody in jail about your case. I mean *nobody*. Got that?"

"Sure, but what's that supposed to . . .?"

"Just remember what I told you," he interrupted. "Don't talk to *nobody*!"

I heard a click on the line. He was gone.

Frankly, I thought he was just a little melodramatic. I should have listened more closely to his warning. There was nothing more for me to do but wait for the ax to fall.

◆ ◆ ◆

Meanwhile, in order to escape the mounting pressure, Darleen and I drove home to Maine to spend Christmas with my family. I was acutely depressed, but I concealed it well and nobody knew how I felt. Tracie, a Christmas Eve baby who had just turned 7, flew up from Maryland the day after Christmas. She was particularly excited because she had never met her family on the Bragan/Rossignol side. We waited until she got there to open our Christmas presents, so she had a double Christmas and birthday. I almost forgot the sword of Damocles hanging over my own head as I watched her interacting with my mother and sisters and then later plowing through all the presents under the Christmas tree.

We went to church on Sabbath. Old friends greeted me with such warmth that I felt like I was really home again. As I sat there on those hard wooden benches and listened to the sermon, I couldn't help thinking of those happier days 15 years earlier when Edie and I had attended this church, discreetly holding hands or singing in the choir together. Those were simpler, less complicated times, I thought.

It was hard leaving my family behind when it was time to go.

✦ ✦ ✦

The weeks turned into months. My caseload continued to climb, so New Year's Day found me working another investigation in St. Louis. On January 11, I celebrated my 30th birthday. It was a lousy day. Darleen wasn't talking to me. She was furious because I'd hired her 22-year-old ex-husband, Ridge Beck, to work for me as an investigator-trainee.

"Why on earth would you want to hire that jerk?" she had screamed when I told her of my plans.

"He's not a jerk," I said. "He's a decent guy who's having a few financial problems right now. He says he wants the job, and I've hired him. Besides, you and I both know he deserved a lot better than what he got during your divorce. We owe him something."

I knew she wouldn't want to pursue that argument.

Ridge proved to be not only a first-rate investigator, but he also became a close and trusted friend. Years later he would write of our friendship and respective marriages to Darleen: "We shared an experience that only two men who have faced combat together would understand."

He has a real gift for understatement!

✦ ✦ ✦

Bill Alt called me when I returned to Chattanooga on February 1. "Dr. Beckman, the Medical Examiner, sent me a copy of his autopsy report on George. They also loaned me some autopsy photographs. They're pretty grim, but I thought you might want to take a look before I send the stuff back."

"What's the bottom line?" I asked.

He hesitated. "I think you'd better take a look for yourself."

I went to Bill's office later that afternoon. We met in the law library. "Do you want to look at the M.E.'s report first or review and sign this claim?" he asked. The claim he referred to was one he wanted to file with the insurance company that held the keyman policy on George and me.

I glanced at the paperwork. "The minute we file those papers, the D.A., screaming for an indictment, is gonna head for the grand jury room," I said.

Bill shook his head emphatically. "No way! If they had any kind of case against you, they'd have already gotten an indictment."

"They don't have any kind of evidence on which to base an indictment," I insisted. "But you can bet your bottom dollar they'll claim the insurance policy was the motive. At least they can try and hang a circumstantial evidence case on that alone."

"You've been playing detective too long," Bill grumbled. "In the first place, you're not the beneficiary of this policy; the proceeds go to the corporation. Second, you're in good financial shape. So where's the motive?" He waved his hand in dismissal again. "They don't have a case. Period! So sign these claims forms, and let's get this over with."

I signed the papers as though they were my death warrant. Bill took the forms back to his office while I turned my attention to the M.E.'s report. I scanned the papers, which described a variety of bruises and contusions found on George's body. Cause of death was given as a three-and-a-half-inch hairline fracture of the skull. His high blood alcohol content shocked me: .23! At that level he would have been barely conscious. I thought maybe Darleen had told me the truth after all. Almost everything I read was consistent with a bad fall down the stairs.

Almost.

I glanced across the conference table to where Darleen sat. She had picked up the autopsy photographs after Bill left the library. She was totally engrossed with what she was doing and didn't notice me watching her. She chewed on the left side of her lower lip as she studied each photograph before turning to the next one. Her eyes seemed unusually bright, almost seductive, and she kept running the tip of her tongue over her upper lip.

"Give those to me before Bill comes back!" I hissed.

"What difference does it make?" she whispered. "I want to see them too."

I reached over and grabbed the photographs. Bill hadn't exaggerated about the grim quality of the pictures. I'd seen autopsy pictures before, but it's different when the body belongs to somebody you know. I quickly shuffled through a dozen of them before something suddenly caught my attention. It was a clearly defined bruise across his throat. I remembered the nightstick I had seen lying beside his body that night. I had a hunch that stick and the bruise would be a perfect match.

"Did you see this?" I asked Darleen, holding the picture out for her.

She glanced at the picture, then turned away with that nervous giggle I'd come to recognize as a cue to deception. "What are you talking about? I don't see anything."

I shoved the picture closer to her face. "I'm talking about that bruise on his throat. It's just about the size of . . ."

I stopped when I heard Bill returning. "Did you find anything of interest in that stuff?" he asked.

I struggled to keep my voice steady and even. "No, I don't find anything that's inconsistent with him tripping and falling down the stairs," I said.

Bill wasn't listening. He was looking at the spot where my hand had been resting on the black laminated plastic table top. I followed his gaze. My hands were sweating profusely. The wet imprint of my hand was clearly visible on the table. I wiped it away with my handkerchief. "This stuff really takes the starch out of me," I muttered.

◆ ◆ ◆

I barely contained my anger until we were on the outskirts of Chattanooga and driving past the police department on Amnicola Highway.

"Well," Darleen asked, "are you going to tell me what you're so upset about?"

I jerked the wheel hard to the right and screeched to a stop. "Upset, Darleen?" I roared. "I'm not upset; I'm almost beside myself with rage. You did it, didn't you?"

"Did what?" she cried, cowering in the corner. "Please, don't hit me, Jerry!"

I realized my clenched fist was drawn back, poised to strike her. I'd never struck her before—or any woman, for that matter. Befuddled and embarrassed by such an unexpected display of emotion, I dropped my fist, then gripped the wheel with both hands for several seconds to regain my composure.

"Tell me again what happened between you and George that night," I rasped between clenched teeth.

"C'mon, Jerry, we can talk about it when we get home."

"No!" I shouted. "You tell me right now, or I swear I'll . . ."

"All right," she said in a placating voice. "Let me think for a minute."

"No, don't think!" I warned. "Just tell me what happened—and just for the novelty of it, why don't you tell me the truth for a change?"

"I told you I went upstairs to your office . . ."

"What for?"

"I think I cleaned your desk off, threw some stuff in the trash."

"You told me you were putting files on my desk."

"Maybe that too. . . . I don't remember," she whined.

"Where was George?"

"He was in his office. . . . Yeah, he was talking to somebody on the phone when I first went up."

"Who?"

"I dunno who it was!"

"Didn't you answer the phone?"

"No. George said he was expecting a call and he'd get it."

"What happened next?"

"Will you just quit with the interrogation? I told you the truth the first time. Why don't you believe me?"

I thought about the bruises described in the autopsy report, and then I noticed the four-inch clogs she was wearing. She had on the same shoes that night. I took a deep breath. "I'll tell you why I don't believe you, Darleen. First, just for openers, you've lied to me about anything and everything since the day I met you. Second, the evidence doesn't fit . . ."

"What evidence?"

"I don't believe George grabbed you. That's totally out of character for him, no matter how much he had to drink. And then there's all those bruises Dr. Beckman described in the autopsy report. I don't believe George got those in a fall down the stairs, especially that one on his neck. You either hit him in the throat with that nightstick or tried to choke him with it after he was down. I think you pushed him down the stairs, and at some point, either upstairs in my office or at the bottom of the stairs, you kicked him or stomped on him with those clogs you're wearing," I said, pointing at her shoes. "Isn't that just about what happened?"

I slumped down in the car seat. I'd finally said it, but, having done so, I felt totally empty, overcome with the absolute pointlessness of it. "George was a good man, Darleen. He didn't deserve that."

"What are you going to do now?" Darleen asked. She sat totally still, looking out the window, slowly drumming her fingers on her thigh.

"I honestly don't know," I admitted. "If you'll just tell me what happened, maybe Bill and I can figure out some way to handle it."

"All right! I'll tell you exactly what happened, but don't you tell me what a nice guy he was!" she shouted. "He did grab me, just like I told you, and I don't give a _____ whether you believe me or not. After I put the handcuffs on him, he started mumbling about having me arrested and how he was going to ruin you for good, run you out of business, and I . . ."

"He was drunk, Darleen. . . . That was booze talking too."

". . . got mad when he kicked at me. I kicked him back, hard as I could. I kicked him until he stopped. I wish I'd kicked his stupid face to death!" she whispered. Her face was chalk-white, and her body trembled. Fear? Anger? I couldn't tell.

"Why didn't you call me at that point?"

She shrugged her shoulders. "I wasn't thinking. . . . I just wanted him to leave. After he calmed down, I let him get up. He asked me to take the cuffs off, and then he got mad again when I said I wouldn't take them off until we got downstairs. He said he'd fix me. Then he tried to kick me again. . . . I . . . just . . ."

The tears began to flow, along with gasping sobs. "I lost it . . . pushed him as hard as I could. . . . He jumped three or four steps . . . lost his balance . . . fell straight down. . . . He hit his head so hard I thought it would split open. . . . Oh, Jerry!" she wailed, ". . . I didn't mean to kill him. . . . I didn't mean to do it. . . . I didn't mean it."

I sat frozen in place while she wept uncontrollably for several minutes. "What about the mark on his throat?" I asked when the tears subsided. "Did you hit him with the nightstick?"

"I think so," she whispered. "It was lying by my desk, and I grabbed it, . . . but I . . . I . . . just don't remember what happened after that. . . . It was like a big, black cloud took over my brain until I went home to get you."

My mind churned. Was she telling me the truth at last? Did she really not remember what she'd done? Temporary insanity? I doubted the police or the D.A. would accept that after three months of stonewalling. I put the car in gear and started to move, but Darleen grabbed my arm, and I stopped. "What are you going to do?"

"I don't know what to do," I admitted. "But I think we need to talk to Bill and get his advice. I can't think straight about this now."

"What happens after that?"

I tried to detach myself from my feelings so I could think objectively about the facts. "If you tell that story to the cops, and if they believe you—a big if, by the way—the D.A. will put pressure on you for a plea bargain:

second-degree murder, maybe voluntary manslaughter. Another option would be to plead not guilty because of temporary insanity."

"That would mean going to prison or a nut-house, wouldn't it?" A shudder rippled over her body as she spoke.

"Probably," I admitted. "If you'd just told me the truth in the first . . ."

"My, but we are testy and self-righteous today," she growled in a heavy, exaggerated Southern accent. I glanced at her and realized that her mood swing was in full gear, that whatever fear she'd felt was gone, and that she was back in control of herself again. "Just who do you think you're kidding?" she continued. "You knew that night what the score was. What's more, this is just as much *your* fault as mine. None of this would have happened if you'd fired him when I asked you to."

Dumbfounded, I just stared at her. "Darleen, don't you understand that even as we speak the cops are doing everything they can to nail me with his death? Do you think this is some kind of game? This is *murder*! Am I getting through to you at all?"

Stubbornly, she shook her head. "Nobody's going to believe you'd kill anybody. Besides, I've given you a perfect alibi."

My anger ran hot again: "You've given *me* an alibi?"

"Yes. Isn't that ironic?" she giggled.

I held my head in both hands, gripping tightly as though to get things back in balance. "This craziness has got to stop. I'm going to tell Bill what happened, and we'll let the chips fall where they may."

"You try that, and we'll just see who the police believe," she said coldly. "I swear to God I'll tell them that you killed George and that I was just being a dutiful wife, providing you with an alibi. Take a good look at me, Jerry—just who do you think they're gonna believe? Besides, they'd probably like to hear what I might say about some of your clients."

She hit a raw nerve—and knew it. Even if the police didn't believe her story—and I had no doubt they would—she'd also cause two former clients untold grief by revealing details about their private lives. But she really didn't need to threaten me. Paralyzed, I'd already caved in, surrendered to the inevitable, unable to act or think clearly in terms of self-preservation.

"Hosea just *thought* he had problems," I muttered.

"Who in the _____ is Hosea?" she snapped.

✦ ✦ ✦

Darleen went to bed early that night. I went to my office, opened a bottle of Scotch, and drank until I was numb.

"There's no genie in this bottle," I muttered when the bottle was empty.

But from that day on I worked myself into exhaustion during the day and rarely drew a completely sober breath at night.

6

"You're Under Arrest"

BY THE end of March, I knew my time was running out. After working for two weeks on a fraud investigation in Asheville, North Carolina, I decided to go to Washington, D.C., to visit my daughter for a couple of days. She was too young to have any conception of what was going on in my life, but I felt incredibly energized from spending time with her during that short period of time.

She blinked back the tears when I had to leave. "You'll come see me again real soon, Daddy?"

"Yes, real soon," I lied.

✦ ✦ ✦

The knock on the door came at 8:00 Tuesday morning, April 5, 1977.

"Tell 'em to go away!" Darleen grumbled from under her pillow.

The pounding got louder. I jumped out of bed and looked out the window. Two carloads of heavily armed detectives and uniformed police officers were outside my door.

"Open up! It's the police! We have a warrant for your arrest!" somebody shouted.

"I'll be right there!" I shouted back.

I turned to Darleen as I scrambled into some clothes. "Get dressed. Now! Call Bill Alt, and let him know I've been arrested."

The pounding was constant by the time I jerked the door open. Chief Davis, followed by several other officers, rushed through the door and pushed me back into the room. Davis grinned as he waved a piece of paper at me. "Jerry, what I've got here is a grand jury indictment charging both you and Mrs. Bragan with the first-degree murder of George N. Urice."

"May I see that?" I asked.

"Sure, you can," Davis chuckled. "Take your time and read it carefully."

I scanned the document dated Thursday, March 31, 1977. Bond had been set at $20,000 for each of us. At 10 percent for the bondsman, that meant $4,000 to get out of jail. I knew I could make that easily enough.

Davis turned to one of the detectives behind him. "Go upstairs and bring Mrs. Bragan down here now," he ordered. "And put the cuffs on Bragan."

"She's getting dressed. She'll be down in just a minute," I said. I was surprised when Dixon cuffed my hands in front of me, instead of behind my back.

Detective Terry Slaughter grinned. "I'll go get her," he said. He started up the stairs just as Darleen came down. She stumbled and nearly fell. I noticed that her face had turned pale. Like a trapped animal, she looked wildly around the room. In spite of everything, I felt sorry for her and protective toward her.

"I'll call Bill and arrange bail," I said. "Just don't say anything to these people until Bill has talked to you."

"That's enough chatter," Davis warned. "Take them in separate cars."

✦ ✦ ✦

"You're under arrest!" Those are powerful words. At some level I knew I was in shock. Irrelevant thoughts wandered through my mind as they put me in the squad car. I noticed it was a warm spring day. *"You're under arrest!"* It was my sister's birthday, but I'd forgotten to get her a card. *"You're under arrest!"* Too warm for the sweater I wore. No matter: *I'm under arrest! Arrest for murder!*

✦ ✦ ✦

I glanced up and saw Chief Davis looking at me in the mirror. He grinned from ear to ear. "Well, Jerry, do you still think we're stupid?"

That snapped me out of it.

"I never said you were stupid; just corrupt. There *is* a difference," I said.

He laughed as though I'd told a huge joke.

I wondered who had quoted me as saying anything about the Chattanooga police one way or the other. Although puzzled by his barbed question, I dismissed it then. I didn't think about it again until a surprise witness showed up months later at my trial.

✦ ✦ ✦

Reporters and photographers were already lined up and waiting when we arrived at police headquarters on Amnicola Highway. "What a nice reception!" I told Davis. "Did you arrange it just for my benefit?"

"Why thank you, Jerry. I'm glad you enjoy it," Davis said pleasantly. "We do like to keep the media informed."

Darleen didn't notice the news people until after she'd gotten out of the car. "How do you feel?" a reporter shouted. Darleen scowled and flashed the internationally recognized symbol of ill will in his direction—her middle finger.

I stepped closer to her. "Don't be stupid," I whispered. "What you just did will be on the TV news tonight."

"I don't care! What are they doing here anyway?"

"It's just a show the cops have arranged. Time to feed the animals in the zoo," I replied. "Don't let them get to you."

✦ ✦ ✦

Actually, it was much more than a show. It was part of what I'd come to recognize as the demonization ritual of prisoners in our society. The process by which our society transforms an ordinary citizen into a recognizable public criminal is an elaborate ritual. It usually begins with a massive display of governmental force that is dutifully recorded by television cameras. A person is declared the "suspect" of a crime. He's photographed in handcuffs and surrounded by heavily armed officers. His mug shot, usually unflattering and of poor quality, is given to the news media for publication. Although the "suspect" retains the constitutional "presumption of innocence," that's largely a technical fiction. Posting of bond is

60

required for release from jail, so guilt is presupposed.

✦ ✦ ✦

The local CBS affiliate made sure the demonization ritual continued for several weeks by prominently featuring film coverage of my arrest in their promo for each news broadcast. Only when I threatened a lawsuit did they pull the tape.

The interim period between arrest and trial is fertile ground for further demonization. Hungry for details, particularly in sensational cases, the news media keep the public informed with tidbits of heavily slanted information leaked by police and prosecutorial agencies. The defendant can feel the noose closing around his neck.

The trial itself is an elaborate ritual. At best, it is a heavily controlled fact-finding process that is designed to separate truth from fiction. At worst, given elected prosecutors who are motivated more by votes and headlines than anything connected with justice and the public fear of crime, a trial can be little more than a high-tech version of tarring and feathering.

I'd get the full treatment in the months ahead.

After we were slowly paraded before television cameras, the police took us to separate rooms at the police station for a search. Detective Booth spent a lot of time twisting and yanking on my shoes after I had taken them off.

"James Bond doesn't work for my agency. There aren't any explosives or secret compartments hidden in my shoes," I said.

Booth shrugged indifferently. "Just doing my job," he muttered as he went over my belt one inch at a time.

✦ ✦ ✦

An hour later we were transported to the city jail, booked, and then placed in the same cell. It was a "tank," a cell designed for eight or 10 prisoners, and the smell of vomit suggested it had been used as the drunk tank. Darleen sat beside me on a steel bunk. She was shaking all over, either from shock or the cold. Maybe both. I put my sweater around her shoulders.

"What happens now?" she whispered.

"They'll take us over to the Hamilton County Justice Building," I said. "That's the county jail. We'll be booked, photographed, and fingerprinted again. I'll call Bill from there, and we'll make arrangements for bond."

A fresh wave of shivering washed over her. "I'm scared. . . . Will it . . . take long to . . . to make bond?"

"It shouldn't, but I don't know," I admitted. "Just keep yourself together and don't make any statements to anybody. That means *anybody*: guards, cops, other inmates."

✦ ✦ ✦

We were separated again at the county jail. She was taken away to Silverdale, the county workhouse, where they kept female prisoners. I was placed in a holding cell next to the booking desk. After an hour of waiting, I stepped up to the bars.

"I need to call my lawyer!" I shouted at the jailer sitting at the booking desk.

61

He leaped up and rushed to where I stood. He waved a huge ring of brass keys near my face. "Listen, you _____ _____ ," he snarled. "Unless you want these keys rapped up side your _____ face, you'll sit down and shut your yap until I get ready for you. Do you understand what I'm telling you?"

Shocked, I stepped back from the bars and stared at the furious man. His purple face was contorted with rage. His eyes were bloodshot, and I could smell the odor of alcohol on his breath. I'd never experienced this kind of abuse from police officers, and I felt the anger bubbling up in my chest. Fortunately, I suddenly realized that I wasn't a middle-class professional person who was protected by status and laws anymore. I was a *prisoner*. He not only could assault me with impunity, he would be quite happy to do so at the slightest provocation. Moreover, I intuitively knew that nothing would happen to him if he did.

That was my first contact with what I came to see all too often in the years ahead in the dark underbelly of jails and prisons: institutionalized violence perpetrated on prisoners. Other jailers heard what their fellow officer said, but they turned away and pretended not to notice. Although I'd eventually discover later that the vast majority of jailers and prison correctional officers are honest, caring, decent people, I'd see too many of them turn their heads and pretend not to see when other officers violate the law or abuse their power over prisoners.

I choked back the bile of my anger and turned away from the bars. It's a good thing I did. I learned later that this particular jailer enjoyed a well-deserved reputation for brutality by savagely beating two kinds of prisoners: drunks, who couldn't physically defend themselves, and Blacks, who knew they would find no protection in the courts. Any complaint against his brutality was deflected by allegations that the victim had assaulted the officer. Although large in physical stature, he was a grotesque little man, consumed by a generalized, ill-defined hatred for people under his control and wearing a badge that freed him to ventilate his vicious spleen on helpless prisoners.

Eventually, another jailer took me out of the cell to a phone. My lawyer was in Atlanta, but one of his colleagues said a bondsman would be over to see me shortly. Back in my cell, I paced the floor, waiting and wondering why it was taking so long to make arrangements with a bondsman.

Two men showed up late that afternoon and identified themselves as bondsmen. They were polite but noncommittal when I asked them about posting the bond. That's when I first knew something was wrong, radically out of focus. Ordinarily, a $20,000 bond would be made quickly because it wasn't that big and I posed minimal risk. I suspected the district attorney's office had asked them to "slow walk" the paperwork. But why?

The answer to that question would show up five months later in the middle of my trial.

At 6:00 that night I was taken out of the holding cell again. An inmate trusty led me to the clothing room, where my free world clothes were taken and I was given an army fatigue shirt and pair of pants. An officer in central control handed me a piece of paper with a cell location on it. "Go to the elevator at the end of this hall. When you get upstairs, give this paper to the officer, and he'll show you where to go."

I wasn't making bond that day!

◆ ◆ ◆

The new Hamilton County Justice Building contained three criminal courtrooms, the district attorney's office, and the jail, which occupied the first, fifth, and sixth floors respectively. The jail held approximately 300 inmates and was state-of-the-art, with all movement controlled and monitored electronically from a bullet-proof control room. Ironically, I'd toured the facility a year earlier just before it opened. The jailer who had shown me and one of my employees around the building met me when I got off the elevator on the sixth floor.

"I never expected to see you in here!" he said as I handed him the piece of paper with my cell assignment.

"Life is full of surprises, but I don't plan to be here long," I replied.

He stood there for a moment, looking at the piece of paper, before speaking again. "You don't wanna be in this cell," he said. "I've got a cell where you'll be much more comfortable."

A comfortable cell? I thought. *Now there's an oxymoron for you!*

He led me halfway down the hall before stopping at a cell on the right side. Despite the modern technology, his keys reminded me of something out of the Dark Ages. They were huge! Each one was approximately six inches long, and he carried a dozen of them on a brass ring. After inserting a key into the heavy steel door and twisting hard, the door swung open. Once inside, however, there was a small trapgate with another sliding door made of bars. I stood in the trapgate while he locked the door behind me, and I waited for him to electronically open the inside door.

The cell was an eight-man tank. It measured 25 feet long and 15 feet wide. Half of the tank was an open area containing a steel shelf and bench for seating that faced a floor-to-ceiling wall of bars that ran along one wall directly across from where I stood in the trapgate. In one corner was a stainless steel commode and sink, plus a shower. A dingy bed sheet served as a shower curtain. I noticed what appeared to be a rolled up magazine jammed down in the sink, with one end wedged against the bowl and the other against the push-button on the hot water. A steady stream of hot water from the sink was running constantly over a large plastic jug.

The other half of the tank reminded me of caves dug into a cliff wall. Actually, there were two separate cell areas. Each cubicle contained two double-decked steel bunks for four men, plus another stainless steel commode and sink combination. Each bunk was covered with a three-inch thick mattress, encased in a tough plastic, that was as hard as the steel—along with an equally hard pillow. If a prisoner didn't bring his own blanket, sheets, or pillow case, he did without.

I did without.

Six inmates occupied the cell—four Whites and two Blacks. They looked at me curiously as I stepped through the door. Five of them were playing cards. The sixth man got up from where he was sitting with his back up against the wall.

"Hi, I'm Buggy," he said, sticking out his hand. It was a limp grip, and his hands were sweaty. But at least he was friendly. "Take this top bunk here," he suggested, pointing toward an empty bunk. "D'ya need anything? A cup of coffee? Cigarettes?"

"Yeah, I could use a cup of coffee."

Buggy was a dark, muscular, heavily tattooed six-footer in his late 20s who obviously worked out with weights. I had to laugh as I watched him lift the plastic jug out of the water and pour a cup of coffee. This was my first exposure to prison ingenuity.

"They only bring us coffee in the morning," he explained. "You can't have a stinger or any kind of a heater so . . ." he shrugged toward the makeshift heater. "We keep it hot the best way we can."

I put my pillow across the commode and sat down to drink the barely tepid coffee. It wasn't anything to write home about for taste, but it slowly cured the caffeine headache grinding behind my eyes, and I was glad to have it.

"I saw you on the news tonight," he said conversationally as he sat down on the bunk across from me. "That's really tough about your wife."

I nodded without comment.

"I know the bunch that busted you," he continued. "Been knowing them all my life. They just don't get no lower than them do, busting a man's wife like that." He sounded indignant. "They probably figure you for a squeeze play."

"Squeeze play? What do you mean?" I asked.

"You know, use your wife to force you to plea-bargain with 'em. Man, they'd bust your mamma if that'd help. That's how they get most guys to cop out, you know? Say, is it true what they said about you on TV, bein' a private eye an' all?"

"I don't have any idea what they said about me on TV, but I do own a private detective agency."

"I watch *The Rockford Files* on TV all the time. What kind of detective stuff do you do?"

I laughed. "Nothing quite as dramatic as Rockford. It's mostly boring stuff: some criminal defense work, some civil stuff, pre-trial preparation, that sort of thing."

"I wish I could afford to hire you," he said wistfully. "They got me on a two-bit truck theft, 'larceny after trust,' they call it. The guy loaned me his truck for a few days. I didn't get it back when he wanted it, so he called the law and tol' them I stole it." He shook his head woefully.

"That's tough," I said.

"Say, you'll probably be getting out on bond anytime. Would you give the guy a call for me?"

"Well, I don't know about . . ."

"It wouldn't take much of your time. I got this Don Poole for a lawyer, but he won't do anything for me."

I recognized the lawyer's name. I'd done a couple of minor investigations for his office. "Give me the guy's name, and I'll see what I can do."

"Rap, I'd really appreciate that," he said sincerely as he scribbled a name and number on a piece of paper. "All you gotta do is talk to him, tell him I was gonna bring his truck back and ask him if he'll drop the charges. If they make this stick, I'll end up convicted as an habitual criminal doin' a life sentence behind the walls."

The guard locked us into the cubicles after 10:00 at night. An overhead light burned throughout the night, so I didn't sleep much. At 7:00 in the morning, the doors were opened by the jailer, and we had to come out into the dayroom. The cubicles were then locked up until early evening.

◆ ◆ ◆

Buggy was beginning to make me nervous by Thursday. He asked too many pointed questions about my charges. It was always in casual conversation, but he kept coming back to the subject every time I changed it. Finally, I asked Bill Alt to check with some of his sources to find out if the Chattanooga Police Department employed a detective fitting his description.

"What's his name again?" Bill asked.

"He calls himself 'Buggy,' but I've heard one of the other prisoners call him Bill Corbin or Corbet—something like that. They all seem to know him, but they avoid any contact with him like he had a dose of plague. The whole thing just strikes me as odd, especially after that jailer changed my cell location the night I came in."

I didn't tell him what I suspected about the delay in getting a bond posted.

Bill laughed. "You worry too much. I'll see what I can find out, but we'll probably have you out of there by this evening or tomorrow morning."

I was released at noon on Friday, April 8. Ridge Beck had my car, so he picked me up at the jail and drove me to Bill Alt's office. Darleen had been released a few hours earlier. She met me in Bill's library. We were alone. It felt awkward. She looked wilted without makeup. Her hair was oily and hung down around her face like strings. I thought she had lost some weight.

"How are you?" I asked, struggling to make some normal conversation.

Her words poured out: "I didn't think I'd ever get out of there. It was like a concentration camp, and they deloused me with bug spray when they took me to Silverdale." She shuddered. "It was awful. And then on Wednesday they took me to Mr. Gerbitz' office . . ."

If she felt any concern for my well-being, she didn't show it. But my rising anger over that indifference short-circuited instantly when I heard what she said. "What are you talking about?"

"They threatened me with the electric chair, and . . ."

"Whoa! Start at the beginning."

"They took me to the district attorney's office. Mr. Gerbitz and some other prosecutor with an Italian name . . . Lanzo . . . something like that, was there, along with Chief Davis, and some other cop. They said that they didn't believe I had anything to do with George's death, that I was just covering up for you." She giggled nervously at the incongruity between what she knew to be true and what they believed.

"I already told Bill about it," she continued. "Anyway, they offered me a deal for probation if I'd tell them what happened and testify against you."

I shook my head in disgust. "What did you say?"

She grinned for the first time. "You would've been proud of me," she laughed. "I didn't say one word from the time I walked in until they took me back. Not, 'How are you?' 'Good morning.' Nothing! You should've seen the look on their faces! They were like happy, greedy little boys when I walked in. So friendly and solicitous about me. I guess they thought I was some kind of a dumb broad they could scare. When I refused to talk, they got mad. That's when they said they'd make sure I got the electric chair, right along with you."

She frowned. "Do you think they'll really ask for the death penalty?"

I slumped into a chair, exhausted from the emotional strain and lack of sleep for three days. "No, we wouldn't have been released on bond if they were planning anything like that. They've got a very weak case, so they tried bluffing you."

Bill heard my explanation as he walked into the room. "I agree," he said. "They took a wild shot in the dark, which suggests to me they must not have much of a case to begin with. But we'll talk about this next week. You both look beat. Go home and get some rest this weekend. We'll decide what to do next after you've had some rest. That will put things back in perspective."

I knew it would take a lot more than rest to put all this in any kind of rational perspective.

◆ ◆ ◆

After taking a long, hot bath, Darleen joined me in our living room at home. She sat on the sofa opposite me. "Jerry, I don't know what to say," she began hesitantly. "I wouldn't blame you if you never spoke to me again. But I never thought this would happen. . . . I wouldn't do anything to hurt you. . . . Give me some time. . . . Please don't abandon me. . . . Don't give up on me."

Her lips trembled, and I knew she was on the verge of tears. At some level I knew that anger and hostility were the only appropriate feelings I should have toward her. But what struck me with such force was an overpowering feeling of empathy. In spite of what she had done, first to George and then to me, I also knew that she had been emotionally abused throughout her life. That wasn't an excuse for what she had done, but it did help me understand her behavior. Moreover, I loved her, no matter how complicated that made my life.

"Please don't give up on me!"

I crossed the room, sat down, and wrapped my arms around her. Tears stung my eyes. "Our vows were for better or worse," I said. "It can't get much worse than this, but I love you and will never abandon you."

It would get a lot worse!

✦ ✦ ✦

In the weeks that followed, Darleen's mercurial mood swings alternated between euphoric optimism that "things will work out OK" and angry defiance toward me about what she had done and grief-stricken remorse. By July I had little patience with her protests of regret.

"I'm so sorry for everything that's happened," she told me one night after we had come home from meeting with our respective lawyers, Bill Alt and Dick Ruth.

"That doesn't do any good now."

She burst into tears. "Maybe I should just kill myself, and then you'd be happy and free of me."

I struggled to contain my anger. "Darleen, I'm weary of listening to your melodramatic threats to kill yourself. If that's what you want to do, help yourself. But I'm not going to worry about it anymore."

Her face turned white. She jumped to her feet. "I'll show you melo-drama!" she shouted as she ran up the stairs. "Listen to this!" She screamed moments later.

The sound of three quick gunshots brought me out of my chair running. I took the stairs three at a time. I yanked the bedroom door open and stopped short. Darleen was lying face-down across the bed. Her feet pointed toward the door. In her left hand she held a .38 caliber snub-nosed revolver that she had purchased a year previously.

I was frozen in place, and several seconds passed before I realized that she was still breathing. I walked to the bed. The pistol dropped to the floor with a heavy thud when I turned her over. Her eyes were closed, and she felt like a limp rag doll in my arms.

"Darleen, what have you done?" I whispered.

At that moment I realized there wasn't any blood.

She opened her eyes and glared at me.

I jumped back. "What did you do?" I demanded angrily.

She sat up and pointed at the floor directly over where I had been sitting in the living room.

"I just popped a few rounds into the floor," she said with a laugh.

I was too depressed to work up any real anger. "It's too bad you missed!"

67

7

Trial: Let's Make a Deal

IT WAS Tuesday, 9:00 a.m., September 6. Our trial was scheduled to begin at 9:15, and I was running 15 minutes late. I knew that my attorney, Bill Alt, would be upset. On the surface I looked perfectly normal as I parked my car in the lot next to the Hamilton County Justice Building. But appearing normal was easy for me—I'd had a lot of practice during the past five months. Deep inside I felt disconnected and indifferent to the events swirling around me.

"I wonder if there will be any reporters here," Darleen asked as we stepped out of the elevator.

"Are you planning to give interviews?"

Those were the first words we exchanged that morning.

◆ ◆ ◆

Bill Alt and Dick Ruth, Darleen's attorney, were already at the defense counsel's table when we entered the courtroom. Dick, one of Bill's partners, had been an assistant district attorney 10 years earlier. Although he was a short man with dark blond curly hair, he had the ruggedly handsome good looks of a Hollywood actor.

Bill looked relieved to see me. I wondered if he had feared that I might disappear at the last minute. At 39, his brown hair was rapidly thinning and receding from his forehead. I could tell he was feeling a lot of stress, because of the blotchy and flakey skin on his forehead.

"You're supposed to be here at 9:00 sharp!" he snapped.

I noticed that the seats behind the district attorney's counsel table were packed with detectives, George's friends and family members, and uniformed police officers. Except for Ridge Beck and a couple of reporters, row after row of seats behind me were empty. The jury would know which side represented the home team!

Moments later the hum of courtroom chatter subsided as Judge Joseph F. DiRisio entered the courtroom through a door just behind the elevated bench.

"All rise!"

DiRisio was a middle-aged man—in his early-50s. His shoulders were slightly stooped, and he walked with an odd shuffle. He reminded me of someone who had spent too many hours poring over law books. I figured that my chances of getting a fair trial from DiRisio were slim at best. "Whenever DiRisio presides at a trial, the state has an extra prosecutor," one lawyer had told me.

"Be seated," DiRisio said.

I turned and glanced toward the prosecutor's table to my left. District Attorney General Gary Gerbitz sat between his executive assistant, Stan Lanzo, and Steve Bevil, another prosecutor. The three prosecutors reminded me of young lions on the prowl: lean, physically fit, and politically ambitious men in their early- to mid-30s, and hungry for power. I'd heard that Gerbitz didn't get directly involved with trials unless he expected to win. He turned and looked directly at me. A faint sneer creased his mouth before he turned away. His wandering right eye gave him a distinctly sinister look.

Judge DiRisio's bench was built into the left front corner of the courtroom. When seated he faced the counsel table for the prosecution directly in front of him. The defense table was to the right of the prosecution. Between the counsel tables, approximately three feet in front, was a small podium. Movie and TV dramas usually show the lawyers walking back and forth in front of jurors, or leaning against the railing and staring at them while asking witnesses their most dramatic questions. That makes for great TV, but has little to do with reality. Very few judges actually permit that kind of contact with jurors. Instead, prosecutors and defense lawyers question witnesses and argue to the jury from a podium. They never approach witnesses or the jury without permission from the judge.

Witnesses sat in a chair directly in front of the defense counsel's table and to the left of the judge. The jury box was against the wall, directly to the right of the defense. The spectator section of the courtroom could seat 100 people comfortably. This area was separated from the rest of the court by a railing just behind the defense and prosecution tables. One row of reserved seating for reporters was directly behind the defense table.

Microphones were mounted on both counsel tables, the podium, the witness chair, and the judge's bench. The court stenographer, wearing headphones, sat in front of the courtroom between the judge and witness chair. Everything said on the record was tape-recorded. Later the tape would be transcribed by a typist for the official trial record.

Judge DiRisio cleared his throat: "Darleen Bragan and Jeris E. Bragan, are we ready to proceed for the state?"

Gerbitz stood up. "The state is ready, Your Honor."

DiRisio turned to the defense table: "Are we ready to proceed for the defendants?"

My attorney, Bill Alt, stood up: "Yes, Your Honor."

I took a deep breath. *Here goes nothing*, I thought.

People who get their ideas about courtroom trials from watching TV are usually quite disappointed with the real thing. There is little drama. The process tends to be both tedious and confusing for an inexperienced observer because of last-minute technical arguments, usually couched in the most arcane language, between the lawyers over procedure. Jury selection, reading of the indictment to the jury, and other pre-trial skirmishes between the lawyers took up the entire day.

Wednesday morning began with more of the same. Bill Alt wasn't satisfied with the prosecutor's responses to several of his discovery motions. He was particularly worried about one witness on the state's list: William Harold Torbett.

"There's something fishy about that one," Bill whispered as Stan Lanzo droned on about what he had previously disclosed to the defense. "Lanzo told us last July that this Torbett character had skipped bond and wasn't available for me to question. Then they gave us a bogus address for him and a lot of double-talk every time we asked them anything about him."

I shrugged. "So what's the big deal, if he's not available?"

"I dunno," Bill admitted. "Something about this doesn't feel right. They might have some kind of deal with that man."

"Now look who's worrying too much," I laughed. "Besides, what's that guy going to say? That I broke down and confessed in jail to a total stranger? Get serious! The jury will laugh them out of court if they try something that clumsy. That's too . . ."

Bill cut me off so he could hear Mr. Lanzo.

"They asked if there was any agreement with any of the witnesses," Lanzo told the judge, "and there is no agreement with any particular witnesses at this point."

"I guess that settles that issue," Bill whispered.

I agreed.

We both were wrong!

The jury was called into court, and Judge DiRisio addressed them: "Members of the jury, at this time the attorneys for the respective parties have an opportunity to make opening statements to you." He explained that opening statements were the lawyers' theories of the case and weren't to be considered as evidence. "Evidence comes forth from the witness stand from witnesses under oath. With that understanding, you may proceed for the state," he informed the prosecutors.

Mr. Lanzo stepped up to the podium. "I want to emphasize one thing," he said. "The State of Tennessee is not here to put these people in the penitentiary. It will be your job to determine if the state proves its case beyond a reasonable doubt. If you find that the state did prove its case, then I'm sorry to say it, but the responsibility is yours for punishment.

"This is going to be one of the toughest cases that the state has ever prosecuted," Lanzo continued, "because it is going to be one of the most complicated cases. There was a question about circumstantial evidence, and that's what the state's case is going to be: circumstantial evidence."

As I listened to Lanzo, I had to admit that he was very good with a jury. He began softly, got their attention by reminding them of their duty, and then admitted the state's case was based entirely on circumstantial evidence. He quickly followed that cautionary note with a long list of loosely connected facts and what he alleged were contradictions in my statement to police. He insisted that all of it put together proved our guilt beyond a reasonable doubt.

He put some real passion into his final comments: "This is one of the most vicious crimes the state will present to you. Vicious in the sense that it is a calculated, premeditated murder of a partner for profit and gain. The state's theory is, in fact the truth of this matter is, that these two defendants killed George Urice for a $200,000 insurance policy."

He turned abruptly and returned to his seat.

"At least we now know for sure what they think the motive was," Bill growled under his breath.

I resisted the temptation to say I told you so.

Dick Ruth addressed the jury next on behalf of Darleen. He was short and blunt: "The circumstantial evidence case that the state plans to present is filled with assumptions, conclusions, and innuendo."

Bill Alt spoke at length. His analysis of the state's case was a blistering commentary on police incompetence and tunnel vision. "This case was open and shut when the police walked in the door," Bill argued. "They knew whom they wanted. After that they only looked for those things that were relevant to their case." He also reminded the jury that the company was the beneficiary of the insurance policy, not I.

After a noon recess, Mr. Lanzo called his first witness for the state, Dewayne Pitts, the EMT I'd talked to at the scene. His testimony was honest and straightforward.

The district attorney's trial strategy quickly became obvious after a parade of police witnesses took the stand. I thought they showed some real talent for creative fiction in their testimony as one witness after another testified that I'd told them a variety of absurd and conflicting statements at the scene. Usually such evidence would be devastating to the defense, but the state's case quickly unraveled under Bill Alt's cross-examination. Police field notes are critically important in a trial because they reflect exactly what was said and done at the time. But three detectives were forced to admit they couldn't testify from their original field notes. One claimed he'd lost his in a car fire. Another insisted his had disappeared when he moved. A third detective couldn't account for his notes. Even more embarrassing, the detectives contradicted one another about what they claimed they over-heard me telling the other detectives.

Chief Davis and Inspector Dixon put the frosting on the perjury cake. Both men testified that at the end of their interview, after the tape recorder had been turned off, that I'd suddenly blurted out an unsolicited comment to the effect that I was "bluffing" them. Under cross-examination, each detective admitted he thought the statement was "significant" in terms of indicating my guilt, but they all admitted they didn't make any notes regarding the alleged comment at the time. Neither had they discussed it with the prosecution until the day the trial began. Chief Davis, however, apparently hadn't compared notes with Dixon before he testified. He claimed that he'd recently read the "bluffing" statement in Inspector Dixon's nonexistent notes.

By the end of the week hostility between defense counsel and the three prosecutors crackled in the air like static electricity. Bill was disgusted when the trial was adjourned for the weekend. "The state will have to offer the jury something better than this collection of clumsy, incompetent liars if they expect to get a conviction," he muttered.

I looked at the three prosecutors as they gathered up their papers and files. Instead of looking depressed and gloomy about the way the trial was going, they laughed and joked among themselves. Attorney General

Gerbitz smiled broadly as I stepped past him. "Have a nice weekend," he whispered. "It's gonna be your last one on the streets."

Fatigue rippled over me. I was too tired and disinterested to conjure up a snappy comeback. All I wanted to do was to get away from the courthouse and drink myself into an alcoholic blackout. Even though I knew a brutal hangover came later, it was less painful than living in the present.

◆ ◆ ◆

The bombshell came on September 12, Monday afternoon. Mr. Gerbitz stood up. "The state calls William Harold Torbett," he said. Once again he glanced toward me, and I caught a glimpse of that sneering grin.

"Looks like they found their wandering witness," Bill muttered under his breath as Torbett took the oath.

"Yeah, and I think I know why I got stuck in that jail for three days without bond," I muttered.

"What do you mean?" Bill asked.

"It's the oldest trick in the book," I whispered. "In order for a witness like Torbett to have any credibility with the jury, the D.A. has to make sure he can put the defendant and the witness against him in some scenario that will make sense to a jury."

People stared at me. "Do you really think they set you up in a cell with him so he could testify against you?"

"You bet your sweet life I do!"

"Now, Harold, I want you to speak up nice and loud so all these jurors can hear you. They want to hear your story," Gerbitz said. "Where do you live right now?"

"In the county jail."

"How long have you been in the county jail?"

"Since March twenty-first."

Gerbitz then went into a long series of questions about Torbett's prior criminal convictions and prison sentences for armed robbery, burglary, drug offenses, and car theft. Getting an unsavory witness to talk openly about his own criminal history is a standard tactic used by every prosecutor. It's a way of disarming a defense lawyer from successfully attacking the witness's credibility.

"Now, you have some cases pending against you right now," Gerbitz continued. "Do you recall what the offenses are that you're charged with right now?"

"One count of burglary and larceny, one receiving and concealing stolen drugs, and one breach of trust."

Gerbitz paused for dramatic effect: "A habitual criminal statute is attached to one of those cases, is that right?"

"Yes, sir."

I leaned toward Bill. "Now we hear about the deal for his testimony," I whispered.

Much to my surprise, however, nothing was said about any kind of plea bargain deal for his testimony. Instead, Gerbitz continued with a line of questions about Torbett's family in Chattanooga and his history of drug addiction before leading to the crux of his examination.

"Do you know the defendant, Jeris Bragan?" Gerbitz asked.

"Yes, sir."

"Is he in the courtroom?"

"Yes, sir."

"Point to him."

He pointed directly at me.

"Let the record reflect that he pointed to the defendant, Jeris Bragan," Gerbitz said.

Attorney General Gerbitz was in no hurry for Torbett to tell his story. As a professional matter, I had to admire his style. His examination of the witness was soft-spoken and detailed as he allowed tension to build. Torbett's demeanor was relaxed and confident. His answers were short and to the point. Whereas I expected him to claim I'd confessed the crime to him in jail, his testimony caught me totally by surprise.

Torbett testified that he'd known me for approximately 18 months. He said he knew me to be a private investigator. He described my car in detail. He said a man named Charles King was with him when he sold me some guns on one occasion. Then came the dramatic thrust. Torbett swore I'd visited him at the county jail on November 20, two days before George's death, and slipped $300 to him under his cell door.

Every word of it was a bald-faced lie! But how could I prove that I'd never met him before?

"What discussion did you have with the defendant? Now these people want to hear you," Gerbitz said, pointing toward the jury.

"He asked me if I would kill somebody for $2,500."

"He asked you *what*?" Gerbitz was a great actor. He sounded genuinely surprised by this dramatic revelation.

"If I would kill somebody for $2,500," Torbett said again.

I was in shock, but the questioning continued. Torbett went on to say that he'd met me later in the week.

"When you first met, what conversation took place? The jury wants to hear."

"I said, 'Well, I see you took care of old George.' "

"What did he say?"

"I guess it stunned him for a minute, but then he started running down the details about how he done it, sort of bragging about it. He said he was drinking in the office and they got in an argument, said that he hit him with a pair of brass knucks, and he stunned him. He said Urice had been prying into his business for a long time, was trying to bust him, said he was fixing to bust him on some charges that he was doing something illegal in his business."

"You said they got into a fight? Just tell us what happened?"

Torbett continued. "He said they got into an argument, and Urice tried to run and he fell, and he said he put some handcuffs on him before he got back up, and then he hit him again. He said he decided to go ahead and kill him himself."

74

"What else did he tell you?"

"He said then he left and he went home and packed his clothes, he was fixing to go . . . he was goin' to go to Washington. He said after he got his clothes packed, he started thinking that maybe they left some prints or something, something that would lead back to him on the murder, so he thought he'd go back. He took a lug wrench. He was goin' to make it look like a burglary, someone broke in on him. He said he broke the side door down, and he thought someone seen him, so he went in and took off his coat. Said he got some blood on his coat or shirt, and he decided to go ahead and call the police. He thought someone had seen him."

I glanced toward the jury. Their eyes were riveted on Torbett.

"Did you ever see Jeris Bragan after that?"

"Yes, sir."

"Where?"

"In jail. He was in the cell with me."

"What was he charged with?"

"This murder."

"Did you have a discussion with the defendant at that time?"

"Yes, sir."

"What was said?"

"Well, he wanted to know what I was up here for. He thought I was there telling on him about the murder, since they busted him for it."

Gerbitz asked Torbett if I had ever talked to him about the Chattanooga police.

"Yeah, he talked to me about Chief Davis and Terry Slaughter."

"What did he say to you about them?" Gerbitz asked in a soft voice.

"He said they were stupid."

I remembered what Chief Davis had asked me the day I was arrested: "Well, Jerry, do you still think we're stupid?"

I turned and looked at Davis sitting in the spectator section of the courtroom. He looked at me and smiled broadly. With a little cooperation from the D.A., he'd set me up with Torbett like a Christmas turkey, neatly wrapped and tied, and he knew that there wasn't a thing I could do about it.

"Now, you've got a lengthy criminal record. We've read it. And that is your record, is that correct?"

"Yes, sir, it's my record."

"Now, Mr. Torbett, you're charged with some offenses here in Hamilton County right now. Has anything been promised you in regard to those charges against you for your testimony today here in court?"

"No, sir."

"Have you been promised to be protected?"

"Yes, sir."

"Have you been promised any leniency in the form of probation or parole to reduce sentences?"

"No, sir."

"Do you feel like you have to come in this court and make this statement, or did you do it because you wanted to?"

"I done it 'cause I wanted to."

A faint smile played around Gerbitz' mouth as he turned away from the jury and spoke to defense counsel: "You may ask him," he said.

It seemed as though the temperature in the courtroom had dropped 40 degrees. Whenever I glanced at the jury, I'd catch various jurors looking at me as though I were an insect specimen. I couldn't blame them. Torbett was the state's most compelling, powerful witness. In less than an hour Torbett had tied up all the untidy loose ends and conflicts in the police testimony.

Bill Alt and Dick Ruth put Torbett through a pounding cross-examination for the remainder of the day. But they didn't lay a glove on him. He wasn't rattled. He kept his story simple, his answers short. He denied repeatedly that his testimony came in exchange for any kind of plea bargain deal with the state. I knew he had, but we couldn't prove it.

Bill was almost beside himself with anger. Totally aside from the district attorney's deception about Torbett's address and unavailability for trial, he was derisive about the convict's credibility with the jury. "They don't believe a word he said," Bill insisted.

But I'd been watching the jury. They *did* believe him. For all practical purposes I knew the trial was over.

My pessimism abated Tuesday morning when I learned that Ralph Janow, another prisoner in the jail, had contacted Dick Ruth after reading about Torbett's testimony in the morning paper. He claimed Torbett had admitted that his trial testimony was "a pack of lies."

Both lawyers were nervous about putting Janow in front of the jury. They were afraid the state was engineering another trick with Janow. "Suppose he gets on the stand and suddenly claims we offered him money or something for his testimony?" Bill argued. "After what Gerbitz pulled with Torbett, I believe they're capable of anything."

Despite the potential risk, we decided we had nothing to lose. The state rested, and we called Ralph Janow as our first witness. Dick Ruth, who as an assistant D.A. had prosecuted Janow 10 years earlier, conducted the direct examination.

Janow was a 36-year-old career criminal whose prior record was similar to Torbett's. He was a short, slender man, with a ruddy complexion and pockmarked face. His brief claim to fame had come two years earlier when he took a young police officer hostage and held him for several hours at gunpoint in the middle of the Walnut Street Bridge. The hostage wasn't just any policeman—he was the police chief's son. The police were not amused when Janow finally surrendered. From what I'd heard he had been nearly beaten to death. The official report said his injuries were sustained while resisting arrest.

After a brief series of questions relating to Janow's identity and prior record, Dick plunged in. "After you read the morning newspaper, did you cause a telephone call to be made?"

"Yes, sir."

"Did you ask to see me?"

"Yes, sir."

"All right, I want you to relate to the jury what you told me at noontime down in the jail."

Janow wasn't well educated or articulate, but he told his story with chilling clarity. Shortly after I was released on bond, Torbett had approached Janow and another convict, Sammy Miller. He told them he'd worked out a deal to get the habitual criminal indictment dismissed by agreeing to testify against me. But he needed at least one other person to substantiate his story. He said that the state would make the same deal with them. Janow, who had known Torbett for many years, and Miller refused to participate in the scheme. But Charles King agreed. Unfortunately, even with coaching, King was so confused about his story that the D.A. didn't dare risk using him as a witness.

"Did Mr. Torbett ever state whether he had met Mr. Bragan prior to meeting him in the jail?" Ruth asked.

"No, he made all that up. He said he didn't even know what kind of car the man had."

Steve Bevil, who had recently prosecuted Janow as a habitual criminal, demolished his credibility on cross-examination. He stuck to his story, but Bevil's jackhammer-style of questioning confused him several times. He forced Janow to admit that Torbett still was indicted as a habitual criminal and that he had risked his life in testifying because the other convicts hated a "snitch." By the time Janow stepped down from the stand, I wasn't sure whether he was telling the truth or simply trying to sabotage the state's case—as Bevil suggested—for personal reasons of his own.

During a recess Darleen decided not to testify.

Earlier that summer Stan Lanzo had informed Bill and Dick that my ex-employee, the photographer, had turned over copies of the pornographic pictures he had taken of him and Darleen in 1975. Lanzo had threatened to introduce the photographs at trial as a "character issue" if Darleen took the stand. The photographs were inadmissible because they were irrelevant, but Darleen was still afraid.

"The jury is going to think you have something to hide if you don't," I said.

"Won't the judge instruct them to ignore that?" she asked.

"Yes, he will," I admitted. "And the jurors will all solemnly nod their heads and agree to disregard the fact that you haven't testified in your own defense in a murder trial. But this is the South. They expect you to take the stand. If you don't, you can bet your life they'll still draw their own conclusions about why you didn't."

"Jerry, I can't do it," she said. "I'll never be able to keep my story straight when one of those prosecutors starts hammering away at me."

Nothing I said could change her mind.

I took the stand in my own defense Wednesday morning. During a lengthy direct examination from Bill, I answered questions regarding my own background and the events of November 22, 1976. I'd had enough prior experience as a witness in court to know I was doing poorly as a witness. In fact, I felt like a spectator at my own hanging. One juror would later say I was "cold, distant, and aloof."

Stan Lanzo conducted the cross-examination. I quickly discovered why lawyers had dubbed him "Gerbitz' attack dog." His tone was relentlessly caustic, hostile, and skeptical to anything I said. He quickly zeroed in on the keyman insurance policy.

"If you are found guilty [of murder] you cannot collect any of the $200,000. Is that correct?"

"I can't collect on that if I'm found innocent either."

"Mr. Bragan, just answer my question."

"You are asking me to agree with facts that are simply not correct."

"Mr. Bragan, if you are found guilty in this matter, you cannot collect the $200,000 on the life of Mr. George Urice. Is that correct?"

I knew I should control my anger, but I couldn't. "I cannot collect the money under *any* circumstances," I snapped. "I am *not* the beneficiary of that insurance claim."

Lanzo got increasingly belligerent. I lost track of his question when I noticed Darleen sitting at the table, playing with her nails. Anger surged up in my throat. I was sitting on that stand, getting my brains beat out under cross-examination because of her, and she was bored with the proceedings. I took a deep breath and focused my attention on the assistant district attorney. I asked Mr. Lanzo to rephrase his question.

"*I'll* ask you the questions and tell *you*. *You* don't tell *me!*" he snapped.

"Objection," Bill said. "I don't think we need any argument between counsel and the witness."

Judge DiRisio intervened. "All right, now. The counsel will ask the questions, and the witness will answer."

"I've forgotten what his question was, sir," I replied.

"You say you forgot the question? You forgot the question I just asked you?" Lanzo's voice bordered on shouting. "Did you forget the question I just asked?"

"Yes, I asked you to repeat it."

"You *did* forget it?"

"Your questions are getting a little confusing."

"You don't remember the question I just asked you?"

Halfway through his bullying cross-examination I suddenly realized his style was two-pronged. First, he hoped to anger me sufficiently that I'd lose my temper in front of the jury. Jurors expect defendants to be submissive and very emotional. Second, his questions were framed so that I was continually saying No to everything he asked. Psychologically, it's a brilliant ploy because jurors frequently begin thinking No *matter what he's asked, he denies everything!*

I spent most of the day on the stand. By the time I stepped down, I was emotionally and physically exhausted. Bill said I did well, but I knew better. I barely listened as our final witnesses took the stand.

Thursday morning, September 15, both sides rested their cases and presented final arguments to the jury. At 5:05 p.m., the jury retired to consider their verdict.

"How long will they be out?" Darleen asked Bill.

"It's hard to say. Generally, you can figure about an hour of deliberation for every day of testimony. We may not get a verdict until late tomorrow."

"They won't be out for very long," I said.

Bill didn't argue. I turned and looked out the window. Rain was pouring down outside.

Darleen put her arm around my waist and leaned against me. "What do you think they're gonna do?" she asked.

"I think they're going to convict me of first-degree murder. I don't know what they'll decide about you."

Two hours and 25 minutes later a bailiff informed us that the jury had reached a verdict. "We did our best," Bill said as we took our seats at the counsel table.

"I appreciate your help, Bill. You've been a good friend and a terrific lawyer. Nobody could have done any better," I replied.

Judge DiRisio cleared his throat. "All right, let the record reflect that all counsel and the defendants are present. We have an indication that the jury may have reached a verdict. I would remind the audience again that there will be no audience reaction to the verdict, whatever it is. Let the jury return."

At 7:46 p.m. the jurors filed into court. None were smiling. None would look our way.

DiRisio turned to the jury. "Members of the jury, do you have a foreman?"

Samuel West stood up. "Yes, sir."

"Mr. Foreman, has the jury reached a verdict in these cases?"

"Yes, sir. The jury has reached a verdict."

"All right, what is the verdict of the jury, sir?"

"The verdict for Jeris E. Bragan: guilty."

"Of what offense, sir?"

"First-degree murder."

"Of what?"

"First-degree murder," Mr. West said again.

"What punishment did you fix?"

"Ninety-nine years, sir."

I felt ice-cold. Off in the distance I could hear thunder crashing as my world came tumbling down.

Judge DiRisio continued with the judicial bookkeeping. "All right, what is your verdict as to Darleen Bragan?"

"The jury finds Darleen Bragan guilty of second-degree murder."

Darleen leaned toward me. "Nice going, hotshot!" she hissed.

"And what punishment did you fix?" DiRisio asked.

"The sentence the jury finds the minimum of 15 years, a maximum of 20 years."

After polling the jury, Judge Dirisio turned to me. "Jeris E. Bragan, would you please stand."

I struggled to my feet.

"Jeris E. Bragan, on the verdict of the jury finding you guilty of murder in the first degree and fixing punishment at 99 years, it is the judgment of the court that you are guilty of that offense. You are sentenced therefore to 99 years in the state penitentiary."

I looked at Darleen as she stood for sentencing. I felt nothing but pity for her. At one level I knew my feelings toward her were totally irrational. None of this would have happened if she had just told the truth in the first place. In spite of everything, I still loved her. I grieved for all that was so pointlessly lost.

◆ ◆ ◆

Moments later I was led into the jail by a bailiff. "Mr. Bragan, I'm so sorry," he said. "You'll probably get that conviction reversed because of Mr. Torbett, so don't give up hope."

I never saw the man again, but I'll never forget the human warmth and compassion he displayed.

Once again I changed into the jail uniform of cast-off army fatigues. Those clothes seemed appropriate as a symbol—I was cast off myself. At 8:45 p.m. a guard on the sixth floor put me in a solitary cell in the clinic. The solid steel door slammed shut, and I heard the lock click in place.

I walked across the cell toward the bars and strained to look out over the dark city skyline I knew so well. Torrential rain swept in over the city. Lightning ripped and slashed like a flaming saber through the night sky. Bone-rattling thunderclaps shook the building that held me, while a furious wind slapped sheets of water against the window. But the raging storm outside was small compared with the tumultuous storm swirling within me.

Another prisoner working as a trusty on the catwalk stopped by the bars and peered in, looking at me curiously as he slowly swept the concrete floor. "They've gotcha on a suicide watch, you know," he whispered furtively. Then he tapped the bars near my head. "The last dude in this cell was a 17-year-old kid. He hung hisself right from these bars."

"Why do they have me on a suicide watch?"

He shrugged. "Who knows why they do anything," he muttered. He looked at the gold watch and wedding band on my right hand. "You wanna sell 'em?" he asked, pointing at the jewelry. "I'll give 'ya 10 bucks or a couple nickel sacks of weed for 'em."

He walked away, whistling cheerfully when I declined his offer, and I was left alone again with my jumbled thoughts. I slipped to my knees and wept. "God, why would You let this happen!" I muttered bitterly. It was less of a question than an accusation toward myself. God hadn't done anything; I'd stepped into this noose on my own.

My melancholy introspection was interrupted an hour later when I heard a radio playing softly from a cell farther down the catwalk. The song sounded vaguely familiar, but I couldn't make out the words at first over the roar of thunder. Then the storm suddenly went silent, and the music seemed to fill my cell—"You'll Never Walk Alone."

The lyrics kept playing over and over in my mind, even after the music stopped. I could hear my Aunt Marion Harris singing that song as she used to do when I was a child attending an old country church in Norridgewock, Maine. I didn't realize it that night, but that encouraging song would come back to me again and again in the coming years as other storms rolled over me. I would not walk alone.

It was after midnight, and the storm had passed by the time I walked back to the bars and looked out over the city again.

"How did I ever get myself into a mess like this?" I muttered.

PART TWO

ROOTS

8

His Hand Is on the Wheel—1949

I WAS tired, but I couldn't sleep that first night in jail. I struggled to relax, to think clearly about the catastrophic tidal wave of events that had rolled over my life. What could I do now? It was too late for that. The hole I'd dug for myself was too deep. Each potential solution I thought about posed half a dozen compounding problems. I felt like a trapped rat in a maze.

A line from Nietzsche kept playing in my mind: "With the death of hope comes the hope for death."

I tried to pray again, but the words—choked off by an overwhelming conviction of guilt and failure—refused to come. "You're on your own, kid," I muttered to myself.

Unable to peer around the corner of my own self-destructive and dysfunctional thinking, I retreated into the past, back to Norridgewock, Maine, searching through the dusty relics of childhood memories. *For what?* I wondered. Comfort? Hope? Perhaps some clue that would help me make sense out of the nonsense that had taken over my life?

"Damned! Damned! Damned!" I was using that word a lot lately. But I *felt* damned—by God, by circumstances, by myself!

"Dear God, how did I ever get myself into a mess like this?" I muttered aloud. It wasn't much of a prayer, but it was the only thing resembling one that I'd uttered in many months. But the words just bounced off the ceiling. Then an unexpected thought filled my mind: *His hand is on the wheel.*

I remembered.

◆ ◆ ◆

It was a crisp fall day in 1949. I was nearly 4 years old. Leaves on the sugar maple trees were already turning to a lush collage of autumn colors in Corinna, a small woolen mill town located in central Maine. My father had taken me with him on this day as he serviced his route sales customers with a variety of patent medicines and household products offered by the Raleigh company.

My memory of the day was particularly vivid for two reasons. First, that was the last time I remember my 25-year-old father in good health. He was a slender six-footer with wavy blond hair and crinkly blue eyes. Although I didn't understand it at the time, he was already in the last stages of massive heart failure. A mild case of strep throat, left untreated when he was a boy of 12, had damaged the valves in his heart. Within days he would collapse, suffering the first in a long series of strokes and heart attacks that would kill him four years later.

There was a second reason I remembered the day so clearly: My father had promised to let me drive the old Dodge panel truck he used in his business.

"Well, son, are you ready for your first driving lesson?" he asked once we turned off the main highway onto an old dirt road.

I was too excited to speak, so I just nodded eagerly.

He chuckled and stopped at the side of the road. "OK, climb over here in my lap and we'll see what you can do." He took my hands and placed them on each side of the steering wheel under his own. My fingers barely closed around it.

"I'll just rest my hand on top of the wheel so my arm doesn't get tired while you're driving, OK?"

"Yup!"

"Are you ready?"

"Yup!"

I gripped the wheel with all my strength and looked straight ahead as the truck started to move, slowly at first and then picking up speed. I was almost beside myself with the thrill of holding that wheel in my hands and driving down the dusty dirt road. "Look, Daddy! I'm driving!" I shouted over the roar of the engine.

"You sure are, and you're doing just fine," he replied. "Keep your eye on the road. . . . Atta boy! . . . You're doing fine. . . . Turn slowly into that curve. . . . Yup. . . . Just like that. . . . No, not quite so hard. . . . Yeah! . . . Just like that!"

Dad kept up a steady patter of encouraging, reassuring words as the miles passed. I felt strong, confident, euphoric as he talked about how to drive in snow, in rain, in traffic. I don't remember any of his counsel. It didn't mean anything to me at the time. But his manifest confidence in my ability to drive this enormous truck—or so it seemed to me as a little boy—left a lasting impression on me.

And one more thing, something that didn't register with me at the time: *His hand never left the wheel!*

Days later he was rushed to the hospital.

My childhood portrait of God was painted in vivid colors with the raw material from my relationship with Dad before his illness. For years, whenever I thought about God, there was a picture in my mind: It was of me as a little boy, sitting in God's lap. His hand was on the wheel, and He was laughing merrily and singing at the top of His lungs as we drove down an old, dusty back road in Maine.

Like any old picture, however, its clarity blurred from my neglect and the passing of the years.

✦ ✦ ✦

My mother, a high school dropout who had married at 16, was a tall, beautiful woman with dark brown hair. She was barely out of her teens when she finally brought Dad home from the hospital. He looked ghastly. The once tall and handsome man seemed withered. His face was covered with a grizzled beard that exaggerated the dazed expression on his face. Looking at me without recognition, he struggled to say something. But the sounds were an incoherent babble. I ran away and hid in the dark security of the toolshed for several hours, wondering why God would allow my father to be so desperately sick.

HIS HAND IS ON THE WHEEL—1949

As the months slowly passed, I watched my mother patiently care for him: feeding and dressing him; constantly changing and washing the soiled bed sheets; talking to him and encouraging him to exercise. Over the doorframe in the kitchen she hung a pulley contraption with clothesline rope threaded through the pulley and two handles on each end of the rope. His lifeless left hand hung limply over one handle while he pulled on the other with his right hand. Up and down went his arms, hour after hour, while the squeaking of the pulley echoed through the house and he stared off into some dark and empty space of his own.

The man who once swept me up over his head, carrying me lightly on his shoulders, wasn't strong enough even to grip the pulley with his left hand. That pulley was an enigmatic riddle to me. I pulled on each end of the rope with both hands, wondering what there was about the exercise that was good for my father.

And then my mother encouraged him to walk again. He lost his balance easily and fell awkwardly to the floor the first time she let him walk without leaning on her arm. His eyes looked wild with fear, and his arms and legs drew up defensively into a fetal position. For a brief moment he reminded me of a peculiarly shaped turtle on its back with arms and legs sprawling aimlessly and helpless in the air.

I burst out laughing at the strange sight.

Mom helped him get up and stumble back to his chair. Then she took my hand and firmly led me into the kitchen and sat me on the table. I was more stunned than hurt when her right hand shot out and lightly smacked me in the face. It's the only time she ever slapped my face, and it got my undivided attention.

"Don't you *ever* laugh at your father again," she rasped through clenched teeth, "or anybody *else* who is humiliated."

I wasn't sure what "humiliated" meant, but I knew for certain it wasn't something to laugh about!

◆ ◆ ◆

Except for two words—"nanna" and "sleep"—Dad couldn't speak. I missed his laughter and boisterous singing, but the crippling illness put him on his back most of the time, and the laughter was gone. My mother had the impossible task of being both mother and father to me and my two sisters.

I never saw her cry or get angry during those days, although she must have done both when nobody else was around. In spite of our poverty, with three small children to raise and a severely disabled husband to care for, her courage and confidence seemed like something chiseled out of stone—sturdy and unshakable. Until I was much older, I never knew we were poor.

My father's life was a brutal study in frustration. Many times I saw him boil over in exasperation when he couldn't communicate something simple to my mother. "Nanna! Sleep!" he would scream, waving his right fist in the air, obviously confused about what he heard himself saying and what his mind was trying to speak. Other times, he simply slumped back in his chair, shaking his head from side to side like a great wounded animal, as though to clear his muddled thinking. And then silent tears of despair rolled down his gaunt face.

There is something terrifying about watching a strong man cry silently.

The bewilderment and frustration of his existence finally exploded in violence. After repeated attempts at communicating something to my mother, his fist shot out, striking her solidly on the left side of her face. Even as her head snapped back from the blow, she stepped in close and tried to control his rage. Twice again I heard the dull smack of hard knuckles smashing into soft skin as she became the focal point of everything empty and debilitating about his life. While blood flowed freely from her lacerated mouth, she continued speaking calmly: "Erwin! Erwin, listen to me! Calm down! Control yourself!"

In the center of this powerful emotional storm, the young woman remained calm and focused. She wasn't afraid of being hurt; her fear was that he would suffer another stroke. Moments later, slumped again in his chair, with his face twisted in confusion and the rage spent like air from a lanced balloon, the silent tears again ran down his face.

Both parents were oblivious to my presence. My mother quickly went about the business of repairing the damage to her face, washing away the blood and applying an ice pack to her swollen mouth, while discreetly watching my father carefully for any sign of injury to himself. A woman who wouldn't have tolerated physical violence from a man for one second under different circumstances, intuitively knew that my father wasn't responsible for his behavior, and she wasn't distracted by anger or bitterness.

The tears passed, and Dad sat quietly in his chair, looking curiously at his useless left hand, picking it up with his right and letting it drop back in his lap like something dead. He kept staring at his hand as though it was a foreign appendage, a strange and distasteful part of himself that he no longer recognized.

Later that day, my Uncle Merlin, Dad's older brother, came to the house. After one look at my mother's battered, swollen, and discolored face, he glared at my father and then exploded. "Jean, this man is dangerous, and it's time you faced that fact!" he roared. "Look at your face. Look at your face! He's going to accidentally kill you one of these days. Do you want your kids to see that? You're gonna have to put him in a state institution for his own good."

Her weary and bruised face tightened, suddenly flushed with deeply felt anger. As though shrugging off the fatigue she felt, she slowly stood up and faced my uncle. Her voice remained calm and steady, but the words shot out of her mouth like the steady fire of a jackhammer. "When I married Erwin, the vows were for 'better or worse.' And it can't get much worse than now," she said, looking at my father slumped in his chair, his face telegraphing great shame and defeat. "But I will *never* have my husband locked up in any institution as long as I can take care of him myself, and you will never bring that subject up again," she shouted. "I will *never* leave him or abandon him. Do you understand that? *Never!*" she hissed through bruised lips.

✦ ✦ ✦

After struggling for two years with the strain of caring for three small children and nursing my father back to some degree of health, Mother moved to Norridgewock, Maine, to live with her parents, Bernard and Lula Whary. They rented a 100-year-old rambling New England farmhouse near the Kennebec River on the north side of town. Despite its size, the house still bulged with children. In addition to my two sisters—Glenice, age 6, and Beverly, age 3, my mother's three younger brothers and one sister also lived there. Philip and Ronald were already in their late teens and would move out on their own soon. Russell and Jolene, although technically my aunt and uncle, were only slightly older than I and seemed more like an older brother and sister.

Norridgewock, named after the Norwock Indians, was little more than a village of 1,500 people in 1952. The community was a mixture of blue-collar Protestants and Catholics, spread over 20 square miles of heavily wooded rolling hills and valleys. Nobody locked their doors, day or night; crime was something that happened in faraway cities. The Alfond brothers employed 300 people in their shoe factory. Others worked at a small canning company. But most of the town's people earned a living farming or working for other shoe factories, woolen mills, or poultry processing plants scattered throughout larger towns nearby, such as Madison, Skowhegan, or Waterville.

Main Street, which ran east/west through the center of town, consisted of a half dozen stores: Pete Cote's grocery store, a hardware shop, a five- and ten-cent store that kept changing owners, the post office, and a volunteer fire department. Mr. Cote, known simply as Pete to both children and adults, was a cheerful, jovial Frenchmen who ran a tab at his grocery store for anybody in town who needed credit. Payment was weekly or monthly, whichever the customer preferred. No interest. No credit applications.

Despite its small size, the town supported two churches. The Congregationalists had a typically New England-style church building on Main Street near the center of town. (Catholics went to church in Skowhegan or Waterville.) My family attended the Seventh-day Adventist church on Upper Main Street.

Although the square wood building still had an outhouse for toilets and didn't offer much in terms of attractive architecture, Adventists were particularly proud of their church's history. Ellen and James White, two of the denomination's founders, had preached at this church several times in the late 1800s. A large antique desk-style pulpit dominated the front of the sanctuary. To the left of the pulpit lay an enormous Bible. The Whites had preached from this same Bible. Though the church had undergone radical structural change in recent years, the same pulpit still faced the same wooden pew benches used 100 years ago.

The Kennebec River ran through the north side of town, which was connected to the south side by a massive four-arched concrete bridge. Pulp wood clogged the river every spring as thousands of cords of wood floated downriver for processing by the Scott Paper Company in Waterville. I hated walking across that bridge when we moved to the south side of town. I thought it would collapse every time a large truck rumbled by. I never mentioned this fear to anyone, especially after my youngest sister, Beverly, began scampering up over the 30-feet high arches every day as we walked to school! Although my lack of courage embarrassed me, nothing she said could induce me to climb up on top of those arches.

Shortly after we got settled in with my grandparents, our family expanded again when Helen C. Franklin, the new teacher at the 10-grade Seventh-day Adventist school, came to stay with us while her husband served a tour of duty in the U.S. Air Force. There was more to their separation than the Air Force. Even though she got pregnant during one of their reconciliations in 1952, she made it clear to everybody that she wanted a divorce. More specifically she wanted a divorce on "biblical grounds" so she could remarry and continue her career as a church school teacher.

Helen had a vivid imagination, so the stories about her husband got more and more colorful with each passing month. At first, she claimed he was verbally abusive toward her. Later she added a touch of physical violence. Then she claimed he also was running around with other women. To that she added additional allegations that he was homosexual, into witchcraft and devil worship. She told these stories about him in a hushed, melodramatic whisper to anybody who would listen. I thought he must be a walking personification of evil incarnate! She left no stone unturned where trashing his name and reputation was concerned. Eventually, to escape her wrathful gossip after his discharge from the Air Force, he quit his job as an elementary school teacher and fled to Alaska, where he worked on a fishing boat for several years.

Years later I'd learn that most adults took what she said with a grain of salt. Nevertheless, she got her divorce on "biblical grounds" because a prominent minister confirmed her allegations. I suspect he did so to escape from her pestering himself!

Helen was obsessed with the demonic. From the beginning she insisted that our house was possessed by evil spirits. According to her, evil spirits occasionally rattled her bed and bumped into her in the hallways at night. All of us kids looked forward to the evening when she'd tell us spooky stories before we went to bed. It wasn't unusual for her to stop midsentence and stare fearfully at the window. Goose bumps would raise up on my arms.

"What's wrong?" somebody would ask. Everybody knew the answer before she spoke.

"Don't look now," she'd whisper in a trembling voice, "but there's a man's face in the window. It's Satan. Don't look! I'll just pray, and God will make him go away."

As quickly as she bowed her head and closed her eyes to pray, we kids would peek at the threatening window. Nothing was there, of course, but our own imaginations conjured up whatever was required to keep the entertaining game going.

In spite of this convoluted obsession, Helen was a dynamic, beautiful woman of 28 from Washington, D.C. She had a four-year college degree, which wasn't that common back then, so people in the church community were happy to have her teaching their children. At four feet eleven inches, however, she wasn't any taller than some of the older boys she taught in the eighth grade. Despite her short stature, her vivacious personality and enthusiasm for teaching children to appreciate everything from math to handmade crafts gave her enough command in the eight-grade classroom to control it.

The boys were particularly fond of Helen—especially my Uncle Russell—and she made little attempt to disguise her preference for him. I discovered just how far that preference went when I opened her bedroom door one morning and found them in bed together.

He was 14.

She was 28.

They both were naked.

"Get out of here you sneaky, little . . ."

Russell clapped his hand over her mouth and cut off her scream. "Get lost! And you keep your big mouth shut!" he hissed.

Two hours later Helen found me in the barn. Her voice was syrupy sweet. "I shouldn't have yelled at you like that," she said. "But you scared the daylights out of me . . . ah, you know, while Russell was giving me a back rub."

Back rub! I was young, not stupid!

She sat down beside me on a bale of hay and put her arm around my neck. For the first time something about her made me feel very uncomfortable.

"You probably shouldn't say anything to your grandmother about Russell giving me a back rub," she purred. "You know how Grammy is. She'd misunderstand, and I'd be in a lot of trouble. You wouldn't want to see me in a lot of trouble, would you?"

Actually, I didn't think Grammy would misunderstand any more than I did. But we were a typically closed-mouthed New England family that never discussed anything of importance together—certainly nothing spelled s-e-x. I promised not to say anything.

Years later I'd discover that everybody in the family either knew or suspected that Helen was carrying on a sexual relationship with Russell. But nobody said anything. In addition to our own inhibitions, I suspect we all were a little intimidated by Helen. Most people simply breathed a sigh of relief when Russell turned 18, followed her back to Washington in 1958, married her, and adopted her daughter, Darleen, who was 5 years old.

Nobody suspected then what a nightmare his life would become before it ended in pain and torment 19 years later.

◆ ◆ ◆

Something snapped inside my father's brain after his first stroke.

Whatever affection he felt for me before evaporated completely later. He'd fly into an incoherent rage whenever I was around him. Mystified by this transformation in his attitude toward me, I avoided him as much as possible. I was convinced he despised me by the time he died in March of 1954. My teacher called me out of the classroom at 11:00 one morning to give me the news about his death. I knew that boys weren't supposed to cry, so I didn't. I just nodded, stuffed my feelings way down deep inside, and went back to my classes for the rest of the day. In fact, I really didn't know how I felt about my father anymore.

Mother took my sisters and me to the funeral home to view his body a couple of days later. He looked odd because of the way his lips were so tightly pursed together. I stared at the handsome young man lying in a dark casket. I'd never seen him dressed up in a suit and tie before.

I didn't cry then either.

Mother sold our home in Corinna for $1,500 and bought her own home on Upper Maine Street a few months later for $2,500. Helen moved with us, along with her daughter, Darleen, born the year before. I felt relieved when Helen moved out a few months later. The house was more than 100 years old and quite run down, but it was ours. More importantly for me, it was just four houses away from our church.

That creaky old church was a special place to me. I loved the feel and the smell of the place. It was God's house, and I liked being close to it. I'm not sure where I got such strong feelings as a youngster for God, church, or religion. My family was religious in the sense that we all went to church every week, but there was little God-talk as such in our family. Nevertheless, God's loving Presence as a heavenly Father became an integral part of my life. It was an experiential thing that was every bit as real as anything else I could imagine. It was something beyond abstract theological doctrines; it was set in concrete.

Ironically, it was my Catholic stepfather who nurtured that faith even further.

✦ ✦ ✦

Shortly before Christmas in 1954, Mom went to Waterville to buy my sister Glenice a watch. She found one at Rossignol Jewelers, owned by Fred J. Rossignol, a 42-year-old bachelor. He recommended a Cinderella watch that came in a glass slipper.

He phoned Mom on Christmas Day, early in the afternoon. That was the first time I'd ever seen Mom really flustered about something. She was smiling when she hung the phone up. I knew from the conversation to whom she was talking.

"What did he want?" I asked.

"Oh, he says he just happened to be in town and wants to check on your sister's watch," she said.

I glanced out the window. A snowstorm had buried our town under three feet of snow. Nobody with any sense was outside, but he just "happened to be in town"?

Right!

HIS HAND IS ON THE WHEEL—1949

I liked Fred the first time I met him. He was a tall, muscular man with a swarthy complexion, who dressed in the most expensive suits I'd ever seen. His shirts even had French cuffs and cuff links, something I'd only seen in pictures. I was fascinated to discover that he traced his family back to Quebec, Canada, and that he spoke French fluently. "In fact," he said, "Rossignol actually means Nightingale in English." Since I'd never met anybody whose name meant something, I was quite impressed.

✦ ✦ ✦

Having Fred for a stepfather was a mixed bag. On the negative side, he understood little about raising children. His own father, a violent and abusive man, abandoned his family when Fred was young. Consequently, Fred tended toward a very harsh, authoritarian style of discipline. My sisters and I weren't allowed to speak at the dinner table; no display of feelings or discussion about them were permitted; and any sign of discontent with a decision he made was squashed on the spot.

Fred possessed a deeply rooted distrust and skepticism about other people. Nobody was allowed to come into our home unless he or my mother were there. That ban included everybody from other children to neighbors. It even extended to my Grandfather Whary! We were, to be quite frank about it, a typically dysfunctional family of the time: We never discussed anything within the family that was important.

As a teenager, I came to loathe my stepfather. Only much later in life was I able to balance out the good with the bad and realize that his less desirable characteristics reflected some of the wounds he had picked up in his own childhood.

On the plus side, it was clear from the beginning that Fred adored my mother. Although I heard some disapproving mutters from people in our church about Fred's being 13 years older than Mom, I knew the real source of concern was something more fundamental: He was Roman Catholic. Still she married him—the day after Christmas in 1956.

Fred was mystified by the disapproval some people felt over his marriage to Mom. A critically wounded hero of World War II, his philosophy was deeply rooted in a sense of honor. There were only two kinds of people in this world, according to him—the honorable and the dishonorable. Honorable people, he said, were faithful in marriage. They were patriotic, showed respect for other religions, took care of their parents, honored the elderly, and worked hard to support their family. They were faithful to God; generous with their money; despised racist, sexist attitudes and dirty jokes; and, of course, didn't curse. Dishonorable people violated these rules. Such people were not trustworthy, he said, and he wouldn't have anything to do with them.

I suppose Fred would have been considered a worldly man by conservative Adventist standards of the time. But he wouldn't tolerate profane or vulgar language in his presence from anybody. It wasn't a front that he put on. He never used such language himself. His frosty stare would freeze a person in mid-sentence if they swore or tried telling him a dirty joke. I saw him bodily throw a friend of his out of his store after the man made some belittling comments about his own wife and laughed while admitting he wasn't faithful to her.

"Get out of my store!" Fred roared, "and don't ever come back!"

"I want you to remember something," he said later after calming down. "A man who will betray and belittle his wife will betray anybody and anything. A man like that can't be trusted. Those jokes aren't funny," he continued. "They trivialize adultery, sneer at marriage, and treat women like a piece of raw meat. Don't tell jokes like that yourself, and you shouldn't permit other people to use such vulgar humor around you. If there's anything funny about that kind of garbage, an honorable man should give up laughing!"

Fred was a feminist long before the word ever became fashionable. He was a strong, powerful man, but he treated Mother with deference and respect. I never heard him raise his voice to my mother in the 30 years of their marriage. He didn't know anything about supposedly "women's work," so he wasn't too good to do the dishes, clean the house, or do the laundry. I thought their honeymoon would end eventually, but it never did. They always held hands while riding together in the car or walking together. He preferred that she sit close to him in the car.

"Marriages aren't made in heaven," he said. "A good marriage is carved out on earth by two people who *choose* to be thoughtful of one another. A wife is a gift from God, so an intelligent man *chooses* to be thoughtful where she's concerned. It's no more complicated than that."

Fred had never encountered Seventh-day Adventists before, so he knew virtually nothing of our faith or world view. Although he never said so, I think he judged all Adventists to be "dishonorable" people because of the way a few reacted to his relationship with my mother. But he wasn't an inflexible man. He changed his mind quickly when presented with new evidence.

Fresh evidence on the issue came in the form of a new pastor assigned to the Norridgewock church: Elder Arnold Swanson, a young, dynamic Swedish man who quickly earned a solid reputation with people in the community for his open warmth and genuine affection.

"That's a good man," Fred announced after Pastor Swanson visited with him a few times at the store. "He's what a real Christian man is supposed to be, so you pay attention to what he says," he told me. I did pay attention. I liked Elder Swanson too. For the first time I began thinking in terms of being a pastor myself someday.

◆ ◆ ◆

Even though Fred was a self-educated man who never went beyond the seventh grade in school, he loved talking about ideas and principles. Any issue was good fodder for an ethical discussion. Being a man, according to Fred, had nothing to do with aggression or being tough. "It doesn't take any brains to be a tough guy," he insisted. "A well-trained monkey with a club can beat up anybody! What makes a man worth something is his compassion for other people and his strength of character during tough times."

But there was another side to the coin that I had to learn. Between my

10th and 11th birthdays, I grew quickly. All of a sudden I towered head and shoulders over all my classmates. Worse yet, because of the sudden growth spurt, I was clumsy and awkward. As a group some of my classmates thought it was great sport to tackle me. The older boys in the eighth and ninth grades, however, began picking fights with me. One in particular made my life miserable.

I ran home crying one day with a bloody nose.

Fred listened to my story without comment until I finished. "It's time you learned how to defend yourself," he said.

"You mean, fight back?" I wanted no part of that!

"That's exactly what I mean," he said. "I'll get you a punching bag and some weights, and then I'll teach you how to fight."

"But I thought you said only fools go around fighting," I protested.

"I didn't say anything about fighting all the time. You'll have to deal with me if you ever take what I teach you and turn into a bully yourself," he warned. "On the other hand, you can't let bullies slap you around either. Life is full of bullies. You have to confront them head-on. Otherwise, they get to thinking they can do anything they want to everybody. You have to teach them a lesson."

For the first time I began to think I could deal with that ninth grader.

Fred got me a rhythm punching bag and weights, and then taught me how to use them. I managed to avoid conflict with the older boys throughout the winter. But then spring came, along with a fresh dose of verbal attacks first, followed by pokes and slaps.

"C'mon, ya big clumsy horse," he taunted one day after trapping me in the bathroom. He slapped me back and forth across the face. I tried to get away, but his friends blocked the exit. "What's the matter? Baby boy need his mommy?" he sneered.

Suddenly my right fist popped out, catching him squarely on the corner of his jaw. I could hear Fred's voice in the back of my mind: *"Hit the body, not the face. The object of the exercise is to teach 'em a lesson, not hurt 'em."* It was all over in a couple of minutes. My tormentor and his three friends were gagging on the floor.

"Don't you bother me anymore!" I shouted before running out the door. I ran across the back field toward home. Halfway there I got sick to my stomach and threw up. Later that night I told Fred what had happened.

"Did you enjoy punching them?" he asked.

"No, I got sick afterward."

"That's good," he said, nodding thoughtfully.

I didn't understand how that could be good.

"It's like this," he explained. "Life is tough. Sometimes, the choices you have to make aren't between a clearly defined good or bad, black or white—your choices are between worse and worser. There are times when you have to do things that you'd rather not do. It's about personal duty—you *have* to do it, regardless of how you feel or what you'd prefer. I didn't like what I had to do in combat during the war, for example. But I knew other men who really enjoyed all the killing. They hated to see the war end because they loved it!"

His voice took on a sharp edge. "Don't ever fight unless you have no other choice. But don't hesitate or back down when it's necessary."

◆ ◆ ◆

Fred never used religious jargon. He didn't believe that Christianity consisted of a set of abstract verbal formulations about reality. It was following Christ in everyday life: helping people in need, showing respect for others, and standing up against bigots or bullies of whatever kind.

One night he brought a calendar home and hung it in a prominent place in the kitchen. It showed two families walking down a street toward two churches on opposite sides of a town square. I was 10 years old at the time, but I've never forgotten the caption under the picture: "You go to your church, and I'll go to mine. But let's walk together."

Fred remained a devout Catholic throughout his life. He always went to mass early Sunday morning. I went with him many times, and he seemed to enjoy teaching me about Catholic rituals and beliefs. But Fred still jealously protected the integrity of my own religious tradition. To this day I feel comfortable in a Catholic church and enjoy worshiping there with my Catholic friends.

"It's a good thing for you to know what other people believe and what their faith means to them," he explained. But he was adamant about my remaining a "good Seven-day Advent"—that was the way he always pronounced it. "That's a good name," he once chuckled. "It means you're Adventist seven days a week!"

Even though he understood little about traditional Adventist Sabbath observance, he was convinced it was generally a good idea. Part of that observance meant I was supposed to be in church on Friday night for what we used to call M.V. (Missionary Volunteers) meeting, Sabbath morning for Sabbath school and church services, and Sabbath evening for vespers. Wednesday night prayer meeting was optional, but he made it clear he thought I should probably take advantage of the option.

"You be faithful and loyal to your church," he once commanded when I protested. "Besides," he added, "it would hurt your grandmum's feelings if you don't go regularly." For him that was the ultimate theological argument. To hurt my grandmother's feelings was equivalent to offending God because God cared about people's feelings. Honorable men were to take that into account and behave accordingly.

I never saw Fred pray except at mass, but no meal began at our home before one of my sisters or I said grace. "*God* doesn't need to be thanked, but *we* need to remember our blessings so *we* don't take them for granted," he explained. "Remember, everything that comes to you in life is a free gift from God."

He encouraged me to attend Adventist schools, and he was pleased when I told him I was going to major in theology at college. He even attended a week-long evangelistic series in which I did some of the preaching. I'm sure my inexperienced preaching left a good deal to be

96

desired, but he insisted that I did well. "I'm gonna tell the priest you preach better than he does," he said, clapping me on the back. "You're gonna be a great success!"

◆ ◆ ◆

Some success! *There's many a slip between the cup and the lip*, I thought years later as I sat on the steel bunk of my jail cell.

I glanced at my watch: 4:00 a.m. If only . . . If only I could go back and do it all over again! Life would be different if people had left Edie and me alone. That, too, was a pointless thought, I knew, because there's never any going back.

Never!

9

What Might Have Been—1959

EDIE!

It was May 1959, and spring had burst through the bitter cold of winter in Maine. Everything was turning green. The pungent smell of lilacs and apple blossoms wafted through the air as I planned a surprise for Edie. She was 15, a tall and slender freshman girl with a pixie haircut and dancing green eyes who had moved to Norridgewock a year earlier to board with my grandparents while attending Riverview Academy, a 10-grade church school.

Competition among the boys for her attention was keen. I was no exception, but I had some disadvantages. For one thing, I'd never had a real girlfriend before, and Edie was two years older than I. Plus she could turn me into a stammering, tongue-tied idiot with her smile and quick wit. But I had one important advantage over the rest of the guys: She loved classical piano music, and I played the piano. I spent hours dreaming up excuses to go to my grandparents' home when I knew Edie was there. Inevitably, I'd end up playing the piano for her, and I'd have her undivided attention for as long as I wanted to play.

May is the time for a teen tradition in Maine: May baskets. Throughout the month kids would get together and target various friends or teachers for a May basket. The "basket" itself was a box—usually a shoe box—to which we attached a handmade handle of some kind. We decorated the box with colorful strands of crepe paper, pooled our money, and then filled the box with penny candy. One person would hang the basket on the doorknob of the house where the recipient resided and then scream at the top of his or her lungs: "May basket on _____" while the rest of us would run for cover.

The object of the game was simple: The person receiving the basket had to chase and tag another person. The tagged person, in turn, joined whoever tagged him in chasing the rest of us in this teen game of hide-and-seek. In a small town like Norridgewock, when televisions were still rare and there were few other outlets for entertainment, this game usually lasted from late afternoon until well after dark because couples particularly enjoyed pairing off and disappearing for as long as possible. Only when every person in the group had been tagged could we come back to the house and pig out on the candy, hot dogs, and roasted corn!

It didn't take long to decorate the box and then round up the money and candy and 20 kids to hang the May basket on Edie. Several guys grumbled when I insisted on hanging the basket myself, but after some heated debate they gave up the argument when I stubbornly refused to budge. I crept up to my grandmother's door. Edie was standing in the kitchen, looking out the window. I didn't see her until I'd hung the basket over the doorknob. Her face lit up in a dazzling smile.

"May basket on Edie!" I shouted.

"This was your idea, wasn't it?" she laughed as she yanked the door open and grabbed the box.

The other kids scattered as I backed slowly away from the door. After looking at the box for a moment, Edie put it down abruptly and charged in my direction. I turned, stubbed my toe on the sidewalk, and sprawled over backward into the muddy driveway. Edie rushed over to me. "Are you all right?" she asked.

"I'm OK," I admitted.

"Good!" she laughed, tapping me on the shoulder. "I gotcha now!" She grabbed my hand in both of hers and helped me up.

"Was this your idea?" she asked as I brushed the mud off my pants.

"Yeah," I admitted. "I hope you don't mind."

"I love it!" She reached up and kissed me lightly on the cheek. "You're so sweet, but now you've gotta help me catch everybody."

I was 13 years old and branded for life with that kiss!

My family spent the summer months at our cottage on Great Pond Lake, so I didn't see Edie as much as I wanted to after school was out. We both planned to go to South Lancaster Academy near Boston the following year, so we had to work that summer in order to earn enough money to pay the cost. She worked in the shoe shop with my grandmother, and I got a job cleaning out the chicken houses for Arbor Acres of Maine. Whenever I could arrange it, I bummed a ride into Skowhegan during the noon lunch hour so I could eat with her in the park.

Teen romance took a lot more time back in the '50s. We wrote letters and notes, but weeks passed before I worked up enough nerve to hold her hand. Once I knew she liked to hold hands with me, I never wanted to let go. My mother tartly suggested once that Edie's hand wouldn't disappear if I let go of it. I was sure she was probably right, but I couldn't think of any good reason to test the theory!

When school started in the fall, Edie was a sophomore at Riverview and I was in the public school's eighth grade. She went home later than I did because she worked as a janitor at her school to help pay her tuition. After school I went across town in order to walk home with her when she finished working. It was only a mile from her school to my grandparents' house, but we could make that trip last two hours. The bridge over the Kennebec River was our favorite place to stop and talk for hours at a time.

◆ ◆ ◆

Things at home were less pleasant. Part of the tension reflected the normal family conflicts that always emerge as children approach young adulthood and begin breaking away from home. But it went beyond that with Fred, my stepfather. He had always been excessively heavy-handed and authoritarian with my sisters and me. We weren't allowed to speak while eating at the table. Our opinions, feelings, or wishes were not only inconsequential, any expression of them was a major source of irritation that he dealt with through ridicule and sarcasm.

My coping strategy, which was sullen withdrawal, infuriated him to the point of violence. As we youngsters approached our teen years, however, his compulsion to dominate and control us took on an increasingly abusive overtone.

"Get that sullen look off your face or I'll knock it off!"

"Quit that sulking or I'll give you something to sulk about."

"I'll have you locked up if you give me any lip!"

My sisters tried to adapt by being submissive and perfect in whatever they did. With Fred anything less than cheerful passivity brought on a stormy scene of shouting and accusations.

The smoldering undercurrents erupted one Monday night. It was December 7. Fred and my mother worked late at his store. Earlier in the day, as he always did, Fred told my sister Glenice that her boyfriend wasn't allowed in the house while he was gone. Glenice wasn't rebellious, so she obeyed. When her boyfriend stopped by, she went outside to talk to him in the driveway. It began snowing, so when Fred came home he saw the boy's tracks leaving the driveway.

"I thought I told you not to have anybody in the house while I was gone!" he shouted.

"I didn't have anybody here," Glenice insisted.

Fred turned livid. He grabbed Glenice's arm and jerked her toward the kitchen door. "Do you think you can lie to me and get away with it? I can see the footprints in the snow out there."

Glenice started to cry, both from fear and frustration, I suspect. "But he didn't come into the house. We just talked outside for a little . . ."

Fred was almost beside himself as he shook Glenice by the arm. It wasn't normal parental anger; he was enraged. His face was white, and he was breathing heavily. "You're turning into a liar, just like your brother. I'm not going to have a worthless tramp living in my house," he roared.

That's when my own temper exploded. "You leave her alone!" I shouted. "Try picking on somebody your own size."

I was leaning against the kitchen sink when Fred turned to me. "What did you say?" he asked softly.

"I said leave her alone."

He charged across the room, seized me by the throat, with both thumbs digging into my larynx.

"OK, wise guy," he hissed. "You think you're a big deal, huh?"

His voice was soft but filled with a fury I didn't understand. Instinctively I did exactly what he'd taught me to do in self-defense. I put my hands together and jerked them straight up, breaking his grip on my throat, and then shoved him away with all my strength. Stunned, he lost his balance and fell backward. I balled my fists, crouched into a boxer's stance and moved toward him as he bounded to his feet. Even though I was just 13, I stood six feet two inches and weighed 160 pounds. I had a longer reach than he did, and I knew I was faster. More importantly, I was scared and determined that he wasn't going to beat me up.

He charged me like a bull. My fist drew back, measuring him as he charged. At the same time I saw my mother out of the corner of my eye as she rushed into the room.

"Jerry, you stop it!" she shouted.

I dropped my fist just as Fred slammed against me and his fingers closed around my throat again. I felt his sharp nails digging, cutting into my neck. His eyes had narrowed to slits. I could smell the alcohol on his breath and realized he had been drinking.

Mother grabbed his wrist. "Stop it, Fred. You stop it right now!" she ordered.

His rage evaporated, and he stepped back. A heavy smoker, he struggled to get his breath back. "You're gonna go to reform school," he rasped. "I'll have you locked up until you're 21, and . . ."

My fists balled again. *In for a penny, in for a pound*, I thought angrily. But Mother pushed between us.

"You kids get upstairs to your rooms. Right now!" she ordered.

Fred and I glared at one another. "Jerry, I'll call the sheriff myself and have you locked up if you don't go upstairs right now!" Mother warned.

I looked at her and then Fred again. For the first time I realized how deeply the hostile currents ran in our family. I suspect that we all had a neurotic love/hate relationship going with one another. I went to my room. Although the overt hostility between Fred and me dissipated within a few weeks, things were never the same again. I was afraid that if I stayed in that house much longer one of us was going to kill the other sooner or later. Nearly 15 years would pass before the alienation that set in that night would be healed.

◆ ◆ ◆

The next day I talked to Edie about what had happened as we stood on the bridge.

"Let me see your neck," she said.

I pulled back my coat and showed her where Fred's thumbnails had cut my neck on both sides. Once that emotional boil was lanced, I ventilated for more than an hour. It was the first time I'd talked to anybody about the nutty stuff that went on within our family behind closed doors. She was shocked.

"I thought I was the only one who grew up in a violent family," she said when I finally ran out of steam.

"Is your father like that?" I asked.

She hesitated. "Worse!" She spit the word out. "Besides the physical violence, he does a lot worse! You wouldn't have anything to do with me if you knew what he did to me. Nobody would," she whispered. Her lips trembled, and tears streamed down her face.

I was as confused by her emotional distress as what she said. "What are you talking about? Nothing could change how I feel about you."

She laughed bitterly. "You wouldn't even be seen with me if you really knew about my life."

She shivered as the cold wind blew up from the river and swirled around the arches over the bridge. I wrapped my arms around her, trying to protect her from the wind below and whatever threatened her from within.

"Why don't you tell me what you're talking about? Then you'll see that it doesn't matter to me in the slightest," I insisted.

"Is that a fact?" she said sarcastically.

"Yes, that is a fact!"

She pulled away from me and leaned against the concrete railing of the bridge, staring intently into the murky water rushing below us. At that moment she was a stranger to me. I didn't understand either her anger or her fear.

"Whatever is bothering you, I promise you can trust me with it."

She took a deep, shuddering breath. "Well, listen to this, and then tell me that you still love me."

I listened as the words poured out. Her voice was flat, impersonal. For years her father had sexually abused her, beginning when she was 5 and continuing until three years ago when she had turned 12 and threatened to tell her mother if he didn't stop. She had pulled farther away from me as she talked. Now standing nearly three feet away, she turned and faced me squarely. Her face, framed by light from the bridge globe, was contorted with anger and bitterness.

"You see? I'm just a common . . . a common tramp. I hear that boys don't like used merchandise," she added bitterly.

Stunned at first, and then angry that she thought I'd think less of her because her father had raped her, I stood there speechless and looked at her. I didn't know what to say. Nobody had ever heard about child sexual abuse back then, or if they did, they certainly didn't talk about it. I couldn't imagine a father doing something like that to his own child. But even at that age I knew, if only intuitively, that it wasn't her fault.

"I knew what you would think. I can see it in your face," she cried.

"You do *not* know what I think!" I shouted. "What he did to you wasn't your fault. *It wasn't your fault!* And furthermore, you are *not* 'used merchandise,' as you put it."

That seemed to be a new thought for her. She didn't say anything for a moment. Then she turned away. "I should have done something to stop him," she said stubbornly.

"Like what?" I demanded in exasperation. "Kids can't do anything when parents act like nuts. Besides, didn't you do something when you were old enough to defend yourself?"

She continued as though she hadn't heard me. "I hate him," she whispered. "I'm never gonna stop hating him, and God won't forgive me for that. For years he told me he'd go to prison if I ever told on him. He made me feel guilty, as though I were responsible for what he did to me. Can you believe that? Now he wants me to forgive him. I can't. I won't!"

She began crying again. "My whole life is ruined!" she wept bitterly.

This was my first encounter with the complicated emotional and spiritual acid bath that a person who has been sexually abused as a child struggles with. I didn't know what to say or do, so I pulled her toward me and held her close. "I love you, Edie. God doesn't blame you for anything. It wasn't your fault." I said it over and over again as she cried against my shoulder. She seemed to accept that, but at some deeply rooted level I realized she didn't fully trust me any more than she did any male. I didn't know it then, but those wounds would nearly destroy her life in the decades to come before any healing would begin.

✦ ✦ ✦

Later that night I walked to the church for a special choir practice. My Grandmother Whary conducted the choir. She was already feeling testy because she was preparing a special Christmas program and several people, including Edie, hadn't shown up. "She says she isn't feeling good," Grandma explained. "Why don't you see if you can get her up here?"

Edie was sitting in the living room when I walked into the house. She barely looked up when I said hello. "Are you still talking to me?" she asked.

Confused, I shrugged. "I don't know what you're talking about."

"I figured you wouldn't want to talk to me anymore once you had time to think about what I told you today."

At first I felt angry because I thought she was full of sulky self-pity. But as I looked at her face, I realized she was both scared and serious. She kept glancing at me, studying me intently, then turning away whenever I looked at her. She really thought I'd change my mind about my feelings for her.

I sat down on the stool in front of her and took her hands in mine. She started to turn away. "No, look at me while I talk to you for a minute, Edie. I don't know what to say about that stuff with your father. When I think about what happened to you, it makes me so mad I'd shoot him on sight if I saw him today!"

She tried to pull away. "I should have . . ."

"There's nothing you could have or should have done," I interrupted. "I don't understand how a father could do something like that to his own daughter. What I *do* understand is that it wasn't your fault. You're *not* to blame. What happened doesn't change how I feel about you. If anything, it makes me love you more . . ."

"Because you feel sorry for me?" she asked. Her voice was biting. "I don't need . . ."

"No, I don't feel sorry for you. At least not in the way you're saying it. Didn't you feel sorry for me when I told you about that fight with Fred last night?"

She nodded.

"Does that mean you're condescending to me?"

"No, but . . ."

"No, but nothing!" I insisted. "We feel deeply for the people we love when they've been hurt. You've been hurt. I love you. And I want you to go steady with me from now on."

Tears welled up in her eyes again. "Play 'Moonlight Sonata' for me," she said.

"If I play that for you, will you go steady?"

She giggled. "I might think about it."

She stood behind me, resting her hands on my shoulders as the soft, haunting melody filled the room. I knew that song would come in handy

104

some day, so I played from memory as though my life hung in the balance!

"I'd love to go steady with you, Jerry Bragan!" she said when I finished.

I breathed a huge sigh of relief and, following the teen custom of the time, slipped my watch onto her wrist.

◆ ◆ ◆

Insofar as it was humanly possible, Fred and I maintained a brittle peace by avoiding contact with one another until, along with Edie, I left for South Lancaster Academy in the fall of 1960.

I felt free for the first time in many years as I unpacked my few belongings in Thayer Hall, an enormous mansion built by the Thayer railroad baron but now used as the boys' dorm. Edie lived in East Hall, the girls' dorm, located a mile away on the other side of campus.

SLA had been grafted into the sprawling campus of Atlantic Union College. The property itself, laid out over scores of acres on gently rolling hills, was dotted with a mixture of old colonial-style and Victorian era buildings. Evergreen trees were intermingled with hundreds of massive oak and maple trees that turned the landscape into a blaze of color by mid-October.

SLA students worked in the morning and went to classes in the afternoon, while AUC students attended classes in the morning and worked in the afternoon. Edie, like most students, worked at the book bindery to help pay her school bill. I worked with the grounds and maintenance crew.

Although my classmates elected me president of our freshmen class, I never felt as though I belonged there. I felt rootless and disconnected from both the other students and the faculty. I certainly knew that many of the teachers were caring, nurturing Christians who were deeply committed to their students. But after years of domination from Fred, I didn't respond well to what struck me as an oppressively controlling environment. I was particularly offended by a couple of faculty members who seemed to have an unhealthy preoccupation with whether or not Edie and I were doing anything more than holding hands. We weren't.

◆ ◆ ◆

Edie and I went home for the summer. She stayed with my grandparents and worked in the shoe factory again, while I went back to my summer job of shoveling chicken manure out of the four-story barns. She didn't like it when I told her that my Uncle Russell, who had married Helen Franklin, had invited me to stay with them in Takoma Park, Maryland, and attend Takoma Academy for my sophomore year. A few days later she handed me my watch. She was angry. "It's time for us to break up," she said.

"Why? What's . . ."

"Listen, can't you take a hint? Do I have to spell it out for you? I don't love you anymore, and I don't want to go steady with you. It's as simple as that."

Stunned, my feelings churning in turmoil before they turned numb, I turned and walked away. I had no idea that she believed I was trying to get away from her by going to TA or that her mother had warned her that she'd have a miserable year if she continued her relationship with me while we were going to different schools. Years later I'd learn that Edie hoped I'd reassure her of my love and try to talk her out of breaking up. That one simple misunderstanding set our lives on an entirely different trajectory, one that would alter our lives forever, bringing each of us more unnecessary pain and suffering than we could have imagined then.

I saw her once more after that. I came home for Christmas vacation in 1962. She was quite brittle when I told her I still loved her. "No you don't," she insisted. "Besides, I don't love you anymore." Unaware of her fear of abandonment or how deep her distrust for men went, I took what she said at face value and gave up.

Twenty-five years would pass before I saw her again.

◆ ◆ ◆

Living with Russell, who was more like an older brother than an uncle, gave me the freedom and independence I craved. I quickly found a job working as a janitor. It didn't pay much, but it was enough to cover the cost of my tuition and books. Helen was, to put it delicately, a little more problematic. She hit on me the first week I was there. I managed to sidestep her bizarre behavior by avoiding being alone with her in the upstairs apartment where she and Russell lived in her parents' home. Finally she gave up and left me alone.

Darleen, Helen's daughter whom Russell had adopted shortly after they got married, was 8 years old. She seemed happy to have me living with them. She was an unusually quiet and withdrawn girl. Except for Russell, I don't think she had much stability in her life. Helen spent hours telling her bizarre stories about her "demon possessed" father. Even if any of these stories had been true—and they weren't—it was a profoundly unhealthy thing to inflict on a child. Every childish prank Darleen pulled was met with dire warnings: "You're gonna turn out just like your father if you don't straighten out." I wondered then what kind of impact this nutty stuff would have on Darleen as an adult.

Fortunately, my own schedule kept me away from Helen most of the time. Besides working and going to school, I saved every extra dime from my job so I could take the bus into Washington, D.C., as often as possible. I couldn't get enough of wandering around that historical city.

I'd been fascinated with politics and Washington ever since I first listened to the Democratic convention on the radio in 1956. Although a lot of people from my religious tradition were convinced that the election of Senator Kennedy meant that the pope would take over the country, I rooted for him in his campaign against Richard Nixon.

Now I lived not far from the White House, the Capitol, and all the historical monuments strewn about the city. I went through the White House tour so many times that a Secret Service agent got suspicious and pulled me out of line one day to ask why I came through so often. He thought I was 18 or 20. It took several minutes to convince him I was just 15. Later I got a pass from Senator Muskie's office and sat for hours in the Senate gallery, totally engrossed as I listened to senators I'd seen on TV as

106

they debated.

✦ ✦ ✦

It was at Takoma Academy that I met Karen,* the girl I would marry. Her father was Czechoslovakian, and her mother's ancestry was French. Although a little shy, Karen got the best of both worlds in terms of intelligence and a classic Slavic beauty. She was slender, five foot three, and easily the smartest girl in school. I loved her thick black hair and the way her skin turned to a rich olive brown under the summer sun. Halfway through our sophomore year, we began walking home together every day after school. Her parents made me feel welcome in their home, which was nice because I spent more time there than anywhere else!

I loved TA and actively participated in a variety of school activities. That spring I ran for vice president of the Student Association. The principal told me I'd lost by a narrow margin to another sophomore. Later one of the teachers who counted the ballots told me I'd won but that the principal had changed the vote count and gave the election to my opponent. I was never sure that was true, much less why the teacher told me. The following year, however, my classmates elected me class president, and I planned to run for president of the SA that spring.

When the principal learned of my plans he called me into his office. He was blunt. "I'll come right to the point, Jerry," he said. "You're not going to run for president of the Student Association this spring."

I grew hot as I remembered what the teacher had told me the year before. "I certainly will run, and maybe the vote count won't get fixed this time," I said.

The color rushed to his face. He jumped forward in his chair and banged his fist on the desk. "I make that decision, and it's final. Do you understand me?"

Flustered by his anger, I looked at him for a long moment. "Why don't you want me to run?"

"Boy, I don't have to explain anything to a smart-mouth like you. You're not running. Period! Now get out of here!"

I never felt like I belonged at TA after that.

Russell and Helen moved to Collegedale, Tennessee, in 1962. For the next two years I rented my own apartment and lived alone while attending Takoma Academy. If school officials knew about it, they didn't say anything.

✦ ✦ ✦

President Kennedy was a powerful symbol for young people my age. Images of the New Frontier inspired our idealism and optimism about the future. Indeed, he convinced us that we could change the world for the better. I fell into a deep depression when he was assassinated on November 22. Three weeks later I dropped out of TA and went back to Maine to finish the last half of my senior year in the public high school. I had little interest in school, so I worked nights at a hospital in Skowhegan and skipped at lot of school. Besides the chance to save up money for college, that night job gave me a lot of time to think and reflect about what I wanted to do with my

---

* a pseudonym

life. Increasingly, I felt a call to the ministry.

Karen wasn't happy about my going back to Maine, but we kept our relationship going long-distance through letters. The depression I'd experienced after Kennedy's death diminished, and I was ready to return to Takoma Park in the spring of 1964 to attend Columbia Union College.

Karen's parents thought we were too serious about one another and gave us an ultimatum in October: Either you get married or break up. Youthful rebellion hadn't swept over our community in 1964, so we got married a few days after Christmas during the semester break.

My plan was to major in theology. I was fascinated by the subject. Within two years, however, I felt overwhelmed by a variety of theological questions and what struck me as a philosophy of majoring in minors. But the last straw for me came with some nontheological conflicts I had in rapid succession with three professors. One professor dropped a solid B I'd earned in literature to a D because I'd been tardy at several classes.

"That D doesn't say I was late for class. It says I don't know anything about American literature," I argued.

"Those are the rules," she said.

A second teacher threatened to have me expelled from the college when he learned that I attended the National Ballet in Washington.

"School policy forbids theater attendance, as you well know, and this is pagan dancing," he said primly.

"Have you ever seen a ballet?"

He would have been no less shocked had I asked him about his sexual habits. "Certainly not!"

A third refused to let me take a final examination until I took off my wedding band. "You know the rules. Take it off, or you're out of here."

"I'll take it off, and then I'm outta here," I snapped.

My sister Glenice arrived that day to visit with Karen and me. Hours later I was still fuming about the conflict over my wedding band as Glenice and I sat on the balcony of my apartment.

"Do you mind if I smoke?" she asked as she pulled a pack of cigarettes out of her pocket.

"Go ahead," I said. "And give me one of them."

"You don't smoke."

"I do now. Give me one."

I'd never smoked before, so I choked and coughed violently after inhaling the first time. But I kept at it until I quit gagging. It was a stubborn, stupid, self-destructive thing to do, but smoking that cigarette was my blunt declaration that I was finished forever with the church and God of my childhood.

Fortunately, God wasn't finished with me! It was a long, convoluted path that lasted for 10 years, but God eventually guided me right back to Him and the faith community of my childhood.

I dropped out of CUC and transferred to the University of Maryland. There I switched my major to psychology and criminology. The euphoria I felt about renouncing my denomination passed all too quickly. It was easy to thumb my nose at the church, but suddenly I felt profoundly rootless and restless. The pastoral goal I'd followed for years disappeared, along with all the meaning and purpose that gave my life direction. My idealism took a beating too as the years slowly passed and all of my political heroes were gunned down, one after the other in a wave of insane assassinations.

Now what?

10

Making of a Private Detective—1975

AFTER DROPPING out of the theology program at CUC, I worked at a variety of jobs in retail and industrial security before I accidentally stumbled into a job working as a private detective. Actually, I don't believe it was accidental at all. Today I think it was the serendipity of God's grace. More than anything else I've ever done professionally, I'd realize years later that working as a private investigator had taught me how to weigh and analyze evidence as I, from behind prison walls, investigated a variety of theological topics.

My daughter was born on a snowy Christmas Eve—in 1969. The doctor had assured me that I could be present in the delivery room, but we discovered on arrival at the hospital that fathers weren't allowed. Frustrated and fuming, I angrily paced back and forth in the waiting room.

"It's a girl," Karen whispered in a groggy voice when they wheeled her out of the delivery room.

I looked down at the baby, wrapped in a pink blanket and lying between her mother's legs. She opened her eyes when I bent over to kiss her on the forehead.

"Welcome to the world, Tracie," I said.

Our eyes met, and she seemed to be studying me. Then she gave a huge yawn and went back to sleep. That was the first time in my life that I experienced a profound sense of wonder.

Her birth—the joy of being her father—and my work as a private detective was the real beginning of my theological education.

Much to my surprise—and delight—I discovered that I made an excellent P.I. Not only was I good at all the required skills: skip-tracing, surveillance, interviewing, records research, and so forth—but clients in trouble seemed to have a lot of confidence in me. I rapidly worked my way up to a management position with several agencies before I realized that I could make more money with my own company.

That's when Jerry Kavanagh and I founded The Phoenix Corporation. Jerry was the first person I talked to when I was ready to set up my own agency. Given our limited financial resources, it was a huge gamble. But he was willing to take it. At age 32, Jerry, who wore horn-rimmed glasses, was a tall and lanky man from Newport, Rhode Island. A graduate of the Wharton School of Finance and Commerce, he'd attended Catholic University's law school for two years in Washington before dropping out.

Our paths crossed when I worked for a short time as the assistant director of security for the Parkview GEM International Corporation. Their security chief and I had uncovered a widespread internal theft ring that involved department managers and senior officials. Jerry, who was a department manager, gave us some valuable tips that led to several arrests. When Tom Huth published the story on the front page of the Washington *Post*, my boss and I got our walking papers the next day.

The Phoenix Corporation's logo was the mythical Egyptian phoenix bird emerging unscathed and reborn from the flames. Jerry liked the symbol because he'd felt like the proverbial downstream drifter ever since dropping out of law school. The symbol also spoke at some deeply rooted level to my spiritual life, but I didn't understand the language then.

We spent several weeks sloshing through the winter snow as we called on lawyers in suburban Virginia before the first cases came in. We were so broke that neither one of us could afford to repair the holes in the soles of our shoes. Our running joke whenever we called on a lawyer was for one of us to remind the other not to cross his legs in such a way that would show the holes in the soles. Initially, we spent most of our time on divorce cases, chasing wandering spouses. I didn't care much for that kind of tawdry work, but it paid the bills. We worked hard, got lucky a few times, and our reputation for uncovering important evidence spread quickly.

The most interesting case came early and proved to be the most challenging. It also gave me my first clue about how people can try to manipulate the criminal justice system and victimize innocent persons.

Our client, represented by one of Washington, D.C.'s most talented and colorful lawyers, was the senior air traffic controller at National Airport. Arlington County detectives had charged Joe with the rape of a teenage girl. Like most people, I have a visceral aversion to sex offenders, particularly those who assault children, so I wasn't thrilled when the lawyer asked us to investigate the charges.

"Personally, I don't care much for helping a rapist get off," I told Jerry after we left the lawyer's office.

My partner was more philosophical. "It's a living," he said.

At 42, Joe was already older than any other air traffic controller in the country. He had started a part-time photography business a few months earlier for something to do when he retired. The girl claimed that he'd gotten her drunk, raped her, and then took nude pictures of her. Despite a thorough search of Joe's home and studio, however, the police had not been able to find the photographs. The evidence was thin, but I knew people had been convicted of rape and sent to prison on substantially less evidence.

We began by interviewing the arresting detective. He didn't try to conceal his hostility toward Joe. "He's just a rich playboy who uses his money to molest kids by taking dirty pictures of them," the detective said.

Aside from the heated editorial commentary, however, his only evidence was the girl's complaint plus Joe's admission that he had shot some portraits of the girl.

"It looks like an open-and-shut case," Jerry admitted.

I wasn't so sure of that after meeting Joe and his wife, Jeanne. They were still wandering around in shock after the arrest. I expected angry denials from Joe. Instead, he was dazed and bewildered. He had difficulty focusing on my questions. Nothing about him fit the profile of a sex offender.

"I think we've got an innocent man on our hands," Jerry said later as we drove away.

"I agree. But why would that girl make those kinds of accusations if it weren't true?"

Jerry shrugged. "That's what they're paying us to find out, so we better get to work."

Joe's wife called us a few days later. She was so excited I couldn't understand her words at first. After several attempts, she gained control of her emotions. "Some guy with a foreign accent called me a few minutes ago," she said. "He says the charges against Joe would be dropped if we paid him $5,000."

I whistled. "So the whole thing is about blackmail," I said. "This is fantastic! We'll nail the buggers when the payoff is made, but . . ."

Jeanne started to cry. "I never thought of that."

"You don't have to cry now. We'll set up a sting with the police. It's just a question of catching . . ."

"But I got mad and told the guy I was gonna call the police," she said.

The wind went out of my sails. I knew her threat would probably scare off the caller.

"It won't do any good to call the police now," I admitted. "They'll assume you're making up a story to help Joe. Just to be on the safe side, in case the man does call back, I'll come over this afternoon and hook a tape recorder up to your phone."

Blackmail as a motive made sense, assuming Joe wasn't guilty. But our investigation of the family's background turned up nothing more than what appeared on the surface: They were a White, middle-class suburban family. There was no evidence to connect anybody in the family with the person who called Jeanne.

After three weeks of chasing leads down one blind alley after another, we put the girl under 24-hour surveillance.

"If that girl is 16, I'm a 12-year-old!" Jerry growled the first time we saw her. She was a tall, willowy brunette who bore a faint resemblance to Sophia Loren.

"She's 16 going on 26," I replied.

It looked like our surveillance was going to be a waste of time and money as we followed the girl back and forth to school for the first few days. But we hit the jackpot late one afternoon when we followed her from school to a squalid storefront photo studio in Alexandria, Virginia. It was little more than a front for prostitution, one of those sleazy places where women pose nude in a back room for men with rental cameras. Any additional "services" are negotiated between the model—using the term loosely—and the man.

"I'll bet you dollars to donuts she ain't the receptionist," Jerry said.

She wasn't.

After a two-week period of intense surveillance and additional investigation, we were able to prove conclusively that she worked as a nude model in the studio, which was owned by an older man from Iran. Her parents didn't know she was dating the man.

When confronted with the evidence we had uncovered, the arresting officer was not impressed. "Maybe your client isn't guilty of rape, but he's guilty of something," he stubbornly argued. I couldn't believe what I was hearing.

Fortunately for Joe, the trial judge thought differently after examining the evidence in a closed-door hearing. The charges against Joe were promptly dismissed. My work had made a difference in another person's life. Nothing I'd ever done in my life had ever given me such an overwhelming feeling of personal accomplishment.

Jerry laughed when I told him about it. "We're just a couple of frustrated priests," he said.

"You're Catholic; I'm Protestant," I reminded him.

"So you're a frustrated Protestant minister."

I knew he was right, but I couldn't admit it for some unfathomable reason.

✦ ✦ ✦

Although the case never generated any publicity, the story about our investigation spread among the lawyers. By summer of 1972 we were up to our ears in work and looking for a third partner. That's when Jim, a friend who used to work for the C.I.A., urged me to talk to William R. Raymond.

"Bill is just the man you need," Jim insisted. "He's had years of experience as a former detective with the New York City police department."

"Why did he leave the department?"

Jim hesitated. "It's a bit complicated," he admitted. "You remember hearing about that cop, Sirpico, who was investigating corruption on the N.Y.P.D.?"

"Sure."

"Well, Bill took over where Sirpico left off. A bunch of cops were busted as a result of his undercover work, along with some Mafia characters. When he testified before the Knapp Commission and the indictments came down, the mob put out a $200,000 contract on his life. The Feds changed his name and put him in the Federal Witness Protection program."

Jim's story was plausible, especially given his contacts in the ubiquitous intelligence community around Washington. I agreed to meet with his friend the next day.

Bill arrived at 2:00 sharp. He wore a conservative brown suit with faint pinstripes, a brown striped tie, and a white shirt with expensive gold cuff links in the French cuffs. At five feet ten inches, he was a muscular 170 pounds and stood ramrod straight. He looked more like a banker than an ex-cop. He was, in fact, an engaging man with a broad Irish smile and a heavy New York accent. His wry conversation was peppered with comical stories about wheeling and dealing with all the pimps, junkies, hookers, and a variety of other colorful scoundrels he dealt with during his 14-year career as one of New York's finest.

We needed help, so I was ready to hire him on the spot. "There's just one problem," I admitted. "How do we check you out? We can't do the usual background check on you because your identity has been changed."

"That's easy," he replied. "Just run my fingerprints through the Alexandria police department. I've got a clean record. But I need to be honest with you; there's one more thing you should know. I've got a murder indictment hanging over my head."

Jerry whistled. "I'm glad to hear it's nothing serious! Is that all?"

Bill hesitated. "No." He hesitated again, obviously considering how much to tell. "You might as well know it all."

Bill had testified before the Knapp Commission in the summer of 1971 after working undercover for nearly a year for them. Wearing a concealed body transmitter, he had developed evidence that led to the indictment of 48 fellow police officers. But his cooperation wasn't voluntary. A Knapp agent, Jack Armstrong, had caught him on tape making a deal with Xaviera Hollander, better known as the "Happy Hooker," to put her on the pad. In exchange for $1,500 a month in payoffs, Bill promised to alert her to any impending raids from the vice squad on her prostitution operation.

Other Knapp Commission agents put Bill's finances under a microscope. In addition to Bill's inability to explain the source of income spent on hundreds of thousands of dollars in stock transactions, the agents also discovered that he owned the Blue Plains Flying Corporation. Bill had organized the company as a business to teach fellow police officers how to fly. It didn't take the agents long to discover that all seven planes owned by the company had been paid for in cash.

"There's no easy way to say it," Bill said. "I was a crooked cop. I got sick of the system. Over the years I took hundreds of thousands of dollars in bribes and payoffs to fix cases."

"What does that have to do with murder?" Jerry asked.

"Shortly after I testified for the Knapp Commission and all the indictments came down, some other cops began looking for a way to take me out of the box. If they could nail me on something, all those indictments wouldn't be worth a bucket of warm spit. That's when John Justy, a detective in the Manhattan D.A.'s office, dug out an unsolved murder case from Christmas Eve of 1968. According to Justy's theory, I busted into the house of a pimp by the name of Jimmy Smith. I supposedly shot and killed Smith and a hooker named Sharon Stango who worked for him. A john named Gonzalez was wounded, but he survived. Somehow Justy got him to identify me as the shooter."

Jerry whistled louder this time. "What's their theory about the motive?"

"They're trying to prove I had Smith on the pad, and I'm supposed to have killed him because he wasn't paying off."

"So where does the case stand now?" I asked.

"I was tried this summer. It lasted eight weeks. In fact, the trial just got over a few weeks ago. F. Lee Bailey defended me. The jury was hung 10 to

2 for acquittal." He grimaced as though in pain. "The two women on the jury hated my guts after they heard about my past. They held out for conviction. The state's case was pretty weak to start with, so I don't think they're gonna re-try it again."

"Where are you at now?" I asked.

He seemed confused. "What do you mean?"

"I mean what's going on in your personal life? Is that life behind you now? Have you straightened your life out?"

He laughed but not from humor. "What you mean is How can anybody trust me now?"

"Yeah, that cuts right to the heart of the matter," I agreed.

He thought for a long time before speaking. "I've paid a pretty high price for what I did wrong. For whatever it's worth, I wish it had never happened. But that life is behind me."

Jerry and I kicked the issue around for the next two days. On the one hand, we both were convinced that Bill had straightened out his life and we needed the kind of expertise and experience Bill had. On the other hand, however, we realized there was some risk in bringing him into the agency if he ever started cutting corners.

"I think we should give him a try," I said.

Jerry disagreed. "You get second chances in the church, but we're not running a church," he argued. "This is the real world. If he ever screws up, it will be our heads on the chopping block."

I knew taking Bill on staff was a gamble, but I pushed the issue. Given Jim's strong recommendation, plus my pressure, Jerry finally agreed that we could give him a chance.

"If your fingerprints clear through the Alexandria police department, we've got a deal," I told Bill a few days later.

His fingerprints cleared.

◆ ◆ ◆

Jerry left the agency a few weeks before Bill and I picked up two unusual cases in October. One involved the owner of a construction company who had bailed two subcontractors out of bankruptcy. They showed their appreciation by embezzling approximately $250,000 from him. Our client knew how much money was missing, but he couldn't prove how it was being done. That was our job.

The second case involved a messy domestic conflict with an unusual twist. Our client, a senior official in the Nixon administration, was also a general in the Army reserves. He was up for promotion to his third star, but unexplainable delays kept putting it off. Recently separated from his wife, the general suspected that she was raising questions about his security status with his superiors in the Pentagon. Our task was to determine to whom she was talking and what was being said.

After reviewing the cases, we decided to have John Lindsey, an electronics whiz kid I'd met recently, place telephone taps (his own design, mind you) in the offices of the subcontractors and on the phone of the general's wife. The object of the exercise for the general was to find out whom his wife was talking to in the government and what she was saying. With the embezzlers, we wanted to determine how they were operating and with whom.

Although there was some ambiguity about the legality of such taps in the federal wiretapping statutes, I knew we were skating on thin ice. But our clients owned the premises and the telephones we tapped, so I thought we were at least arguably within the law.

Lindsey made a mistake in installing the tap on the general's wife. When he went back to install it a second time, she saw him and called the Arlington police. A uniformed officer stopped him a few blocks away. John promptly made a deal with the police and told them everything he knew or could imagine before they turned the matter over to the FBI in Alexandria. Bill had left the agency after an angry conflict with me a few days earlier, so he was happy to talk with the FBI when they questioned him.

In February of 1973, FBI Special Agent Bill Coopman and several other agents raided my office, looking for evidence that we were engaged in wiretapping. I was the only one arrested and tried. Although I argued that the tapped phones belonged to our clients and that they had a right to know what was being said on those phones, the U.S. Attorney argued for a very narrow interpretation of the law. He prevailed and the jury found me guilty of two felony counts of wiretapping. It's unlikely a similar case would even go to trial today, but the Watergate break-in and wiretapping scandal was underway, and I was sentenced to six months at Allenwood, a federal minimum security facility in Pennsylvania.

"Look on the bright side," my lawyer joked. "You need a vacation anyway, and you'll get to spend it with all the former White House employees."

I was not amused!

Neither was my wife, Karen. She was devastated when my appeal was denied. I thought it was ironically appropriate that I drove myself to Allenwood and began serving my sentence on September 13—Friday the thirteenth—1974.

Within days of my arrival I received a wedding announcement from Darleen, Russell's adopted daughter. It also contained a depressing letter in which she described what struck me as a rather bleak and forlorn existence. From reading between the lines I gathered she had gotten married primarily to get away from her mother, Helen. That didn't surprise me, but I thought the strategy might be hard on her young husband. She ended the letter by asking me to come and visit her soon. I wrote back, promising to do so.

Allenwood was built in the middle of 18,000 acres. The housing units, mounted across the top of a small hill, consisted of four dormitories. Each dorm had two wings that held 50 men and faced the administration building at the bottom of the hill. There were no walls or barbed wire to identify the facility or to keep inmates from escaping. We were free to walk anywhere on the property as long as we didn't cross clearly marked boundaries. The staff was courteous, and the environment was pleasant. But it wasn't the "country club" that many critics claimed at the time. There were no golf or tennis courts. Inmates wore green fatigues from Army surplus. All phone calls were monitored, and incoming or outgoing mail was censored.

Most of the prisoners were highly educated professional men who had been convicted for a variety of white collar crimes. Intermingled with judges, congressmen, doctors, police officers, White House officials, and a few Mafia dons who were getting ready for parole after serving longer sentences behind walled prisons was a colorful assortment of paperhangers, loan sharks, con artists, gamblers, and drug dealers.

If there was one single thing that surprised me about the people incarcerated at Allenwood it was the lack of embarrassment about their crimes. They talked easily—to the point of bragging—among themselves about the charges that brought them to prison. This was especially true of those convicted for forgery, embezzlement, counterfeiting, and drug dealing. The social pecking order was determined by who had bragging rights on the most money stolen! Of course nobody liked being there. A few were angry about the inconvenience, and they worried about how a felony conviction would affect their future. But there was no real guilt or shame—just irritation about having gotten caught.

Shortly after arriving at Allenwood, I discovered that the prison library had a large number of books on religion and theology. For several weeks I immersed myself in reading the work of theologians Paul Tillich, Richard and Rhinehold Niebuhr, Karl Barth, Martin Buber, and many others. I would read for a few hours, and then I'd walk for several miles, thinking about what I was reading. Ironically, I slowly found my way back to my own conservative spiritual roots by reading the works of these liberal to radical theologians.

One Tuesday night I went to the Yokefellows meeting after another prisoner told me that one of the free-world volunteers knew me. Yokefellows is an interdenominational Christian organization that targets prisoners for ministry. I was delighted to discover that the person who knew me was Pastor J. M. Clemons, husband of my former English teacher at South Lancaster Academy, Doris Clemons.

Pastor Clemons was a warm and nurturing man. "How are you?" he asked.

"Truthfully, I'm a little embarrassed for you to see me here."

He squeezed my shoulder. "Don't be," he urged. "Everything will work out for the good."

Before I could reply, he asked if I'd like to go to church with him the following week. "The superintendent has already approved it if you want to go."

I don't remember what Pastor Clemons preached about that week. What I do vividly remember, however, is being deeply touched as I listened to his congregation singing hymns I hadn't heard in nearly 10 years. I felt at home in that old country church in Pennsylvania. I felt the need for God's healing grace, for reconciliation with my faith community, for forgiveness for my anger and resentment toward those who I felt had driven me out of the church with their judgmental attitudes. Once again I felt God's call on my life to ministry.

I never saw Pastor Clemons again.

✦ ✦ ✦

In late January I was released after having served four and a half months. It was time to pick up the loose threads of my life. On the bus home I made a commitment to God to return to college and finish my degree in theology. God was in His heaven and all was well with my world at last.

Then the world caved in on top of me!

My wife picked me up at the Trailways bus station on New York Avenue in Washington, D.C. She acted like she was glad to see me, but I knew something was wrong as soon as I got in the car. She appeared jumpy, distracted. Over breakfast I'd glance up and find her staring at me.

"Is there something you want to talk about?" I asked.

Karen shook her head. "No, I guess it just feels strange having you home after being away for four months."

I accepted her explanation. Later that afternoon I went to see Dr. M. K. Eckenroth, chairman of the religion department at Columbia Union College.

"I guess you never expected to see me again," I said after talking to him about my life since dropping out of college in 1966.

He laughed. "Actually, I thought you'd be back sooner or later," he said. "I'm just glad it's sooner."

I breathed a sigh of relief. "Do you think there's a place in parish ministry for an ex-detective turned theologian?"

"I think you have a bright future, and I'd love to have you in our program."

I felt euphoric when I left Dr. Eckenroth's office. For the first time in many years my life seemed to be back in clear focus.

But the tension with Karen continued. It finally came to a head when she asked me to meet her at a restaurant after work. After several minutes of awkward conversation, she blurted it out: "I don't know any easy way to say this, but I'm in love with another man, and I want a separation. I'm moving out of our apartment until you can find a place of your own."

Stunned, I didn't know whether to laugh or cry. I knew the character she was talking about.

"He'll break your heart," I warned.

"He says he loves me."

✦ ✦ ✦

The emotional and spiritual high I'd felt after returning home dissipated quickly. My wife's boyfriend proved to be an intensely jealous and insecure man who continually interfered with visitation between my daughter and me. Even though Dr. Eckenroth urged me to continue with my plans to finish my degree at CUC, I slowly drifted into a deep depression. It happened so gradually that I didn't recognize any of the signs. When my Uncle Philip invited me to spend some time with him and his family in Tennessee, I quickly accepted.

On Wednesday, March 20, 1975, I packed my clothes and books into a

U-Haul trailer and left Takoma Park for an unknown future in Tennessee. I had promised Tracie the night before that I would stop by her nursery school to say goodbye. But when I reached the intersection of Flower and Carroll avenues, I knew I couldn't do it. I clenched my teeth and drove straight ahead. Philip was out of town when I arrived, so I drove over to Collegedale, Tennessee, to see Uncle Russell. Angie, his mother-in-law, told me he was having dinner at Darleen's house and gave me directions.

I arrived just as they were sitting down to dinner. Darleen heard my car in the driveway. She burst through the door, raced across the lawn, and jumped into my arms. I hadn't seen her since she was 10, so I barely recognized her at age 22. Her unbridled joy at seeing me was like a tonic. I suddenly felt energized, at home again as I joined the family for dinner.

Ridge Beck, Darleen's husband of seven months, played host to a borderline sullen family. Helen, who had grown quite overweight since I'd last seen her, talked nonstop, but her cheerfulness was forced and brittle. Russell, who was always a quiet man, rarely spoke. Darleen's contrived gaiety stood out in sharp contrast against the gloomy, oppressive atmosphere that hung over the dining room as we ate. I'd clearly walked into the middle of something unpleasant.

"Did I walk in on a family fight in progress?" I asked Russell when we talked privately after dinner.

"No. Angie called before you came over and said that you'd been up to see my brother," he said.

"So what?"

"Well, you might as well know that Helen says she had an affair with him while he lived with us a few years ago. She also says he sexually abused Darleen."

Philip had already told me about the accusations. Knowing Helen as I did, I didn't believe a word of it.

"Do you believe that's true?" I asked.

"No, I don't," he admitted. He shook his head as though that would clear the air. "Things have just been a mess, and I don't know how to straighten any of it out."

I didn't know what to say. I'd always thought of Russell as my big brother, the "strong, silent type" who had everything under control. Instead, I would soon learn, he suffered from bleeding ulcers and heart disease. He was addicted to liquid Talwin and trapped in the quicksand of a destructive marriage to a woman who was slowly sucking the life out of him.

"What are you going to do now?" he asked, changing the subject.

"I'm thinking about going to Southern Missionary College and finishing my degree in theology."

"Do you have a place to stay?"

"Not yet."

He put his arm around my shoulder. "Jerry, my home is your home. I've got an extra room you can use, so why don't you stay with me until you get back on your feet?"

◆ ◆ ◆

A few days after I moved in, Russell collapsed in the bathroom while getting ready for church. He called for help, but the door was locked. I forced it open when I heard him gagging. He had fallen into the tub fully clothed. His face was gray and dripping with cold sweat. Blood covered the walls from projectile vomiting.

For the next 45 days Darleen and I spent days and nights together in the hospital as Russell fought for life. Twice surgeons rushed him to the operating room to surgically repair the bleeding ulcers in his stomach and intestines.

Darleen moved home during the second week of the vigil at the hospital and announced that she was getting a divorce. According to her, Ridge was physically violent and abusive. She also claimed he was homosexual. I assumed it was true. It never occurred to me that she would lie about something like that.

I had a lot to learn!

PART THREE

INTO THE
WILDERNESS

11

Breaking Point

"NINETY-NINE Years for Him, 15-20 for Her." That's what the editorial page headlines chanted the next day. Prosecutors and police were praised for their diligence in prosecuting me.

The demonization process—my transformation from an ordinary person into a heinous criminal, deserving of scorn and punishment—was nearly complete with my conviction.

Appeals would be filed, of course, but very few appeals are successful. Conviction by a jury radically changed my status within the criminal justice system and in terms of public perception. I was no longer cloaked with the presumption of innocence. Even though I was, in fact, not guilty of murder in any degree, I was "legally guilty" because a jury said so. That simple fact carries great weight with appellate courts, which are loath to overturn a jury verdict. All subsequent appeals of my conviction would begin with the presumption of guilt. Protests of innocence were irrelevant. The only relevant issue for the higher courts to consider was whether or not prosecutors had secured my conviction by properly dotting all the *i*'s and crossing all the *t*'s.

The stripping away process began immediately. My clothes, wallet, money, belt, and identification were taken at the jail. I was given a green Army fatigue shirt and a matching pair of trousers. Neither had seen an iron in many years. A trusty gave me a blanket.

"They don't provide you with sheets, pillows, or pillow cases," he explained. "You'll have to get those from home."

It was a long night!

Ridge Beck brought me a pillow, plus sheets and a pillow case Friday morning. He also included a hand-held, battery operated Panasonic radio in my package. Somebody broke the antenna off before it was sent up to me on the sixth floor.

"You can't have an antenna because it might be used as a weapon," a guard said.

"You've gotta be kidding!"

The guard stared at me through steely eyes. "Do I look like I'm kidding?" he snapped.

He didn't. I tried a new approach.

"I'm not going to make any weapons," I insisted. "Besides, the radio isn't worth two cents without an antenna."

"I don't imagine you would," he said agreeably. "But others might. We have to treat everybody exactly the same here. No special privileges for anybody."

"The lowest common denominator for everybody," I muttered.

"I think you've got it figured out! Now listen up: the rules around here are real simple. Follow the rules, and things will be fine. Violate the rules, and your life is gonna get real hard. All inbound mail to you is opened and read before you get it. Stamps are cut off . . ."

"Why?"

"To make sure you don't try smuggling any drugs like acid in under the stamp," he replied. "All outbound mail from you is to be left open so it can be inspected. You can't have hardcover books—might conceal weapons. No after-shave—prisoners drink the stuff. No razors—prisoners cut one another. No metal ink pens—prisoners stab one another. We don't do laundry here, so you can either wash your stuff in the sink or send it out through your visitor for cleaning."

I felt a giant vice clamping shut around my neck as he continued with a growing list of things I couldn't do or have.

The radio was useless until a trusty brought me a two-foot piece of copper wire that night. It wasn't a gift; I had to pay him with two packs of cigarettes. I quickly learned that prisoners almost never do anything for one another unless they receive payment—usually in the form of drugs or cigarettes. Cash was contraband. I didn't appreciate having to fork over two packs of cigarettes for two cents' worth of wire, but at least I could listen to the radio.

Batteries were hard to obtain, however, so I didn't turn the radio on until Friday night. I tuned it to WSMC-FM, Southern Missionary College's frequency, and tried to relax as I listened to the sacred music broadcast from the college church. Only six days earlier, I'd sat in the back of that same church and listened to Pastor Jere Webb's preaching. My earliest possible parole date wouldn't come for 30 years: September 2007. By then, if I survived, I would be 61. I knew, deep in my heart, that it was quite unlikely that I would ever again set foot in a free-world church.

◆ ◆ ◆

The stripping away process continued a few days later when Bill Alt came to see me. I had to sign everything I owned over to him, including the stock in my company. Except for the stock, which he would hold until he collected on George's life insurance policy, everything else would be sold to pay my mounting legal bills. The judge refused to set an appeal bond for me. Bill said he would appeal that decision to the Tennessee Court of Criminal Appeals, but he never did.

"What difference does it make?" he asked when I pressed him on the issue. "You couldn't afford to make bond now if they set one."

Darleen was freed a week later on September 22, after posting a $20,000 bond, so I had to pay $2,000 to the bondsman, and that cleaned out my checking account. For the first time since I could remember, I didn't own anything, not even the shabby clothes I wore, and I didn't have a dime to my name.

Darleen came to visit me at the jail for the first time on Saturday. I thought she had lost weight, and she looked pale. Her mother, Helen, was with her. Helen reminded me of a nervous bird as she stood, wringing her hands and glancing about with jittery eyes, a few feet behind Darleen. I remembered something my mother had told me years earlier: "If you want

126

to know what your wife will be like in 20 years, take a long, hard look at her mother." That was a depressing thought! Both women were dressed in black. Black widows, I thought. To love either one was to take your life in your hands. Russell got off easy, I thought, by escaping in death.

Darleen picked up the phone on her side of the bulletproof glass. "I'm so sorry," she whispered.

"What for?"

"When I said 'Nice going, hotshot' at the end of the trial."

"You were upset."

"Yeah, but I didn't have any right to blame you. This isn't your fault. I should . . ."

"Watch what you say on these phones," I warned. "The guard sitting in that control booth behind you can hear every word you say."

She ignored my warning. "I don't care," she said stubbornly. "This is all my fault, and I'm not gonna let you suffer the consequences. Just give me a little time to get myself together, OK? I promise I'll get this straightened out."

I appreciated the sentiment, but I knew that was all it amounted to as a practical matter. After that our conversation was strained and inconsequential. I think we both felt relieved when the hour was up and she had to leave. In fact, despite many conflicting feelings, I realized I mostly felt relieved during those first few days in jail. I wasn't happy about my sentence, just relieved that the pressure was off. I didn't have to make any more decisions about what to do with my marriage or anything else connected with it.

I sobered up fast after the initial shock of conviction and imprisonment wore off. My body and mind hungered for a drink. For months I'd used alcohol to escape dealing with anything that made me uncomfortable. My current situation was just about as uncomfortable as I could imagine, but I had to confront it by standing on my own two legs—no matter how wobbly—without booze.

As my thinking cleared and the finality of my sentence began to dawn on me, I drifted into a deep depression. I couldn't eat anything. The jail food was bad enough to begin with, but it wasn't the quality of the food—I simply lost my appetite.

I went to the Saturday evening chapel program when I heard that Southern Missionary College's only Black professor, Dr. Lorenzo Grant, was going to preach. I'd never met him personally, but I'd seen him at the Collegedale church. In any event, like most of the other prisoners, I wanted to get out of my cell for a couple of hours.

Bill Hughes, who had published several instructional books for accordion music, led the song service as he played his accordion. He was a gifted musician. Within minutes he had the prisoners singing at the top of their lungs. But it was hard to hear Dr. Grant when he began preaching. He was a soft-spoken man, and prisoners routinely ignored preaching in order to catch up on their conversations with one another.

Suddenly, Grant's voice barked out like a drill sergeant: "Hey, you there

127

in the back doing all the talking! Yeah, you!" he thundered, pointing at a man in the back row. "If you've got something more important to talk about than I have, get up here and share it with everybody."

Everyone froze. Prisoners weren't accustomed to a preacher who got confrontational with them. A heavy, nervous silence hung in the air.

"Well, have you got something important to say?" Grant demanded.

"No, sir."

"Good! Keep quiet until I've finished."

Some resented Grant's blunt style, but most of the prisoners appreciated the courage it took to demand their respect.

With attention focused on the pulpit, Grant continued telling the story of Elijah's heroic confrontation with the priests of Baal on Mount Carmel. "It's hard to believe, but as soon as Queen Jezebel threatened him, this brave man took to his heels like a little, scared rabbit. He ran for days until he dropped. An angel found him hiding out, belly-aching and moaning: 'Life ain't fair! Oh, my, ain't it awful! I wish I'd never been born!' Does any of that sound familiar?" Grant asked.

A sprinkle of nervous laughter.

I knew exactly how Elijah felt!

"But do you know what the angel said to Elijah?" Grant asked. "He asked him a simple question, and it's a question I'm gonna ask you tonight." People leaned forward to hear because Grant whispered the question in a soft voice: "What are you doing here?" He slowly looked over the congregation until he stopped where I sat on the third row. His eyes locked on mine. "What are *you* doing here?" he demanded.

I couldn't look him in the eye. *You wouldn't believe why I'm here,* I thought bitterly.

Grant's voice slashed through my thoughts. "I didn't ask *Why* are you here. I asked *What* are you doing here?"

I glanced up. He was still looking directly at me. "Don't confuse the question with an accusation from God. It's not an accusation. God wants you to know that no matter where you are, no matter what your circumstances, you still can make something meaningful out of your life. Hear the question! It's the most important question you will ever answer. And believe me: God expects an answer."

I heard Grant's words, but the reassuring content of his message got lost in the rubble of my own internal conflicts and bitter feelings. I understood Elijah's feelings a lot better than I understood God's question.

✦ ✦ ✦

On October 20 a trusty brought me his newspaper. "I thought you might like to see this," he said, pointing at a short news blurb. In terse fashion, the story announced that a plea bargain agreement had been reached between the D.A.'s office and William Harold Torbett. In exchange for a guilty plea on two minor felonies before Judge Joseph DiRisio, the habitual criminal indictment was dropped, and Torbett was sentenced to a five- to eight-year term in prison.

"The plot thickens!" I said, whistling softly.

The century-old prison known as "The Walls," where I spent a third of my life.

Inmate Work Card

INSTITUTION: Main Prison NO. **3·0714**

ISSUED: 8-21-85 EXP. 8-21-86

NAME: Jeris E. Bragan

NUMBER: 88856

JOB PLACEMENT Newspaper Editor

APPROVED: _____
Job Placement Officer

Work Supervisor _____
Security Official

CR-2424 (3/83)

January 11, 1960; I'd just turned 14. A few weeks earlier, Tuesday, December 8, 1959, I'd asked Edie, the girl with the dancing green eyes, to go steady with me.

"Ole Sparky," Tennessee's electric chair. Had the crime for which I was convicted been committed a few weeks later, I would have been sentenced to death.

My mother, Jean Rossignol, during our first visit together at the prison in 1981. That pained look on her face isn't from squinting into the sun!

Valerie Dick interviewing me for program on WSMC-FM, summer 1982, one of my best friends to this day.

I'm with Elder Conn Arnold (center) and Tony Larson (right), the subject of my first published story. We wanted Conn to feel right at home in the midst of a den of thieves!

Cross-examining Tony Larson on the Hot Seat shortly before he was paroled in June 1983. "Are you finished with drugs, Tony?" "Man, I'm clean!"

My daughter, Tracie, summer of 1984, the first time we'd seen each other since 1977.

Elder Arnold's secretary, Rashalle Stirewalt, watches as Eddie McMillen signs to join the Adventist Freedom Fellowship at the end of Arnold's revival in 1984.

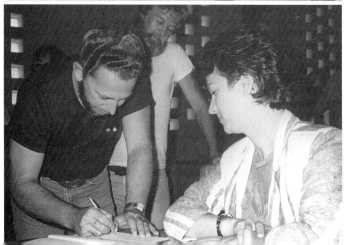

Jim Vandever displays a pistol and silencer discovered in the prison metal shop. Nearly 100 men were murdered—shot, stabbed, or beaten to death—during my 15 years in prison. I didn't know it at the time, but Jim Vandever was the man who asked Fred Steltemeier in 1988 to look into my case after the parole board turned me down in 1987.

Elder Conn Arnold baptizes Rick Bettner shortly before Rick was murdered at the prison.

133

Actress Sissy Spacek shown talking to inmates during a break in shooting the movie *Marie* behind the walls of Tennessee State Penitentiary. During the shooting of this film a serious stabbing took place. The cameramen didn't realize this wasn't part of the script "action," and kept shooting pictures as the wounded prisoner rushed past them.

Ron Patterson, Methodist churchman and senior editor at Abingdon Press, grades papers for a creative writing class he taught at Tennessee State Penitentiary.

Bishop James Neidergeses greeting "Pop," the man who danced naked around a bonfire in the middle of a prison riot. Bishop James always had time for anyone who needed to talk to him.

Elder Arnold (center) with Billy Buford (left) and Jerry Long (right). Jerry Long was murdered shortly after this picture was taken. Edie arrived at the prison just as the ambulance arrived. "What's happening?" she asked. "Some guy by the name of Jerry was just killed in Unit II," the guard said. Edie thought it was me.

Kentucky-Tennessee Conference president Clay Farwell shown talking with prisoners Pepper Carrol (left) and Eddie McMillen (right).

Wardens Mike Dutton (left) and James L. Vandever (right), two of the finest men I've ever known, meet with inmate council to discuss problems. They brought three critical hostage situations to a conclusion without any violence during their years together at Tennessee State Penitentiary.

Conn Arnold arranges a country music concert at the prison with Grand Ole Opry star and SDA Roy Drusky.

Adventist volunteer chaplain Ken Whalen stops by my cell late one night to talk.

Randall Dickman, high school teacher and nursing home administrator, crippled from the neck down in an auto accident three days before his eighteenth birthday. Randy tells inmates, "When life hands you a lemon, find a way to make lemonade!"

Tennessee's governor Ned McWherter and state legislators getting a tour of Tennessee State Penitentiary and learning why federal judge L. Clure Morton declared the prison system to be unconstitutional—"a place where terror and violence reign," the judge said.

Arnold shown with Dr. Amos L. Wilson, a Presbyterian churchman, chief of chaplaincy services for the Tennessee Department of Corrections, and a Christian brother in Christ who did much to nurture my faith during some very difficult years behind the walls.

I'm with Chaplain Cleveland Houser (center), an SDA church-man, and Dr. William Johnsson, editor, *Adventist Review* (right).

October 1990—I wonder if I'll ever get to change my address! (This picture was taken by Al Trace while I'm being interviewed for Dan Matthews' *Christian Lifestyle Magazine.*)

After 25 years Edie and I met again on Sabbath, February 8, 1986, when she came to visit me at Tennessee State Penitentiary.

F. C. "Doc" Wallace, founder of Goodwill Industries in Nashville and longtime free world supporter of the 7th Step Foundation, taken shortly before his death. Doc lent me the money to buy an electric typewriter for my writing.

1986 was a good year for me: I met Edie again; *Scandalous Grace*, my first book, was released; and I earned my B.A. degree.

Visiting on the picnic area, summer 1987.

Edie and I spent hundreds of hours "together" on the phone between 1986 and 1992.

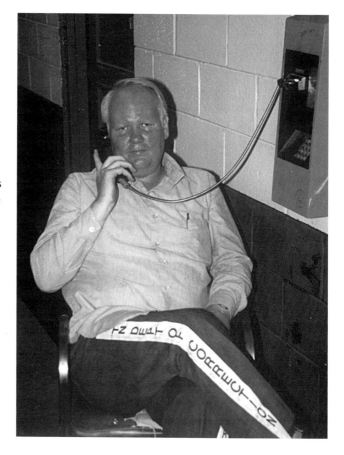

Next to me is an old friend, Ed Ley, a former police officer and parole officer who helped Fred Steltemeier track down William "Buggy" Torbett in October 1988.

Our marriage, April 8, 1989, one of the most bitterly cold days of the year!

It was Edie's birthday, May 22, 1992. Edie shown with federal appointed counsel Tom Bloom (left) and volunteer lawyer Fred Steltemeier (right) moments before I was released from prison.

May 22, 5:15 p.m., Edie and I shown following lawyers as we walk away from entrance to prison, followed by TV news cameraman from WTVF, channel 5.

This beats prison stripes! By the pond behind our home.

Edie and
Jeris Bragan,
1992

"But you ain't heard the best part," the trusty laughed. "He ain't goin' to the joint. They sent him out to the workhouse and gave him a cushy minimum security job as the barber and commissary man."

I shrugged. "So what?"

"Man, you really are a square-john citizen," the trusty growled. "First off, you don't go to the workhouse with anythin' more 'n' six years unless somebody with real clout pulls strings to arrange it. Buggy ain't got that kind of clout anywhere. Second, you don't get no cushy trusty job when you first walk in, 'specially with a record like Buggy's. An', third, he's tellin' everybody it's all been set up for him to 'escape' as soon as your appeal is shot down."

"So what?" I said again. "They'll just put out an arrest warrant, charging him with escape, and pick him up later."

"You don't get it, do you? Rap, there ain't gonna be no warrant chargin' him with escape."

"I don't care what they do with him," I said. "This proves they had a deal with that punk, just like we said. DiRisio will have to order a new trial, or the newspapers will eat him alive."

The trusty looked at me and shook his head. "Look, I don't wanna bust your bubble, but the fix is in on *you*. This is Chattanooga, and those folks downstairs [in the judge and D.A.'s office] do whatever they want. I don't know what you done to make 'em mad enough to do what they done to you, but I don't wanna see you goin' off the deep end when they stick it to you."

Typical convict paranoia, I thought. Few prisoners have confidence in any part of the social system, largely, I believe, because they tend to view the rest of the world through their own predatory eyes. I'd worked as a private detective long enough to know that every system is only as good as the people who manage it, and Chattanooga had some serious problems with corrupt officials in the police department and in the attorney general's office who played fast and loose with the rules. But I also believed that what they had done with Torbett was too blatant for even Chattanooga's standards.

Bill Alt agreed with me when I called him on the phone and told him about the newspaper story. "You're absolutely right. That alone will get you a new trial," he said. "I'll get a hearing date set up for early January. The trial transcript won't be ready by then, but we won't need that now."

He was wrong.

I spent a long time looking out the window that night and thinking about how to handle my appeals. Despite that pressing problem, my mind kept wandering off to Maine, Edie, and May baskets in spring. Again, I wondered where she was and how life was going for her. I had no idea that she was only blocks away, attending a convention at a nearby hotel, or that her life was almost as empty as my own.

✦ ✦ ✦

In spite of the good news about Torbett, I still couldn't shake off the depression that had closed in around me. My weight plummeted. By the time I walked into court for the new trial hearing, my waist had shrunk from 44 inches to 34. I'd lost nearly 60 pounds in four months.

"The jail must have a great weight reduction program!" Bill joked when I joined him at the counsel table.

"Yeah, it's all in the food. You ought to try it!"

We both laughed.

It was the last laugh of the day. The hearing was a farce in which all the actors kept a perfectly straight face.

Bill opened by reminding the court that while the state had a legal right to make any deal they wanted with a witness, they were required to disclose those agreements prior to trial. It is the exclusive task of the jury to weigh the credibility of each witness, he argued, and Torbett had lied to the jury about being an indicted habitual criminal. Even worse, District Attorney General Gary Gerbitz had knowingly solicited perjured testimony from his witness. Stan Lanzo and Steve Bevil then used that perjured testimony in closing arguments to the jury in order to bolster the credibility of their witness.

Stan Lanzo, representing the state, was incensed at the suggestion his office had deceived defense counsel, the court, or jury. He took the stand and swore under oath that prior to trial he had disclosed everything connected with their plea agreement with Torbett.

Bill turned livid with anger. He took the stand and flatly denied Lanzo's claims. The only thing Lanzo had ever disclosed, he said, was a statement to the effect that Torbett had fled while on bond and would not be available to testify at my trial. As proof, Bill showed the court where the state had given as Torbett's address an empty parking lot.

Lanzo smiled. "That must have been a typographical error," he said. He went on to describe Torbett's testimony as "crucial" to the state's case, and his participation in the trial was a "unique situation." The D.A.'s office was so concerned about Torbett's safety that they assigned him a code name. Even other prosecutors weren't informed about Torbett's testimony. Nor had Torbett's attorney, Don Poole, who coincidentally had once been Gary Gerbitz' law partner, been informed of what was going on with his client.

Bill called Don Poole as a witness. Poole admitted that the state had kept him in the dark about their private meetings in which arrangements had been made for his client's testimony. He admitted that a plea bargain between the state and Torbett had been reached on February 23, 1977, more than a month prior to my indictment. He referred to an October 18, 1977, "Agreed Order" that he had in his file which he said disposed of the case exactly as agreed to earlier in February. (Another 15 years would pass before I would see a copy of that "Agreed Order." It had been signed by Judge DiRisio, Don Poole, Gary Gerbitz, and Stan Lanzo. Had we examined it that day, we would have been able to prove our claims. Instead, we got sidetracked and forgot to review the document.) Poole said he couldn't understand why Torbett had testified contrary to the agreement, because he had discussed it with his client on at least two separate occasions during meetings with Torbett at the jail. Poole couldn't explain why Torbett's case had been leapfrogged on three different occasions past my trial date.

Lanzo argued that Mr. Gerbitz hadn't really solicited perjured testimony. Nor had Torbett intentionally lied. He simply "misunderstood" his pending status.

There was no misunderstanding, Bill insisted. The state simply held that indictment over Torbett's head like the proverbial sword of Damocles until after he provided the state with the testimony they expected.

As I listened to the lawyers arguing back and forth, I felt as though I'd suddenly tumbled down the rabbit hole of *Alice in Wonderland*, where up meant down, white meant black, yes meant no, and nothing made any sense whatsoever. Any lingering doubt I had about Judge DiRisio's complicity was put to rest when the lawyers finished their arguments and the judge issued his ruling.

"Firstly, in regard to the matters testified to, in connection with Torbett, I do find this fact," DiRisio said, "that there was no misleading of the defendant, or misrepresentation to the defense counsel, and find further as fact that there was no failure to disclose exculpatory evidence. Motion for a new trial is denied!"

The trusty had been right when he said "the fix is in" on my appeal.

Bill was seething with barely controlled fury as he stuffed papers into his battered briefcase. Not once had either of the lawyers directly accused the other of deceit or criminal wrongdoing, but the implications, couched in glittering legal generalities, weren't the least bit subtle to those who understood the jargon. At best, according to Lanzo's position, Bill had been incompetent in his cross-examination of Torbett; at worst, he lied and committed perjury on the stand when he denied that Lanzo had told him everything about their "deal" with Torbett.

Despite my own predicament, I still felt empathy for Bill. He was—and is—one of the most brilliant, honorable lawyers I've ever met. There was no way Judge DiRisio didn't know that the state had intentionally solicited perjured testimony from Torbett. Even though we didn't have the trial record available and failed to examine the "Agreed Order," DiRisio still had heard Torbett's testimony, and there was nothing ambiguous about it. He simply let the district attorney get away with it.

"This isn't over by a long shot," Bill insisted. "I'm gonna stick with you to the end. We'll appeal this all the way to the United States Supreme Court if we have to. So you hang in there and don't do anything stupid."

"I'd be hard-pressed to do anything more stupid than I've already done," I muttered under my breath.

◆ ◆ ◆

Darleen came to see me a few days later. I could tell something was wrong the minute I saw her step off the elevator. She was aloof and evasive when I tried to talk to her.

"OK, out with it. What's wrong?" I asked.

"Nothing is wrong," she snapped.

"Look, Darleen, we don't have hours to play this game. Our visit will be over in just a few minutes. Something has got you upset, so why don't you talk to me about it."

She hesitated, then took a deep breath. "Well, you'll probably find out about it anyway, so I might as well tell you. I'm dating a guy . . . actually, a couple of guys. It's nothing serious. I just can't stand being cooped up in the house all the time."

I felt like I'd been slapped in the face with a wet, dead fish. "You can't stand being 'cooped up,' " I said, stretching my arms to encompass the jail.

Her face turned red. "I can't do anything about your circumstances. I've got my needs, so I've gotta get on with my life until you get out of here."

There was more than one reason for the bulletproof glass in the visiting booth! I glanced at the control booth. The guard was out on the floor, so I didn't have to worry about him listening to what I said.

"I've got to ask you one simple question, Darleen. How can you do the kinds of things you've done to me when you supposedly love me?"

She looked me straight in the eye without blinking as she spoke. "Actually, to be honest about it, I don't think I ever loved you, Jerry. You were a meal ticket. I was tired of being poor. I wanted out of my crazy family and out of my marriage to Ridge. You made it easy for me to get away from both without losing a thing."

I winced with each word.

"I imagine that's the most truthful answer you've ever given me."

She shrugged. "You asked for it."

"Yeah, I guess I asked for it all right."

Later, back in my cell, I discovered that the day light had burned out. The light fixture over my sink had two lights, both of which were controlled by the guard in the control booth. The brightest light was turned on at 6:00 each morning. At 10:00 at night this light was turned off and a much dimmer one was turned on so the night guard could see into the cells.

The guard couldn't replace it, so he turned on the dim night light. I paced restlessly from one wall to the other in the gloomy darkness. As I thought about my life I felt increasingly damned with guilt and failure, utterly condemned and abandoned by God. Everything I'd ever done wrong, great or small—every failure, large or small—raced round and round in my mind like gerbils. The fragmented thoughts ran faster and faster until they began crashing into one another, tumbling wildly across the track before they disappeared into the boiling cauldron of my subconsciousness.

In spite of my agitation I stretched out on the bunk and fell into an exhausted sleep. The same nightmare came as it had scores of times during the past four months. Again, I saw a body stretched out on the table, the unblinking eyes staring out of my face straight up at the ceiling. Lights from a control panel near the body furiously blinked on and off in an erratic fashion, and I heard a beeping sound that grew louder and beeped faster and faster. That was *me* paralyzed and suffocating on the table, but I couldn't do anything to free my impotent twin. My pulse pounded in my ears in time with the frantic lights and beeping monitor.

I couldn't watch anymore.

148

BREAKING POINT

I had to wake up.

I began thrashing against the invisible cords that bound me.

I screamed something.

A word.

It was always the same word.

This time I heard it.

"*Help!* Dear God, please *help* me!" I cried. I woke up panting for breath, with tears running down my face, thrashing and muttering, "Help! Help! Help!"

It was a futile plea. Nobody could help me now. I'd thrown my life away, and there was no getting it back—not now, not ever. It was midnight. I had reached the breaking point.

I glanced at the bars where the teenager had hung himself a few months earlier. I'd thought of suicide many times during the past few months but had always dismissed the idea. For the first time, however, I realized just how tired I was: tired of living, tired of thinking, tired of being. I wanted to die. It was my only means of escape from what had become an unbearable existence.

Method was the problem. I couldn't think clearly enough about how to hang myself without botching the job or taking so long the guard would discover me before I was gone. Then I spotted the plastic disposable razor the guard had given me to shave with that morning. He'd forgotten to come back for it. I dropped it on the floor and crushed it with the heel of my boot. It took some time, but I finally extracted the blade from its protective plastic cover. It was thin and bent easily. But it was sharp enough if I made the incision just right on my wrist.

I scrambled onto the bunk and stretched out under the blanket when I heard footsteps from the night-shift guard coming down the walk in front of my cell. He stopped at the bars and peered in at me through the gloomy darkness. I held the blade between my thumb and forefinger under the blanket.

"Are you having a bad night?" he asked.

I wondered if he had heard me thrashing around. I struggled to focus on his face. I'd never seen him before. "Can't seem to sleep tonight," I mumbled.

"You've been through some rough spots during the past few months," he said. His voice sounded sympathetic. "But you can't let it get to you. Things are gonna get better if you don't give up hope."

I hope things are gonna get a lot better for me as soon as you leave me alone, I thought.

"Since you can't sleep anyway, how about I bring you a cup of coffee?" he suggested. "It's instant, but I know it's better than that boiled-sock brew they give you to drink from the kitchen."

"Not tonight, thanks. I think I'll try to sleep."

"OK, but you bang on the door if you need anything." He started to walk away, but then turned back. "Don't forget that God loves you, and you've got a lot of friends who care about you," he said. "This thing with your appeals may take a long time to clear up, but I believe you'll win in the end if you don't give up hope or lose your faith in God."

Hope! I didn't have any hope left. I thought about my daughter, Tracie, and how miserably I'd failed that little girl as a father. Tears stung my eyes. I squeezed the blade. The sharp edge nicked my finger.

That didn't hurt much, I thought. *It's time to do it and get this living nightmare over.*

Suddenly a strange sound filled my head. It reminded me of water rushing over a waterfall. Briefly I thought I was having a stroke or heart attack. But then a bright light filled the room. My eyes were closed. I don't know why, but it didn't occur to me to open them. I could see the light getting brighter and brighter through my eyelids. A firm hand closed over my left hand, clasping it as a friend does when shaking hands. Both the light and the hand felt strangely healing, warm, comforting.

Vaguely, I wondered if I was dreaming again. I fingered the blade in my right hand. It was still there, sharp, and waiting.

The sound of rushing water receded, replaced with music. It was my Grandfather Whary, singing in his high tenor voice. It was too distinct to be memory. It sounded like a new cassette tape playing inside my head. I remembered reading about a neurosurgeon who had discovered that a patient's memory of past events had the effect of being an immediate, present experience when electrodes were touched to different parts of the brain. The words to Grandpa Whary's song had that quality of present tense. They were clear and pristine:

> My life goes on,
> Some days are good, some ill;
> O Father, let Thy loving Presence fill
> Both day and night;
> O hold me so I cannot fall,
> For Thou art Life and Strength,
> And All in All.
> Hold Thou my hand, dear Lord,
> Hold Thou my hand;
> And when temptations come
> Help me to stand.
> Constantly near to Thee,
> All shall be well with me,
> Holding Thy hand, Dear Lord,
> Holding Thy hand.

If this is madness, it's rather nice, I thought. *No wonder crazy people resist getting well.* Laughter? I thought I heard laughter in the distance. Maybe God enjoys a good joke!

Tears slowly ran down my cheeks.

Then I heard a voice. It was my voice! It took several moments before I recognized the words. I was reading aloud from my favorite passage in Paul

Tillich's book *The Shaking of the Foundations*: "Grace strikes us when we are in great pain and restlessness. It strikes us when we walk through the dark valley of a meaningless and empty life. . . . It strikes us when, year after year, the longed-for perfection of life does not appear, when the old compulsions reign within us as they have for decades, when despair destroys all joy and courage. Sometimes at that moment a wave of light breaks into our darkness and it is as though a voice were saying: 'You are accepted, accepted by that which is greater than you, and the name of which you do not know. Do not ask for the name now; perhaps you will find it later. Do not try to do anything now; perhaps later you will do much. Do not seek for anything; do not intend anything. Simply accept the fact you are accepted.' "

It was nearly dawn before the Light dimmed and the Hand withdrew from mine. For the first time in my life, despite all my past theological study and speculations, I suddenly understood grace on a deeply personal level. Correction: I didn't "understand" it in cognitive terms; I felt it at some deeply personal level that transcended words.

I sat up on the side of the bunk when I heard the guard's footsteps approaching.

"I see you got a good night's sleep in spite of all that extra light," he said cheerfully.

My jaw dropped. "You saw the light?"

"It was hard to miss," he said, glancing up at the light fixture over my sink. He looked puzzled. "I could see the light through the window in your cell door. I tried to turn it off several times, but I couldn't. I guess something must be busted in the circuit."

I was confused. "What are you talking about?"

"Your day light," he said, pointing at the light fixture over my sink again. "It went off a little while ago. I tried to turn it back on a few minutes ago, but now it won't come on at all. I'll have to put in a work order so the morning shift can get it fixed."

"No hurry," I said. Apparently he didn't know the day light had burned out the day before.

"Well, I'm off," he said. "Just don't forget what I told you last night. No matter how tough things get, God loves you. That's all that matters."

I smiled. "You're absolutely right about that!"

The first light of dawn crept into my cell before I got up. I walked to the bars and looked toward Lookout Mountain, where shadows of the night were in full retreat. Nothing had changed in those few short hours as far as my circumstances were concerned, yet I knew a radical shift had taken place in my life, setting in motion a series of cause-and-effect relationships that would play out during the coming years in ways I didn't even begin to comprehend at that moment.

I remembered being in the fifth grade. Eva Perry, my teacher, was leading the class in reciting Psalm 121. Rolling gently down through rough canyons of memory, I could almost hear the childish voices: "I will lift up mine eyes unto the hills, from whence cometh my help. My help cometh from the Lord, which made heaven and earth. He will not suffer thy foot to be moved: he that keepeth thee will not slumber. Behold, he that keepeth Israel shall neither slumber nor sleep. The Lord is thy keeper: the Lord is thy shade upon thy right hand. The sun shall not smite thee by day, nor the moon by night. The Lord shall preserve thee from all evil: he shall preserve thy soul. The Lord shall preserve thy going out and thy coming in from this time forth, and even for evermore."

I didn't know what the future held for me, but at least I knew one critically important thing: "My help cometh from the Lord."

12

Choose Ye This Day

THE INTENSITY of my late-night encounter with God's grace lingered on with the coming of day. When the spiritual euphoria passed, it was replaced with subdued, introspective feelings of wonder on two levels about this powerfully intimate experience.

First, there was that kind of wonder that left me dumbstruck, in awe about both the goodness of God and the intimate way in which He had touched my life. My sense of wonder was much like the small child's first experience in seeing a fully decorated Christmas tree—something beyond words: pure, speechless joy! All my abstract theological formulations about a God who was remote, disengaged, and unapproachable dissolved in the mist of something profoundly personal.

Second, came the wonder of the irrepressible private detective full of questions. Mystical encounters with God in the form of invisible light and hands was manifestly not a part of my daily experience! I had to wonder: Was the experience real? Did I just dream it? Under the strain of depression and discouragement in the barren wilderness of a jail cell, had my thinking and emotions gotten so twisted out of shape that my brain was playing tricks on me?

For days I reflected on the experience and the questions that naturally followed. On the one hand, I had to grapple with a phenomenon that seemed too unreal and foreign to take seriously. On the other hand, I knew the experience had been too concrete to be ignored or dismissed. At the very least I knew something had happened because I *felt* different. Although nothing had changed in terms of my predicament, the desperation and despair about my circumstances had dissipated almost entirely, replaced by the oddest of feelings: a desire for laughter, of all things, and an appreciation for the comical!

Either I'm nuts and on the verge of a well-deserved nervous breakdown, or there's something to this miraculous comedy of grace, I thought.

Years earlier I would have readily agreed that God does indeed perform miracles. But I couldn't honestly say I was intimately acquainted with any on a personal level. But I wondered if I hadn't been so busy with my career and responsibilities that I simply had not noticed God's acts in my own life. Perhaps it's harder to hear God's voice clearly amid the clatter and clamor of a busy life. I noticed that in the earliest Bible stories men and women lost God in the Garden of Eden and then found Him again later in the wilderness. Prosperity and good times pose serious hazards to spiritual faith. It's a seductive temptation to believe that we are quite self-sufficient and that God can be fitted in around the edges.

As I was thinking about the miracle of grace, an officer in Central Control called me to say that a special agent for the Internal Revenue Service wanted to see me in the lawyers' visiting room.

The agent didn't stand up or offer to shake hands as I walked into the room. He was a tall, slender man—graying at the temples—and had squinty eyes. His polyester suit hung on his bony frame like a bag. I thought his costume would be complete if he had worn a green sun visor perched on his forehead.

"I was just thinking about comedy, and the IRS shows up!" I said.

He didn't smile. "I don't think you'll find this . . . ah . . . comical, Mr. Bragan. Our records show that you failed to file either a personal or business income tax return for last year or 1976."

"What can I say? I've been a bit preoccupied with more pressing problems."

"This is a *pressing* problem," he barked, jabbing his finger on the documents spread out before him. "Do you understand that there are severe penalties—fines, even jail terms—for failing to file and pay your taxes?"

If he expected an argument from me, he was disappointed. I started laughing. I laughed so hard I started rocking back and forth in my chair. The agent pushed his chair back a few inches away from the table and watched me with a mixture of suspicion and alarm. His voice was stiff and indignant when I finally quit laughing: "I'd like to know what you think is so funny about this."

"Look, I'm sure you're a nice guy, and I don't want to hurt your feelings," I said, "but take a good look around you: I'm sitting here, convicted with the use of perjured testimony for a murder I didn't commit and facing 99 years in prison. I'm ruined financially, and there is virtually no likelihood whatsoever that this conviction will ever be reversed. Here you are threatening me with fines and a jail term because I didn't file tax returns last year. Now doesn't that strike you as just a little bit funny?"

The agent glared at me for several seconds. Then his face broke into a broad grin. Before he could stop himself he burst into laughter. "Mr. Bragan, I do believe you have an irrefutable point," he said as he stood up and shook my hand. "I won't be troubling you again."

◆ ◆ ◆

The days slowly turned into weeks and months at the jail. Generally, I would have been transferred to Tennessee State Penitentiary in Nashville shortly after Judge DeRisio denied my appeal. With the massive overcrowding problems at the prison, however, the state agreed to have me remain at the jail until my appeals were exhausted in the state courts.

Margaret Sharp, an elderly friend, came to visit me one day. After a few preliminaries, she came right to the point: "Well, what are you gonna do here, boy?"

Her blunt question irritated me. I'd been wrestling unsuccessfully with the same question ever since I had heard Dr. Grant preaching on the subject months earlier. Although I tend to be a task-oriented sort of man, I felt frustrated because I couldn't find a creative way to get around the obstacles posed by a jail environment.

"Margaret, you've gotta be kidding," I snapped irritably. "I'm in jail!

What am I supposed to do in a place like this?"

A person who loved me less might have indulged that flash of self-pity. Not Margaret. Then in her late 60s, she had faced too many problems in her own life to accept defeatist self-pity.

"You can do anything you put your mind to," she retorted. "Why don't you use some of that intelligence you've got and finish college? You've got time to read, study, and think. I've seen your writing, so get to work and *write!*"

In less than five minutes she had ticked off enough work to keep me busy for the next 15 years! "And remember this: 'Whatsoever your hand finds to do, do it with all your might,' " she added, quoting Ecclesiastes 9:10.

"Right, Margaret! I'll see what I can do."

✦ ✦ ✦

An unexpected opportunity for study and reading came with the arrival of spring. I was moved at my own request from an eight-man tank into an isolation cell. Most prisoners viewed the isolation cells as punishment, but I relished the solitude and privacy. I could read, think, or write for hours at a time. I missed the clinic cell I'd once had because there were no windows in isolation. But I didn't miss the chaos and bedlam that characterized the tank where I'd spent nearly two months. Radios and TV ran 24 hours a day. Even with ear plugs I had difficulty sleeping.

Without windows as a reference for day or night, however, I lost all track of time after a few weeks. I didn't have any pressing appointments or obligations, so it didn't matter when I slept or woke up, and time gradually lost all significance. I read, thought, or wrote letters until I got tired. I'd sleep until I was ready to wake up. After a few months I noticed that I usually slept for eight hours, and then stayed awake for 20. My sleeping/awake cycle slowly moved around the clock every two weeks.

The jail didn't have an area for exercise, so I worked out doing sit-ups and push-ups. Walking required some ingenuity, but I finally developed a system. My cell faced a 21-foot enclosed walkway. Since the guards generally left my cell open during the day, I took advantage of the limited freedom I had and walked five miles each day: 21 feet in one direction, about face, and 21 feet in the other. It took approximately 20 minutes or 126 round-trips to equal a mile. After a while I got so used to the rhythm that I could think about other things while I walked and still keep track of the miles.

After walking each day, I plunged into reading. During my first year of imprisonment, friends sent me hundreds of books and a couple dozen different translations of the Bible: the *New International Version*, King James, Revised Standard, *The Jerusalem Bible*, Amplified Bible, *The New English Bible*, *The Living Bible*, even the Cotton Patch translation of the New Testament, and many others.

Years earlier I'd read the Bible through a couple of times when I was in school. But then I read either because I had to for a class requirement or just so I could say that I'd done so. Now I read in huge gulps, several hundred pages a day, for the pure pleasure of the reading experience. As soon as I finished one translation, I plunged into the next. For the first time in my life I read the Bible with purpose: I was looking for themes, much like a detective who immerses himself in a case in order to absorb the big picture.

Given the recent experience in my own life, I was particularly interested in the miracles God performed. I noticed that miracles happened more frequently in the desert wilderness than in paradise. It was in the midst of the worst kinds of desolation that God invariably brought consolation to desperate people—unexpected springs of water, manna, little oases that came just when they were least expected but most needed.

Perhaps because our culture is so saturated with the stunts and special effects of Hollywood, we'd like our miracles to come with more dramatic pronouncements. But I noticed that most miracles are really quite hard to describe. More often than not they have quiet beginnings and come in the most obscure places. Years ago, for example, when Caesar dominated center stage in Rome and Herod ruled in Jerusalem, the most important Baby in human history was born in the most unlikely place—Bethlehem. It was the most extraordinary miracle of all time. All of human history would be transformed forever because of this single event that only a few noticed.

Of the principle players in the Bethlehem miracle, few were less important than Joseph and Mary, a poverty-stricken young couple down from Nazareth to register for the census. The shepherds were common, ordinary laborers. We don't even know the innkeeper's name, nor do we know for sure how many of those obscure strangers wandered in from the East after following a star.

Even the prophets of the Old Testament, called to a life of service by God, were quite ordinary. And God's call on their lives usually came in the most mundane ways. Only Isaiah had a vision in the Temple. All the others were busy with quite ordinary tasks when God called them. One was hunting cattle, one was tending sheep, another was gathering crops, one was mending a wall, and one was struggling with marriage to a woman who reminded me of Darleen!

Far from the spectacular, I noticed that God's greatest miracles were usually discovered in very commonplace experiences that left people with a profound sense of wonder. It was in the small things that Jesus saw the great truths of God—the miraculous itself. He saw a woman drop a coin into the treasury box. He told about a Samaritan who stopped to help a wounded traveler, a prodigal son returning home, and a woman who lost a coin. He saw each of these incredibly ordinary events as a gift-wrapped container for God's greatest revelation: the miracle of grace.

As I reflected on the biblical view of miracles, I didn't feel at all special because of my own recent experience. On the contrary, I realized that the intensity of the experience revealed just how far God had to go to get my attention because I'd distanced myself from faith in Him! More important, however—and reassuring—was the realization that God met me where I was spiritually, not where I should have been. My modesty wasn't an abstract virtue; I realized I had a great deal to be modest about!

CHOOSE YE THIS DAY

✦ ✦ ✦

I expected abusive treatment from guards after my first encounter with the booking officer on the day I was arrested. But I was mistaken. For the most part the guards remain memorable for their uncommon kindness and decency. Technically, jail rules were quite restrictive and the guards weren't supposed to let prisoners out of their cells except for visitation, commissary, and twice each week for a 10-minute phone call. But the guards rarely refused to let me use the phone when I asked for it. Occasionally they even stopped by my cell during rounds and asked if I wanted to use the phone or get out to stretch my legs for a while. I'll never forget the thoughtfulness of men like Sergeant Sanders or deputies Shelby Rogers, Bob Johnson, Bill Williams, and many others whose names I've forgotten with the passage of years.

Officer Bill Williams, who worked the 2:00-10:00 p.m. shift, was particularly helpful. He usually stopped by my cell in the evening. I'd fix us both a cup of coffee, and we would talk about everything from fly-fishing to politics and religion. One evening he asked me if I would talk to Kevin, a teenager he had locked up in my old clinic cell.

"It's against the rules for me to bring a kid back here, but he needs somebody to talk to him," Bill said.

"What's the problem?"

"He's scared. It's a two-bit charge, but the kid has never been arrested before. I'm afraid he's suicidal because he's convinced his life is over."

"Bring him back," I said.

Kevin was a tall, skinny 17-year-old who reminded me of the typical class nerd, right down to a piece of white tape holding the bow of his glasses to the frame. Although he came from a Baptist home and parents who practiced their Christian faith, he'd broken into a neighbor's house on a dare from other kids he wanted to impress. Nothing had been taken, but a routine police patrol had spotted him when he came out. He wouldn't tell the arresting officers what he was doing, so they charged him with burglary.

"What did you tell your parents?"

"I can't tell them. They'd tell the cops about my friends, and then I'd be labeled a snitch," he said stubbornly.

"So, in order to avoid being a snitch, you're gonna kill yourself, is that it? Does that strike you as being very smart?"

He wouldn't look me in the eye, so I knew I'd struck a nerve. "Let me tell you something, Kevin. You're acting like you took a whole bottle of stupid pills for breakfast. What you did was stupid, but that doesn't make you a criminal. You already know what's the right thing to do. Get this thing straightened out before it gets any worse than it already is."

"But my friends . . ."

"Are these friends, as you call them, doing anything to help you out? Would you let a friend take this kind of heat? With friends like them, you don't need any enemies."

"What am I supposed to do?"

I pointed down the hall toward the phones. "Get down there and call

157

your parents. Tell them what happened. Then call the officers who arrested you, and do the same thing."

"Just like that?"

"Son, are you good at math?" I asked.

"Yeah, sure . . ."

"Did you ever hear that the shortest distance between two points is a straight line?"

He thought for a minute. Then a faint smile. "Get it over and done with, huh?"

"That's the bottom line," I replied. "Don't screw up your whole life like I've done because of some well-intended but misguided values."

He looked at me curiously. "How much time have you got?"

"Ninety-nine years."

His jaw dropped. He glanced at the stack of books and Bibles on the floor of my cell. "Are you still a . . . a Christian?"

I laughed. "Yes, I am. But you sound like the word embarrasses you. What's that all about?"

"I dunno exactly," he admitted. "It just seems that being a Christian is all wrapped up in a bunch of dumb rules and regulations that keep a person from having a good time."

"Are you having a 'good time' now?" I asked.

He shook his head.

"Kevin, being a Christian isn't about 'rules and regulations,' as you put it. It's not even about religion, either, when you get right down to the bottom line. All those things are important, but they're secondary. First, being a Christian means that you're a follower of Jesus. He's your personal Saviour, the Lord of your life. You stand for something that matters—love for other people. You know the old rule: A man who doesn't stand for something will fall for anything. You forgot that rule when you broke into the house."

"You mean a burglar can't be a Christian?"

"No, that isn't what I mean! A burglar is about rules and regulations again; that's secondary. Breaking into the house was, first and foremost, a failure to act in love toward your neighbor! Christians love other people like Jesus loves them."

"I always thought of Christians as being weak people."

"You've got it reversed. Only a truly strong man can admit his mistakes, admit his need for God's forgiveness and grace. To put it another way: only a strong man can confront his own weaknesses. The weakest man is one who wanders through life, believing in the illusion of his own power and self-sufficiency. The typical bully, for example, isn't a strong man. He's a coward who hides behind his fear by terrorizing people who can't stand up to him. A strong man never has to bully other people. A strong Christian man reaches out to lift others up, not put them down."

Soon it was time for lock-down, and Kevin had to leave. "Nobody ever talked to me like you have," he said before he left.

"Are you gonna make that call?"

He grinned. "Yeah, and I think I'm gonna look for some new friends, too. I appreciate your talking to me." He shook my hand and left. Later that evening Bill told me Kevin's parents had picked him up. I never saw him again.

◆ ◆ ◆

Although Bill wasn't well educated or a member of any church, he was a deeply spiritual man who liked to talk about what he described as "moral conflicts." Typical examples were dilemmas that a police officer faced, such as ignoring the criminal acts of a snitch while using the information he provided in order to arrest others.

"On the one hand, a good cop has to use snitches in order to make other cases," he'd argue. "But to do that you've gotta ignore criminal acts the snitch is doing, even bail him out if he gets in trouble with another cop. How do you reconcile the oath of office, which says you'll enforce the law impartially, with doing your job?"

The debate usually went in circles. As the weeks turned into months and he kept returning to the same topic, I began wondering if he had something else more important on his mind that he wasn't talking about. Toward the end of my second year at the jail, he finally told me what was really bothering him.

"I've got a confession to make," he said as he sat down on the foot of my bunk. "You may never want to talk to me again, but I've gotta get this thing off my chest."

"I retired as emperor of the universe a couple of years ago," I joked. "I'm not in the business of judging people anymore."

He took a deep breath. "You may want to change your mind when you find out I withheld an important piece of evidence at your trial."

The skin on my arms prickled. "What are you talking about?"

"I don't remember the exact details, but I think Buggy Torbett testified at your trial that you came to the jail to see him on November 20, just two days before your partner's death, and that you'd slipped him some money for his bail underneath his cell door?"

"Yes, he said that. He also said I offered him money to kill some unnamed person. But what does that have to do with you?"

"I knew Buggy was lying when he testified at your trial because I was the officer on duty that Saturday. I remember the day because I'd gotten a tip from another prisoner that Buggy's wife was gonna try to slip some drugs to him. I stood right beside his cell door during the entire visiting period."

I tried to choke back my anger. "Why didn't you say anything?"

"I couldn't," Bill said. He leaned forward on the bunk, clasping his head in both hands. "My boss, the sheriff, was a Republican, just like Gerbitz. He would have fired me 10 seconds after I got off the stand for messing up the D.A.'s case."

"I don't know what to say, Bill, I . . ."

"I don't expect you to forgive me," he interrupted. "I just wanted you to know that I'll give you a signed affidavit if that will help you any now."

159

I didn't want an affidavit or to forgive him. I wanted to bounce him off the wall! Fortunately, I didn't. Instead, I realized what he had said was probably true. Law enforcement was his only ambition in life, and he probably would have been fired. Chattanooga was a tough town for an honest cop. Besides, better than most, I knew that what had been done couldn't be undone. I decided to let him off the hook.

"I do understand your predicament, so I appreciate your giving this information to me," I said. "I'll talk to my lawyer about the affidavit. Maybe he'll have an idea about how we can use it."

Bill Alt came to the jail a few days later and reduced Officer Williams' story to a sworn affidavit. "We've got a catch-22 here," Bill told me. "His statement won't do us any good on appeal because it hasn't been presented to the trial court. We'll just have to hope we get a new trial."

Officer Bill Williams was killed in a car wreck just before the Court of Criminal Appeals denied my appeal. I felt bad over the loss of a real friend.

◆ ◆ ◆

Like Bill, most of the jailers were good men. There were a few exceptions. Only one is memorable.

A particularly vicious and sadistic jailer walked up to me one day while I was talking on the phone. Without warning, he jerked the phone handset out of my hand and slammed it down on the receiver.

"What are you doing?" I shouted, struggling to control my anger. He thrust his mottled face close to mine. The sour smell of alcohol and tobacco slapped me in the face. "You think you're such a big deal, but you ain't nothin' anymore, Bragan," he hissed. "You're just another stinkin' convict, and I'll rip your _____ head off if you ever give me any trouble."

He shoved me back against the wall, cursed me in the most colorful terms, challenging me to respond to his baiting provocation.

The guard stepped back, taunting me. "C'mon, big boy," he cackled. "If you don't like it, take a swing."

Other prisoners stood nearby, snickering, watching in amusement, eager for a fight. My fists balled. Blood pounded like bass drums in my skull. I wanted to slam that grotesque human being through the wall.

Suddenly, in a microsecond of time, I experienced one of those rare, almost blinding flashes of illumination. I realized in that moment that everything could be taken away from me in that demented, demonic place—even my life. But there was one thing no one could take away from me: *No one could take away my freedom to choose how I responded to what happened to me!*

That realization lanced the boil of my anger. I turned and walked back to my cell. Later, while sitting on my bunk and reflecting about what had just happened with the irrational guard, I remembered a story I'd heard a preacher tell once about a major league baseball umpire who had a reputation for taking his time when calling a pitch behind the plate. Seconds would tick off before he bellowed, "Ball!" or "Strike!"

The manager of the losing team finally exploded one day as the delays got longer with each inning. Livid, he stormed from the dugout and screamed, "Are you blind? Don't you know the difference between a ball and a strike?"

The umpire thrust his face close to the furious manager. "It ain't nothing until I call it something!" he roared.

I laughed because I suddenly felt profoundly free as I thought about the guard and the umpire. But I knew real freedom comes with two sharp edges: One is the exhilaration that comes in boldly confronting radically new and exciting possibilities. At least I could own my feelings, if nothing else. I was free to choose how I wanted to respond to whatever happened to me, regardless of circumstances. I didn't have to dance on the puppet strings of any external provocation.

But the other side of freedom can be scary because of the responsibility that comes with it. Gone are all the excuses. Whatever my response to life's blessings or blisters, it was mine to do with as I pleased. I didn't have anybody to blame for what I did or didn't do or how I felt. That was a particularly energizing experience of empowerment in the jail when things were going well, but it was a demanding taskmaster when things went poorly. This was particularly true in 1979, when the Court of Appeals denied my appeal. Then I wanted to blame either circumstances or other people for how I felt. Fortunately, I didn't indulge those feelings for long. I'd made my decision, and I refused to let it go.

Whatever else I'd lost because of the poor decisions and choices I'd made prior to my trial, I knew I would never again surrender the freedom to make positive choices about how I would respond to whatever I confronted. The words of Joshua helped me keep that commitment when I was tempted to forget: "Choose ye this day whom ye will serve." I drew those words in bold letters on a piece of paper and taped it to the stainless steel mirror so I'd see them at least once each day. The words reminded me that my choices weren't between a variety of theological and philosophical propositions. It was a choice between either an utterly meaningless and purposeless existence in this barren wilderness of prison or a profoundly liberating, meaningful existence that was worthwhile because of my personal relationship with the God who loved me and called me into discipleship with Him. I had no idea where my choice would lead, but I chose discipleship.

◆ ◆ ◆

Darleen continued visiting me at the jail. She apologized for her behavior, but nothing really changed. Except for the formality of divorce, I knew our marriage was over.

◆ ◆ ◆

As the months turned into years, I got to know some of the professors in the religion department at Southern Missionary College. They not only shared their time and books with me, but they also offered me their friendship. Dr. Jerry Gladson, who earned his doctorate in Old Testament studies from Vanderbilt University, was particularly helpful in guiding my thinking and reading on the subject of religious faith and human suffering. He even loaned me the doctoral dissertation he'd written on the subject of suffering as he found it in the wisdom literature of the Old Testament. Dr. Norman Gulley introduced me to Karl Barth's *Church Dogmatics*, and Dr. Lorenzo Grant helped me think more systematically about grace and righteousness by faith within the Christian tradition.

In 1979 Jerry Gladson brought one of his students to the chapel program. His name was Ed Ley. A former police officer in Florida, Ed had abandoned a career in law enforcement when he became a Christian. He moved to Collegedale so he could finish a degree in theology at Southern Missionary College and prepare for the ministry.

After some idle chitchat, Ed came directly to the point: "I'd like to hear more about your case."

"Why?" I wasn't eager to discuss my case with any police officer, ex- or otherwise!

"To be perfectly honest, the chairman of my department, Dr. Doug Bennett, asked me to check you out."

I bristled. "Why?"

"I don't know," Ed admitted. "But maybe there's something we can do to help."

I was skeptical about Ed's interest. I figured he just wanted to look good by pretending to be interested in my predicament, but I didn't want to be rude. "Maybe I can call you on the phone when we can talk about it at some length," I suggested. I thought that would end the conversation.

"Great! Here's my number. Call me tomorrow."

Despite my skepticism about Ed's motives, I did call him. It was the beginning of a long and close friendship. I don't think Ed or the professors at Southern Missionary College had any idea what a powerful impact their friendship was having on my life. But they were living mediators of God's grace for me when I needed it most.

Margaret Sharp's son, Rick, was another. Rick was a gifted pianist who worked for me part-time as a private investigator when I first opened my agency. He loved the work and was good at it. But when Darleen made it clear she had targeted him as one of her conquests, I fired him without telling him why. I knew he felt a lot of anger toward me because of that. Shortly after my conviction, I called him on the phone and apologized. "I still can't tell you why, but I didn't fire you because of anything you did wrong," I explained. "Maybe someday I can tell you more."

He accepted that.

A few months later Rick began providing special music during the jail chapel services. By this time Rick and his mother knew Darleen was doing a lot of "dating." One night in early 1980 he pulled me aside before the program began. "Jerry, Darleen and I've been friends for several years. I know she's doing a lot of self-destructive stuff right now, so I'd like to take her out to dinner—if you don't mind—and see if I can't help her get her act together."

I didn't doubt his motives, but I was concerned for his safety. "Just be careful," I warned. "Make sure you go to some very public place, and don't let her get drunk. Otherwise, you might get a lot more than you bargained for!"

Two weeks later she told me she had accepted an invitation for dinner with him. "Yes, he asked me about that. I told him I didn't object."

"That's big of you," she snarled, "not that you have much to say about it."

Rick was furious when I called him the following morning. "You lied to me!" he shouted.

"What are you talking about?"

"She drank a little too much rosé wine last night, and she told me everything about what happened to George. Have you lost your ever-loving mind! Why did you let her get away with something like that?"

"Maybe you'd better tell me what happened," I suggested cautiously.

After having a few drinks and striking out when she tried to seduce Rick, she had alternated between seductive tears, bragging about killing George, and laughing about how she had fixed me.

"I'm gonna talk to Chief Davis about this. Then maybe we can get you out of there," Rick said.

"I wish the system worked that efficiently, but it doesn't work like that, Rick. In the first place, she'll deny it, so it will be your word against hers. Second, you can bet your last dollar that the cops and the prosecutors couldn't care less. I'd appreciate it if you would just keep that information under your hat for right now. Don't even tell Margaret about it. Maybe if I get a new trial . . . well, who knows what will happen then?"

He wasn't happy about it, but he agreed.

By May 5, 1980, my final appeal was exhausted and so was I. Two weeks earlier Darleen's appeal to the supreme court had also been denied. Her appeal bond was revoked, and she was sent to the women's prison on May 4. It was time to begin my sentence at the Tennessee State Prison in Nashville.

13

Bloom Where You're Planted

"BRAGAN! ALL the way to Music City—bag and baggage!"

I smiled ruefully at the gallows humor as the message boomed three times over the loud speaker. That's the way a prisoner's transfer to the state penitentiary is announced. Although Nashville, Tennessee, is known as "Music City," I knew that wasn't the part of town I would soon see.

A jailer tipped me off the night before about my transfer, so I had my few possessions—mostly books—packed and stacked in boxes in front of the cell door.

I looked over the steel womb in which I'd lived for nearly three years while waiting for my appeal to inch its way through the Court of Criminal Appeals and the Tennessee Supreme Court. It wasn't much, but leaving meant the real beginning of my 99-year prison sentence in one of America's most infamous prison systems. Also, the transfer was a brutal reminder of all the loss and personal betrayal I had experienced since George's death, nearly four years earlier.

Will this movie never end? I wondered bitterly. On some days I felt like I had accidentally wandered into some bizarre time warp, a living episode of *The Twilight Zone.*

I took a deep breath and let it out slowly, shaking off those angry and resentful feelings. I'd watched too many young men in the jail destroy themselves by indulging such feelings. I wasn't about to get trapped in that emotional, spiritual quicksand. Besides, in spite of my grim predicament, I still believed God was with me. That conviction made a radical difference in how I felt about what was ahead.

The jailer wasn't happy when he saw me packed and ready to go. He knew that meant someone had tipped me off to the transfer. Even though most of the officers liked and trusted me, they also knew that an ex-detective like me would know all the tricks of escape if I had this in mind. I didn't, but they couldn't be sure. Fear of ambush is a legitimate concern for every officer who transports convicts to the state pen.

First, a guard wrapped the belly chains around my waist, snapped handcuffs on my wrists, and locked the belly chain securely to the cuffs. Next legs irons, which looked like handcuffs for the ankles, were locked tight around my ankles. Barely able to walk, stumbling awkwardly with the cuffs and chains around my ankles, I was led toward the black police van, where my property and two other prisoners were waiting.

"I wish we didn't have to do this," one officer whispered to me, "but you know how it is."

I nodded and smiled. Seeing myself in chains was more than a little ironic. "St. Paul wore his chains with dignity," I replied. "I guess I can do the same thing."

It was early spring. I was startled momentarily when I stepped outside

165

the jail door and felt the cool, crisp morning air wash over my face. It was a delicious feeling! I stopped and looked up toward the sky. It was the first time I'd seen the sun or felt real air on my skin in nearly 1,000 days. The honking, blaring sounds of a busy city coming to life were exhilarating to hear—and strangely depressing at the same time.

I hobbled across the sally port and cautiously climbed into the van. The leg irons restricted movement of only a few inches per step. I misjudged my mobility, stumbled, and barked my shins painfully on the metal step. Two heavily armed officers were sitting in the cab, separated from us prisoners by a steel-mesh screen. One was young and obviously nervous. He kept fidgeting with the automatic pump shotgun across his lap.

I hadn't been in any vehicle since September 15, 1977, so my sense of balance was off. Nervously, I looked through the grill at the speedometer. It felt as though the driver was racing through the city, but the dial read 15 miles an hour.

"Is that thing working?" I asked.

The guard riding shotgun laughed. "It always feels like that when you haven't ridden for a long time," he explained. "You'll get used to it in a few minutes." I understood why some skeptics a century earlier had been convinced that speeds of 50 miles an hour would kill a person!

Once on the freeway, however, speed wasn't an illusion. I felt sick to my stomach as the speedometer steadily climbed under the nervous driver's foot. At 85 to 90 miles an hour, I figured we would make the 120-mile trip between Chattanooga and Nashville in record time—if we didn't get killed first.

Delo Brock sat beside me. I'd met him a few months earlier when another inmate told me that Delo had some information about Buggy Torbett for me. He said he had talked to Torbett at the county workhouse. "He told me that everything he said at your trial was a lie," Delo said. "Let me know if you ever get a new trial. I'll be glad to testify."

I didn't think a new trial was likely, but I thanked him for wanting to help.

At 40, Delo was a career criminal with a 110-year sentence. Actually, he didn't really have much of a "career" as a criminal perpetrator. An alcoholic and drug addict, most of his convictions were for being with others when they committed various crimes. It wasn't unusual for him to wake up in jail after an alcoholic blackout, facing serious charges, and have no recollection whatsoever of the events. Now, after years of wandering in and out of prison on short sentences, he had made the big time with a first-degree murder conviction. Worse for him, his codefendant believed Delo had snitched on him. He swore he would kill Delo the minute he stepped behind the walls.

"Jerry, I didn't tell on that boy," he complained, offering me a smoke. I waved off the cigarette and nodded. I wasn't indifferent to his feelings, but I'd already heard the story several times, and I had other things on my mind.

"I'm not a new buddy [a new inmate who has never been to prison, sometimes called 'fresh fish'],'' he continued bitterly. "People ought to know me better than that.''

"What are the walls like?'' I asked, changing the subject. Like most men who spent their lives working a life sentence on the installment plan, Delo could deliver a detailed, colorful, and anecdote-strewn monologue on the history and culture of the state pen. I'd already heard many of the stories before, but I figured it would keep his mind off his troubles, and I could enjoy watching the familiar Tennessee countryside while he talked.

People in other cars usually did a double take when they saw the police van and recognized it. I saw children excitedly pointing their fingers at us, and I could easily imagine what their parents must be saying about us. It was disconcerting to know that people were afraid when they saw me dressed in prison clothes. *I guess clothes do make the man*, I thought sourly.

✦ ✦ ✦

With a skyrocketing crime rate, prisoners were rapidly becoming society's official scapegoat as the decade of the seventies ended. This was particularly true in Tennessee after the "clemency for cash" disclosures brought down Governor Blanton's administration. I'd been approached in late 1977 by another prisoner and told my sentence could be commuted if I had $20,000. The F.B.I. and other law enforcement agencies were already buzzing around the Tennessee Department of Corrections like a swarm of angry hornets, but I wasn't interested in that anyway.

Although the governor was never implicated directly in the scandal, he had commuted hundreds of sentences in order to meet a court-ordered reduction in TSP's bulging population. Several of his senior aides, however, were convicted and sent to prison for selling pardons to inmates who had been convicted for serious crimes. To prevent Blanton from signing any more pardons or commutations, Governor Lemar Alexander was sworn into office several days early and locked Blanton out of his office.

The public was outraged at the thought of inmates buying their way out of prison. Prosecutors and other elected officials quickly climbed on the "lock 'em up and throw away the key" bandwagon. The once popular racist demagoguery was replaced by heated rhetoric about crime and criminals. Hundreds of newspaper stories fueled public hostility. Funding for rehabilitation programs dried up, but the prison population climbed higher. More than 2,500 men were crammed into a space designed for 900 at TSP. Like rats driven mad in a crowded cage, prisoners turned on one another, and the murder rate behind the walls climbed steadily higher.

I was not looking forward to life behind the walls at TSP!

✦ ✦ ✦

As we began the climb over Mount Eagle I tuned everything else out in my mind. I watched the scenery speeding by and tried to remember the number of times I'd driven this same route on business only three years earlier. It seemed like a century had passed since I had taken my 7-year-old daughter to Opryland on the same highway a month before my trial. I wondered if I would ever see her again.

Alexandr Solzhenitsyn once said that a prisoner's life was cut in half, and forever after a convicted man always thinks of the world in terms of what happened before prison and what happened afterward—if an afterward ever came. No other place in the world reveals the depths of human cruelty, depravity, or barbarism like a prison environment. It's hard to remain enchanted with humankind after watching what they do to one another in the bitter prison arena.

The van sped over the mountain, and the humming tires sang a mournful song for me: Ninety-nine years! Ninety-nine years! Ninety-nine years! *Is God merely the Eternal Bystander, as Camus had described him?* I wondered. But I didn't want to think about that just then.

❖ ❖ ❖

Suddenly, I realized Delo had asked me something. "Sorry, my mind wandered. What did you say?"

Delo chuckled. "You're entitled to be on mind-escape after what you've been through. But I asked if you were afraid?"

Puzzled, I looked at him. "Afraid of what?"

"Prison! They've got men packed into that zoo like sardines now. I've heard that stickings [stabbings], rapes, and robbery are as common as the cockroaches up there. Aren't you scared?"

"No, not really."

"I am," he admitted softly. "I don't know what I'm facing up there, but I ain't gonna check in [seek protective custody]," he added fiercely. We rode in silence for several minutes, each of us locked into his own dream—or nightmare!—before he spoke again. "It's none of my business, but I know you've never been to the joint before. I'd like to know why you aren't afraid?"

Actually, his questions startled me. I'm not the macho type, and I don't have any more courage than the average person. Even though I knew Tennessee State Prison's grim reputation for human savagery, it hadn't even occurred to me that I had anything to fear. But how could I explain that to him without hurting his feelings.

"Do you know why you're afraid?" I asked.

He looked at me like I was an idiot and swore. "Of course I do! That place is a lunatic asylum, and some people think I'm a snitch. Somebody's gonna try and kill me, and there's not much I can do about it. Isn't that enough?"

I shook my head. "You do have a problem," I admitted. "But that's not the *real* reason you're scared. You're afraid right now because you're going into the prison wilderness alone and on your own. You don't have Anybody with whom you can trust your life."

"Maybe so, but you don't either," he snapped.

"Actually, I do. I've got God with me, so there's nothing to be afraid of behind those walls or anywhere else on earth. Haven't you heard: 'Although the Lord gives you the bread of adversity and the water of affliction, your teachers will be hidden no more; with your own eyes you will see them. Whether you turn to the right or to the left, your ears will hear a voice behind you, saying, "This is the way; walk in it." ' Or: ' "I know the plans

I have for you," declares the Lord, "plans to prosper you and not to harm you, plans to give you hope and a future" ' " (Isa. 30:20; Jer. 20:11, NIV).

Curiously, he looked at the miniature gold cross I wore on the tip of my collar. It was a gift from my Grandfather Whary. "D'you really believe all that faith stuff?" he asked suspiciously.

"Absolutely!"

"It doesn't look like God has been doing you any favors lately," he said pointedly. "Why would God allow a skunk like Torbett do what he did to you?"

"I don't know about that," I admitted. "But I don't believe God gives us any special immunity from pain, unfairness, or adversity just because we're Christians. God isn't a cosmic vending machine in which we put in our 'faith-prayer' coins, pull a lever, and some goodie pops out."

"Then what's God good for?" he asked bluntly.

"Delo, do you love somebody like a wife or a child because they're your personal servants or because of the special relationship you have with them?"

He shrugged without comment.

"I don't know why some things happen the way they do," I continued. "But I do know this: when you *know* God is with you, that He is on your side, offering support and encouragement even as you walk into a modern-day lions' den, you've got nothing to be afraid of, no matter what your circumstances."

"That sounds good," he admitted, "but what *proof* do you have that any of this is true?"

I thought long and hard before answering. "Delo," I said quietly, "you're afraid and I'm not."

"You mean you don't care whether or not God does something to get you out of prison? I thought all you Christians depended on miracles."

"Let me ask you a question: Isn't it a greater miracle for me to be relatively contented and happy *in* prison?"

We rode the rest of the way in silence, but he left me wondering: What proof did I have of God's love and care in my life, especially after all I'd been through in the past three years? The question was insistent and disturbing. Even though I was guilty of obstructing justice, I didn't deserve what I was facing, not by any stretch of the imagination. Was God setting me up for a big letdown?

✦ ✦ ✦

"Welcome to your new home, boys," the driver called out cheerfully as he parked in front of the decrepit-looking reception center.

It certainly didn't look like any home I'd ever lived in! The building had once served as the state prison for women, but it had long since been condemned. It *looked* doomed. Most of the windows were broken out. Bricks were falling off the walls—literally. And the dirty-yellow paint was cracked and peeling everywhere. It was even worse inside. The sour, stale smell of unwashed human bodies and disinfectant smashed into my nose like a boxer's vicious right hook as I stepped through the door. The stench was overpowering. As the belly chains and leg irons were unlocked, I heard what seemed like a mocking voice from deep within: *So God is with you huh? Sucker!*

The next three hours were spent in a flurry of institutional activity: filling out endless forms, answering questions, turning left and right for mug shots, cell assignments, strip searches, and dressing out in the shabby prison clothes. Everything that was colored—towels and washcloths, sheets and pillow cases, even my colored jersey shirts were confiscated.

"Either send 'em home, or we'll give the stuff to the Salvation Army," a trusty said.

I didn't have a home. I learned later that the trusties kept anything that was of value. The junk they gave away.

I looked at the prison I.D. card I'd been issued. *Now I've got a number: triple eight, fifty-six,* I thought.

I looked into the mirror as an inmate barber trimmed my shaggy hair. It was the first real mirror I'd seen in three years. Except for polished stainless steel, we had no mirrors in the jail. I barely recognized the grim-looking, pale man staring back at me. I *looked* like a criminal, and I shrank, feeling the metaphorical doors slamming shut behind me. I was swallowed up in the mindless oblivion of prison: cut off forever from family, friends, colleagues, and the world as I had known it for the first 34 years of my life.

I got another bitter taste of prison when I returned to my cell after lunch. Everything I owned had been rifled and flung about the filthy cell. Everything of value—if only marginally—was gone. A young guard snickered as he locked the door behind me. I'd been warned that the only difference between prisoners and some prison guards was the color of uniform each wore. I knew that was grossly overstated, but I hated them all at that moment as I looked at the wreckage in my cell.

"Is everything all right?" the guard asked, still smirking.

I looked him in the eye until he nervously looked away. "Yes, everything is just lovely here in Camp Run-Amok," I replied.

It's easy to have faith during the days of wine and roses, when one is surrounded by loving family, friends, and symbols of success. Why not? What does faith cost then? All the good things of life sustain faith as a pious idea: God is in His heaven and all is well with the world. But suddenly, like Job, I didn't know *where* God was, and almost *nothing* was well in my world. I wondered if Delo didn't have more sense than I had—and I just didn't want to see it or admit it. Maybe my experience with God's grace back at the jail had just been a fantasy of some sort. Maybe my beliefs about God in general were little more than pathetic, infantile illusions, an immature refusal on my part to come to terms with the utter meaninglessness of my life and my predicament. Yes, a fair question: What *proof* did I have to the contrary?

I slumped on the bunk and struggled with the bile of anger bulging in my throat. "Thanks a lot, Lord," I muttered sarcastically. "I really do appreciate all the help You've been since I was arrested, but I don't think I can stand much more of it!"

I will be with you always . . . .

170

I dismissed that intruding thought with disgust and stretched out on my bunk.

✦ ✦ ✦

The next day my side of the cellblock was called out for exercise in the yard at 10:00 in the morning. It was a small, chain-link enclosed yard, measuring approximately 75 yards by 30 yards. Rolls of razor-sharp concertina wire were strung over the top of the fence. A man would be ripped to bloody ribbons if he tried climbing over it. Just for good measure, however, a shotgun-toting officer stood outside the fence, warily watching the 180 convicts crowded into the pen.

Some men scattered immediately to the center of the yard where a half basketball court was located. Others played a rough-and-tumble game of volleyball, and a few pitched horseshoes. Most of the inmates who had been to prison before knew one another. Each game was played with violent intensity, each man pouring his frustration and hatred into attacks on the balls and horseshoes. I could have cut the smoldering hatred hovering over that field with a knife.

The perimeter of the yard was surrounded by a crusty, foot-worn path from the feet of tens of thousands of inmates who had walked it through the years. It was a single path for those solitary men who didn't want company.

I found a small patch of scruffy grass in a corner of the field and sat down, wearily leaning back against the fence. I closed my eyes, and the angry feelings slowly passed as I absorbed sensations I hadn't experienced in years. The heat of the sun and the cool breeze felt wonderful on my skin. I knew I'd burn to a crisp within minutes, but I didn't move. Even the scruffy grass felt new and good. I stroked it like a pet with my fingers. Cars and trucks hurried back and forth on the busy highway in front of the prison. Everybody seemed to be in such a big hurry. I smiled: I didn't have to worry about being in a hurry for the rest of my life! The smell of diesel fuel and the sound of humming tires reminded me that the world was still very much alive and breathing.

On a nearby hillside I could see cows from the prison farm placidly grazing. I remembered my uncle's farm in Maine as the smell of cattle and manure wafted over the yard each time the wind direction changed.

All at once I noticed a tiny purple weed flower peeping out over the clump of grass near my hand. Something about that insignificant weed captivated my attention. In the midst of all this filth, chaos, and human wreckage, a lovely, delicate flower struggled for life. I picked it and held it up close for inspection. It looked like a miniature orchid, exquisite and fragile, but tough and sturdy at the same time. Soft hues of the color purple splashed over the petals. A deeply rooted intuitive wisdom within knew that the still, small voice of God was speaking to me through that flower. But I didn't understand the message.

I put the flower in my pocket when the yard was cleared.

Several new prisoners like me were driven to TSP that afternoon for chest X-rays, dental exams, and a brief physical. As the transport van pulled into the parking lot, I understood why convicts had sardonically dubbed the prison: "Disneyland" or "The Castle." The administration building was, in fact, an enormous plantation mansion, built in the mid-1900s. With turrets and gun towers, it looked like an old castle—complete with dungeons and dragons, I suspected.

We drove around the side of the building. That's when I saw the 20-foot high walls that surrounded the penitentiary. The walls had been constructed at the turn of the century, built with convict labor out of massive granite slabs. A huge gate was built into the wall halfway down the southeast side of the wall. It was big enough for a tractor trailer to drive through.

"That's what they call the 'vehicle gate,' " another inmate explained. "That's the picnic area you can see off to your right. It's open year-round. Your family can spend all day with you on the weekends. Plus, it's open from 3:00 in the afternoon until dusk during the week."

The guard got out of the van and put his pistol in a bucket that another guard dropped down from the gun tower overlooking the gate. Once the bucket had been pulled up, the massive gates slowly slid open. We pulled into a trapgate and stopped inside. Once the trapgate officer had collected our prison I.D. cards, the second gate opened.

"You men stand by that wall until I process the rest of your paperwork and they call for you at the hospital," the driver said.

I leaned against the stone wall and watched what seemed like hundreds of convicts walking to and fro inside the walls. Out of the corner of my eye I noticed something between the cracks on the wall. I turned to inspect the wall more closely. The granite slabs had been laid down in a crisscross fashion, with mortar between the slabs. But with the passage of time, compounded by decades of freezing and thawing, the mortar had slowly cracked and crumbled in many places. Birds took advantage of larger holes to build their nests. Driven by wind and rain, dust and seeds had slowly accumulated between the smaller cracks over the years. I smiled when I saw several of those miniature purple weed flowers sprouting from cracks in the wall.

How could something that fragile and vulnerable manage to bloom so gloriously in the cleft of these rocks? I wondered.

Bloom where you're planted!

That uninvited thought pressed in upon my mind as I went through the process of being probed and X-rayed that afternoon. Was God speaking to me through this tiny weed flower.

Bloom where you're planted!

I pulled from my pocket a small New Testament and turned to Jesus' words in Matthew: "Look at the birds of the air; they do not sow or reap or store away in barns, and yet your heavenly Father feeds them. Are you not much more valuable than they? . . . See how the lilies of the field grow. They do not labor or spin. Yet I tell you that not even Solomon in all his splendor was dressed like one of these. If that is how God clothes the grass of the field, which is here today and tomorrow is thrown into the fire, will he not much more clothe you, O you of little faith? So do not worry, saying, 'What shall we eat?' or 'What shall we drink?' or 'What shall we wear?' For the pagans run after all these things, and your heavenly Father knows that you need them. But seek first his kingdom and his righteousness, and all these things will be given to you as well" (Matt. 6:26-34, NIV).

Bloom where you're planted!

I put the small Bible back in my pocket. The command sounded both challenging and reassuring. It felt like God was saying, "Sure, you're in a tough spot. But My grace is sufficient. You can bloom where you're planted, just like that flower."

As we drove back to the Reception Center later that afternoon, I remembered some of the lyrics from an old hymn by Fanny Crosby:

> A wonderful Savior is Jesus my Lord,
>   A wonderful Savior to me,
> He hideth my soul in the cleft of the rock,
>   Where rivers of pleasure I see.
>
> A wonderful Savior is Jesus my Lord,
>   He taketh my burden away,
> He holdeth me up, and I shall not be moved,
>   He giveth me strength as my day.
>
> With numberless blessings each moment He crowns,
>   And filled with His fullness divine,
> I sing in my rapture, Oh glory to God
>   For such a Redeemer as mine.
>
> When clothed in His brightness, transported I rise
>   To meet Him in clouds of the sky,
> His perfect salvation, His wonderful love,
>   I'll shout with the millions on high.
>
> He hideth my soul in the cleft of the rock
>   That shadows a dry, thirsty land;
> He hideth my life in the depths of His love,
>   And covers me there with His hand.

✦ ✦ ✦

Showers were the last order of business for the day before lock-down. We had to take our showers in a large stall that had three nozzles—one per man. Men stood in a long line, waiting their turn for a strictly timed five minutes under the spray. The process was unnecessarily degrading and humiliating for some, especially younger men who had never been to prison. Threats, catcalls, whistles, and a variety of perverted propositions were hurled at them every time they stepped into the shower.

Some of the guards standing nearby laughed.

I stood at the end of the line. Nobody else was left when my turn came. At 6 feet 2 and 220 pounds, I didn't have to worry too much about any of the

173

penitentiary predators, but I still enjoyed the time alone. The last guard left to lock up some cells, telling me he'd be back in five minutes.

Just then I happened to look out the window. The color purple screamed out of the sunset sky. A frothing frenzy of purple, blue, red, gold, and orange gripped my eye. Transfixed, in awe, I walked toward the window, vaguely aware of how Moses must have felt when he encountered the burning bush. I felt as though I'd never really seen a sunset before. The sky looked like a magnificent canvas upon which some cosmic Painter had joyfully hurled billions of gallons of passionate-colored paint.

A fragment from Isaiah 43:10 danced in my mind: "He will spread his royal canopy above them" (NIV). The purple hues in the sky and on my tiny weed flower were the same.

"Bragan! You're out of place!" the guard shouted. "What do you think you're doing at that window!"

I told him. Suspiciously, he looked at me and then at the sky. "I'm a Christian too," he finally said. "You can stay until the sun goes down if you want."

Tears stung my eyes as I absorbed the majesty of God's moment with me. Purple is the symbol of a king, and I knew that no matter where I went or what my circumstances, I could still claim kinship with God, the ultimate King, through Christ. As Noah had found comfort and reassurance in the rainbow as God's sign for him after a great storm, this sunset and flower—splashed with the royal color purple—was my *proof* of God's presence and abiding care. Somehow I *knew* that God's grace would be rich in measure as I faced the many and difficult years ahead for me in prison.

✦ ✦ ✦

Two weeks later a guard stopped in front of my cell. "Bragan, you've got a visitor out in the lobby."

A slender man with iron-gray hair and an infectious grin stood up as I entered the lobby. "Hey, it's great to meet you, Jerry!" he said, pumping my hand. "My name is Conn Arnold. Margaret Sharp told me you were here and asked me to visit you."

I liked Conn at first sight, but I had gotten increasingly uncomfortable and withdrawn whenever I was around free-world people, especially people I liked. I didn't seem to have much in common with "normal" people anymore. Or perhaps I was jealous of their freedom to come and go. In any event, I tried to be cordial with Conn, even though I didn't feel like it. I learned that he'd been a pastor for many years before being elected to the position of Personal Ministries Director for the Kentucky/Tennessee Conference of Seventh-day Adventists. Our visit lasted about 30 minutes. He expressed some interest in prison ministry and prayed for me before he left.

"I'll be back to see you again, Jerry," he said. "Straight ahead!"

Straight ahead, indeed! I thought.

Frankly, I never expected to see him again.

14

Trail of Blood

I TALKED to one of the staff counselors shortly before I was transferred from the reception center to the main prison. "What's the best way to survive at TSP?" I asked.

"Survive? That's a good choice of words, because that's just about the best you can hope for over there," he said bluntly. "Keep to yourself. Mind your own business. Don't see anything you're not supposed to see. Don't stare at other convicts. If you don't get killed in the first couple of years, you'll probably survive."

"My, but you're full of optimism today!"

"Yeah, sure. I'm sorry to say it, but there's nothing in that place for a man with your background or education. In fact, the less you let people know about you, the better off you'll be. Convicts resent other prisoners they consider square-John citizens."

"But I've got more time than most of them!"

"That doesn't matter. Regardless of your conviction, you'll always be a square-John to them, and they'll look for a chance to carve you down to size. I hope you make it."

Make it? I thought. *What a delicate way to tell somebody you hope they don't get killed!*

◆ ◆ ◆

I knew the score when I walked through the trapgate at Tennessee State Prison that Friday evening, July 18, 1980: Lions everything, Christians nothing! Even though the prison had a hard-earned reputation for human savagery, I was more tired than afraid when the steel gate slammed shut behind me. It's an unnerving sound. I knew that once those gates closed, there was no way back. I was swallowed up in the belly of an evil beast, finally cut off for good from the free world, isolated in an arena in which men routinely preyed on one another like killer sharks in the sea.

"Hey, Bragan! Is that you?"

I turned around. It was Erwin, a man I'd met two years earlier at the jail. He was a former student at Southern Missionary College. Although Erwin was a couple of years older than I, Dr. Gladson had been concerned about his welfare at the jail and asked me to look out for him. It was good to see a friendly face. He grabbed my hand and slapped me on the back.

"Let me help you carry your stuff down to the block," he suggested. "It's almost time for lock-down, so we can't talk tonight. C'mon up to the chapel services at 9:00 tomorrow morning, and I'll show you around the joint."

I stepped into Unit IV, the housing unit I'd been assigned. It had been built a hundred years earlier—and looked like it, too! In trying to make the prison environment more civilized, prison officials had renamed all the blocks as "units." But prison traditions don't die that easily. I quickly learned that most of the older prisoners still called it "D Block." The cellblock smelled of disinfectant, dust, and the sour odor of human fear trapped in a cage.

Four hundred men, two in each seven-foot-by-six-foot cell, were crammed into space designed for 190. I glanced around. One guard sat at a desk on the main floor, known as the "Rock" in penitentiary jargon. Another officer was patrolling the walks, letting men in or out of their cells. Nearly 200 inmates were out milling around in small groups. The noise was incredible. Screaming radios, TVs, shouting voices, the crash of steel on steel, the rattle of heavy industrial fans. It came at me from every direction, surrounding and assaulting my senses with pummeling force.

The cells were built into the center of the block. Each one had a door with grill-style bars running from top to bottom. The unit was five stories high. Each side of the building had five walks, with 19 cells on each walk. I felt scores of eyes watching me as I climbed the five flights of stairs to nine walk, nineteenth cell

I might as well have had a sign painted on my back: New buddy! I thought.

I was glad to be in the nineteenth cell—it was the last one on the tier. That gave me fighting room, if it came to that, without having to worry about my back. My new address would be: Jeris E. Bragan #88856, Station A—Unit IV:19/9. Translation: Station A was the prison. Unit 4:19/9 meant cell 19 on 9 walk in Unit IV.

My cell partner, Jim, was already in for the night, stretched out on the lower bunk and watching *20/20* on TV. The space was too small for more than one man standing on the floor at a time, so he stayed out of the way while I shoved my box of books and other property under his bunk. The block wasn't air conditioned, so the cell was sweltering. Sweat poured off me. I climbed up on the top bunk and tried to cool off while I looked around. I was astonished by the creative way in which Jim had fixed his cell. In the midst of incredible filth and squalor, his cell had matching quilts on each bunk, carpets on the floor, and a curtain hanging over the door. Several small lamps provided excellent lighting.

"I never expected to see a cell looking like this," I admitted.

Jim laughed. "It took me 10 years of scrounging bits and pieces to get it this way."

His cell partner had left earlier in the evening on parole. Before he could arrange for another cellee, operations had assigned me to the space. I knew he wasn't happy with a stranger in his cell, but at least he didn't show it.

Given the massive overcrowding, space was at a premium, and penitentiary rules about "cell ownership" were clearly spelled out within the convict population: the senior man "owned" the cell. He decided who lived in the cell with him. If the price was right, he could sell the entire cell, or the second bunk, to another man. Any disputes on the issue were quickly settled with clubs or knives! Prison administrators didn't officially sanction this "homesteading" policy, but there were too many prisoners and too few staff members to do much about it.

Arriving new prisoners quickly went on a merry-go-round of cell changes, bounced from one cell to another until they either forced the senior man out, bought their own cell, or lucked into an empty one. Jim let me know, politely, that a friend of his would be moving in on Monday. I wasn't looking forward to the cell-hopping journey. I just wanted to sleep.

Every morning began the same way at 6:30—the ringing of a hand-held bell and a guard bellowing through a bullhorn: "Chow call! Chow call! Five minutes to first chow call!" In order to feed more than 2,000 men in a short period of time, a second call came 15 minutes later, followed in another 15 minutes by the third and final call. As each call came, a second guard at the end of the walk would pull a huge lever and all the doors would open at once. The doors were supposed to be individually locked, but that was done only at night because it took too much time for two guards to lock and unlock each individual door. The lever was efficient, but I soon learned it also allowed cell thieves to break in and steal anything they wanted when the cell was empty.

It looked like a swirling sea of blue as hundreds of men dressed in blue denims poured out of five cellblocks, plus the hospital and SDC (the honor dorm located on the west side of the ball field), all rushing toward the chow hall at once. I spotted Erwin and ran to catch up with him.

"I see you got through your first night," he said.

"Sure. One down, 10,000 to go."

The dining room was actually two huge rooms, each containing approximately 80 tables with four chairs bolted to the table. Each side had a separate entrance and two serving lines. I thought I'd stepped back in time to 1950 when I entered the room. An invisible line ran down the center of each dining room: Blacks sat on the left side of the room, and Whites sat on the right. Only a small handful of White men were sitting with the Blacks.

Erwin followed my gaze. "It's quite a sight, isn't it?"

"Is there much racial conflict here?" I asked.

"Surprisingly, there's very little. The population is about evenly divided in terms of numbers, so both sides make sure interracial squabbles don't blow up into something more serious."

"Who are those White guys sitting with the Blacks?"

Erwin shook his head. "Those are what they call 'gal-boys' or 'punks.' They're homosexuals. A few are whores, but most of them live with their . . . ah . . . boyfriends. You'll see a lot of that kind of stuff around here, but after a while it's so common you don't even notice it anymore."

"This place would be paradise for a cultural anthropologist," I joked.

I heard several people complaining about the food, but I thought it was pretty good for institutional food: scrambled eggs, grits, sausage, jelly, and toast. After years of eating jail food, however, I wasn't much of a critic. In any event, after watching prisoners work themselves up into a rage over the food they ate, a studied indifference to food was one of the choices I made early in my incarceration. My only requirement of food was that it kill an appetite. Rarely was I disappointed!

Unlike the jail or reception center, where prisoners spent most of the time locked up in cells, the penitentiary was wide open.

I asked Erwin about that.

"According to policy, people are supposed to be in their cells unless they're at work, in school, or on the ball field," he admitted. "In theory, you need a written pass to go anywhere. But those rules are impossible to enforce with more than 2,000 prisoners and a limited number of staff. As long as the violence is kept down to a dull roar, the convicts pretty much run the penitentiary and do as they please."

"How do you protect yourself in a place like this?"

He shrugged. "You really can't. You just have to use your best judgment and hope for the best."

"By the way, where's the hospital?"

Before Erwin could reply, another man at the table spoke up: "The hospital is easy to find. Just follow the trail of blood."

I thought he was joking. I soon learned he was serious. Stabbings were so common that the sidewalk running north and south between the cellblocks and the hospital usually had a trail of blood sprinkled on it each day.

✦ ✦ ✦

I got my first good look at the prison that morning. Drab, dreary, depressing, and run-down, I thought. The prison occupied approximately 15 acres, surrounded on three sides by that massive granite wall. The four main cellblocks that ran across the front of the prison acted as the fourth wall. Several strands of barbed wire, carrying 5,000 volts of electricity at high amperage, ran along the top of the walls. For additional security, 10 gun towers on the walls looked down into the compound. It wasn't escape-proof, but only a few men successfully made it over those walls.

As a person entered the compound through the administration building's trapgate, Units I (used as the "hole" and protective custody) and II were directly to the right. Units III and IV were to the left. Directly across from the units on the left side was the chow hall. Unit V, which had four men stuffed in each cell, had been built on top of the chow hall. Directly across from the chow hall, separated by a concrete sidewalk that ran north and south between the administration building and the ball field, was Unit VI—death row, which held 30 condemned men at the time. As I looked at the bunker-style building, I realized that except for timing I might very well have been sitting in the block myself.

Beyond the dining room and death row were four more three-story brick buildings, two on each side of the sidewalk. The ancient plants were slowly crumbling—quite literally. Warning signs were posted on the facilities: "Stay Back Ten Feet—Falling Brick." On the right were two buildings used for the metal plant, where highway signs and metal desks and chairs were manufactured by inmates for state office buildings. That's also where inmates produced a steady supply of deadly shanks, homemade knives measuring from six to 12 inches in length and sharp as a razor on both sides. They cost between $3 and $5.

I knew it was only a question of time before I got to meet one of those shanks.

In front of the metal plant were the offices for the inmate newspaper, *The Interim*.

Across from the newspaper, on the left side of the sidewalk, two more dilapidated buildings housed the wood shop. Anything the state needed made of wood, whether desks or shelves, were manufactured there.

Moving north on the sidewalk, on the left was the commissary and laundry—still known as the "bathhouse" from the days before showers had been installed in the units and men were marched to the bathhouse twice a week for showers. Behind that was the school building, where inmates had access to adult basic education, a GED, or college classes provided by TSU's "College Behind the Walls" program. Directly across from the laundry stood the chapel. The school building, chapel, and hospital were the only new facilities—at least new in the sense that they'd been built in the past 20 years—behind the walls.

Scraggly lawns around the chow hall, Unit VI, the plants, and school were kept up by an inmate yard crew.

Another granite wall, bordering a narrow road that ran around the interior of the compound, ran east and west between the "vehicle gate" and the hospital. It also divided the prison into two equal halves by acting as a security buffer between the upper ball field area and the lower compound. Halfway along the wall was another gate, known as the "green gate" because it had once been painted green, that allowed entry to the ball field. In the event of a riot or serious disturbance, the gate could be pulled shut and locked. The front entrance to the hospital actually completed the end of that wall. The hospital itself jutted out into the ball field.

Directly behind the hospital, bordering the west wall, was the three-story honor dorm, commonly referred to by the initials SDC (Self-determination Center), which was located in a fenced-off compound. Other inmates weren't allowed to enter the compound. A person had to be at the "walls" for at least a year, employed for a year, and have no disciplinary write-ups for 12 months before he could apply for admission to SDC. Then the applicant had to meet the inmate governing board of SDC. He was admitted if the other inmates approved. There was no appeal if they didn't. Not surprisingly, this system was characterized by favoritism, bribes, and every other form of abuse imaginable in the prison.

Despite the problems, however, the program had a long waiting list because of the advantages SDC offered. Each floor had several pay phones that residents could use 24 hours a day. They had single rooms they could lock with their own key. Each week they could order food from a nearby grocery store—which they paid for with their own money. They weren't locked up at night. In fact, they were free to sleep out on the grass in the enclosed compound if they wished—a practice that was halted in 1983 after three men escaped during a heavy fog. While confined to the building at night, they still weren't locked up.

I decided to apply for admission as soon as possible!

✦ ✦ ✦

Before going to the Adventist chapel services, Erwin took me by the 7th

Step Foundation office to meet some of the leaders. The organization, modeled after Alcoholics Anonymous, had been established in the early 60s by Bill Sands, an ex-con from San Quentin. Instead of AA's 12 steps, he wrote what he called "The Seven Step Pledge to Freedom." Sands believed that only hard-core convicts could help other cons who wanted to get their lives straightened out.

James "Buster" Collins, the organization's assistant chapter coordinator, talked to me for a few minutes about the program and invited me to come to their remotivation class that afternoon. He was in his early-20s, convicted for murder and sentenced to life. His cheerfulness and warmth surprised me until I learned he was a Christian. Prisoners who were Christian didn't have any special immunity from the hardships of prison life, but those who were genuinely committed to their faith were generally happier than those around them.

"I was raised in the Church of God, but I go to most of the services," Buster explained. "It don't matter to me whether they're Catholic, Baptist, or Seventh-day Adventist. There aren't that many Christian brothers in this joint, so we tend to cross over denominational lines and try to stick together."

After the decrepit appearance of most buildings behind the walls, the beauty of the chapel surprised me. It was relatively new and seated 150 people in modern wooden pews. A piano and organ were available for music. But only six men attended the service.

"That's about average for most of the services," Erwin said.

The service was short and perfunctory. I wasn't surprised that few men attended.

After dinner I went to the school where the 7th Step Remotivation class was held. More than 100 inmates, family members, and free-world volunteers crowded into one of the classrooms. The first free-world person I met was Doc Wallace, a paraplegic who had been wounded in World War II. In spite of his disability, he was a wealthy retired businessman who practiced his Catholic faith with particular elegance. In addition to founding Goodwill Industries in Nashville, he also had helped establish the 7th Step Foundation. He invested a great deal of his money and time in helping prisoners get their lives straightened out in prison and on the right road when they finally left. Each week he purchased 100 pints of ice cream for those who attended the 7th Step classes.

Next I was introduced to another founder of the program, Dr. Barbara Wallston, Ph.D. Her glasses looked like the bottom of a Coke bottle. She was a short, plump professor at Vanderbilt University's graduate school of psychology.

The class began when everyone stood in a circle and recited the Seven Steps to Freedom. The class coordinator led the group:

"Step One: Facing the truth about ourselves and the world around us, we decided we needed to change.

"Step Two: Realizing that there is a power from which we can gain strength, we decided to use that power.

"Step Three: Evaluating ourselves by taking an honest daily appraisal, we examined both our strengths and our weaknesses.

"Step Four: Endeavoring to help ourselves overcome our weaknesses, we enlisted the aid of that power to help us concentrate on our strengths.

"Step Five: Deciding that our freedom is worth more than our resentments, we are using that power to help free us from those resentments.

"Step Six: Observing that daily progress is necessary, we set an attainable goal toward which we work each day.

"Step Seven: Maintaining our freedom, we pledge ourselves to help others as we have been helped."

I thought the pledge contained a pretty good philosophy.

Beating drug addiction was the topic for the day.

Although Barbara was Jewish, she was, by her own definition, an agnostic who was intensely skeptical about anything remotely connected with religion. She was blunt as a brick wall when it came to confronting convicts she thought were hiding out behind religious clichés in group discussions.

"I don't want to hear all that god-talk," she told one man. "What I want to know is this: When are you going to quit sticking that needle in your veins? All your talk about prayer, plus a quarter, will get you a cup of coffee—nothing else."

Doc Wallace gently chided her: "Of course he has to make a decision to quit using drugs, but I believe prayer and faith in God gives us the strength to make the decision, then keep it," he insisted.

"Rubbish!" Barbara snorted.

I didn't share Barbara's point of view, but I liked her blunt honesty.

In addition to 7th Step, I soon discovered that there were several other inmate clubs behind the walls: the Lifer's Club, which was open to all lifers; the Pirates, open to inmates who worked in the braille class; and Parents in Prison, open to inmate parents who wanted to improve their parenting skills. For alcoholics and drug addicts, there was A.A. and N.A. Even the American Legion had a post behind the walls. Each year the clubs put on several banquets, picnics, and engaged in fund-raising activities. It looked good on paper, but there was a serious down side. Except for Alcoholics Anonymous, I quickly learned that all of the organizations were used to some extent by some inmate leaders as fronts for various forms of racketeering. In front of free-world volunteers, leaders maintained a "rehabilitated" front. Behind the scenes they continued their predatory lifestyle, using their position to wheel and deal in drugs.

On the plus side, however, savvy prison officials made sure the clubs had sufficient incentives to preclude more serious problems. Consequently, gangs, which plagued other prisons around the country, never gained a toehold at TSP. I noticed that many inmates took advantage of the rehabilitation programs available and got their lives back on track. The social activities allowed some, who had spent their entire lives in the criminal subculture, to establish real friendships with square-John free-world people like Doc, Barbara, and Conn Arnold for the first time.

181

BEYOND PRISON WALLS

Despite the problems I saw with 7th Step, that was where I decided to focus my energy. But first I had to establish myself as a "solid con" behind the walls. I knew that would be a neat trick, because I had resolved that I would not compromise either my Christian or free-world values.

◆ ◆ ◆

When a new prisoner first steps behind the walls, he *knows* he's going to be tried on for size by somebody within a few days of arrival. There's no maybe about it for those who don't have friends there already. The only law in the concrete-and-steel jungle of any prison for a new buddy is survival of the fittest, hammered and hacked out in the most barbaric, cruel, and ruthless terms. Consequently, when I moved to another cell, 4/10, I kept a wary eye on everybody around me as I moved my few belongings. When nothing happened during the first week I began to relax.

I ran out of luck on Friday. Three men stopped in front of my cell door shortly before the evening chow call. I didn't recognize them. One man pulled a shank out from under his shirt and held it up for me to look at. The blade had been polished and sharpened. My cell partner cowered out of sight on his bunk. I figured he'd set this up. So much for wishful thinking.

"Ya see this, chump?" he growled, lightly running his finger over the wicked-looking blade. From years of experience in working the streets as a detective, I suspected he was flying high on some dope, probably speed.

I nodded without speaking.

"Wassa matta, chump? You don't talk too good?"

"I can talk all right."

Another kid pushed his face closer to the door. He looked about 19, with long, stringy brown hair. His arms were covered with crude prison tatoos. Later I learned his brains were scrambled from sniffing too much glue. "Ya eitha set out ya watch and ring, or we're gonna cut ya heart out and bite it while it's still pumpin'," he giggled.

Colorful! A blizzard of conflicting ideas and feelings roared through my mind. I remembered an old convict telling me back at the jail: "There ain't no God behind the walls except a shank and a lead pipe. Stand on your own two feet, and don't *ever* back up from anybody. Not even an inch! If you back up one time, you'll spend the rest of your life in the joint traveling in reverse."

I glanced at my wedding band. Although it had long since lost any symbolic value to me, I kept it as a reminder of values that should never change. Staring at the three thieves, I tried to sort out my feelings. How is a Christian supposed to respond to such an encounter? If I gave them my property, I'd never have another peaceful day in prison. Ethical issues debated in high school and college didn't prepare me for this kind of nightmare.

"I think you lads would be better off going somewhere else," I suggested, trying to keep the bile of anger out of my voice.

The crazy one began to cackle in a high-pitched voice, "Did ju hear 'im? He thinks we oughtta go away."

"I'm personally gonna cut you up bad if you don't hand that ring and watch out here now," the first man snarled.

I nodded. "Maybe so."

He looked puzzled. "Are you crazy or somethin'? I'm gonna cut your head off and set it in the sink!" he screamed, waving the knife in the air.

"You might," I admitted, stalling for time. "But you know as well as I do it's not that easy to kill a man with a knife when he's not real thrilled with the idea. You *might* kill me. But then again, you might just lose that blade. Who knows what might happen in a donnybrook?"

The crazy one peered at me suspiciously. "What's a donnybrook? You gotta piece?"

I didn't answer.

The three men looked at one another, confused about what to do next. The robbery wasn't going right. I was a new buddy, supposedly an easy mark for the robber gangs that roamed the prison. The three thieves left the walk, promising to get me when I came out for chow.

I turned and looked at my cell-partner. "Man, I don't have nothing to do with those guys," he protested.

I shrugged. It didn't matter either way.

I stepped out onto the walk when the guard pulled the lever to my cell 30 minutes later. I kept my right hand stuffed in my pocket. Although I wasn't holding anything more deadly than a handful of sweat, nobody else knew that. The guard looked at me curiously when I remained standing in front of my cell, waiting for the 400-man mass to exit the cellblock. I'd heard stories about men being dropped in a crowd by an unknown assailant, the rest unaware he was stuck until he fell over with a piece of steel hanging out his back.

I knew the prison system well enough to know that the guard wouldn't be of any help, so I ignored him. Even if he was willing to interfere, I couldn't yell for help from a guard and expect to walk the prison yard later—at least not and live to tell about it.

As I stepped through the entrance to the cellblock, I saw the crazy one about 20 yards ahead, leaning against the wall of the chow hall. The second man lurked near the entrance, about 10 yards to my right. I didn't see the third one, but I knew he wouldn't be far away. Curtly, I nodded to the one standing near the door. He looked straight ahead, pretending he didn't see me. The handle of the shank stood out against his shirt. Briefly, I flirted with the idea of nailing him right where he stood, getting it all over and done with once and for all. Instead, I took a deep breath and began walking toward the chow hall.

The distance between the main dining room and the cellblock was the longest 100 yards I've ever walked. I could visualize my own trail of blood on the sidewalk leading to the hospital. Halfway between the two men I heard the sound of feet scuffling on the concrete behind me. The man hadn't moved—he just wanted to see me run. I didn't. I stopped and waited, looking directly at the kid leaning against the wall. Five seconds passed in silence. Ten seconds. Twenty. I had both hands in my pockets again. The kid stared at me owlishly, trying to focus his drug-soaked brain on me.

Men in prison seem to know, if only intuitively, when something is "going down," and they stay away from the scene of the action. But I could feel a hundred curious eyes watching. Silently. Waiting.

The crazy one got fidgety, changing his slouch from one foot to the next, until he began moving away, crablike, keeping his back to the wall until he was well past me. By the time I turned back to the cellblock, both men had ducked back inside.

I didn't see Buster or Erwin, so dinner was a lonely affair that night. Most prison killings take place inside the chow hall, so nobody sat beside me or even *at* the table I so conspicuously occupied in the crowded dining room. I would have been a lot happier if a legion of those proverbial angels had shown up about then. Instead, I suddenly remembered an obscure passage from Isaiah: "See, I have refined you, though not as silver; I have tested you in the furnace of affliction" (Isa. 48:10, NIV).

I chewed my food slowly, then wiped the sweat off my forehead. "Talk about a furnace!" I grumbled silently. "I need a small army, and You give me riddles!"

Nine-walk was deserted when I returned to the cellblock after dinner. Most of the population had gone to the ball field to escape the stifling heat inside the block. Thirty minutes later the same guard came around, opened my cell door, and let me go inside. After putting a tape of the Heritage Singers on my stereo, I leaned back against the cool, concrete wall, waiting for the Three Musketeers to return. I had no doubt they would be back.

I seem to be caught in a real bind, Lord, I prayed silently. *I don't want to hurt anybody, and I'm not real eager to get killed over something as trivial as a watch or wedding band. But if I just hand over what they want, I'll have to go through this exercise again and again. I won't be able to walk the yard safely, at least not without constant conflict.*

Silence.

As the following hour passed with only the Heritage Singers for company, I felt more than a little forlorn. What was I doing in this human sewer, I wondered, a million miles away from anything human or sane, trapped in some nightmarish time warp straight out of the *Twilight Zone.* I looked at my watch. Seven-thirty, EST. Once more I could hear the voices of old college friends singing in the Sligo church, even the good-natured grumbling about compulsory chapel attendance. That seemed like a century ago. "If the old gang could see me now," I chuckled sardonically, "they wouldn't believe their eyes!"

"Hey, man! Lemme talk at ya for a minute."

I leaned forward on the bunk. Standing at the door was the man who had flashed the knife at me earlier. "Here we go again," I sighed.

"Lookie here, we gotta straighten this thing out," he stammered. "Some friends of yours just talked to me, and said they'd have ta do something about me if I didn't lay off you, see?"

"No, I don't see. And I don't know what you're talking about. What friends?"

He looked agitated, fumbling around for words. "Look, this joint ain't big enough so's I gotta be lookin' over my shoulder all the time, wonderin' if you're comin' afta me, or your road dogs is gunnin' for me, too. So far, ain't nobody got hurt or lost nothin', right? You got heart—I can see that—and you ain't gonna let nobody rob you. I respect that. Let's say you and me call it a draw, OK?"

"I still don't know what you're talking about, but that suits me fine. No hard feelings either way."

"I got ya word on it?" he asked suspiciously. "You'll call off your friends?"

"We're square."

He stuck his hand through my cell door, a gesture of trust and goodwill, and locked his wrist and thumb with mine in a penitentiary-style handshake.

"Those homies of yours are the biggest and baddest-lookin' dudes I ever seen in my life! I don't want nothin' to do with 'em!" he said, backing away.

I sat down on the bunk, thoroughly puzzled. Then I remembered another fragment from the Psalms: "The angel of the Lord encamps around those who fear him, and he delivers them" (Ps. 34:7, NIV).

My evening prayer was brief: "Lord, nice timing!"

◆ ◆ ◆

I didn't see the man with the knife again, so I always wondered what had happened to him. Several years later Eddie McMillin, a solid Christian brother I'd once celled with, told me that Tim Kirk wanted me to come see him where he was housed in Unit I. Tim was Tennessee State Prison's most notorious prisoner, second only to James Earl Ray, convicted of killing Dr. Martin Luther King, Jr. In 1983, during an outbreak of racial violence in D-Block, Brushy Mountain Prison's maximum security unit, he used a pistol he'd smuggled into the prison to hold several guards hostage. Several Black inmates were wounded. Two were killed. Shortly before he went to trial for the shootings, his lawyer-turned-girlfriend smuggled another pistol in to him and helped him escape. He was captured in Florida several months later.

I had no idea why Tim wanted to see me.

It was 3:00 when I entered Unit I. Security was massive. After a thorough searching, a guard led me to an enclosed security cage for visitors and locked me inside. The cage was divided in half by a thick steel screen. Moments later I saw another guard leading Tim toward me. He had long, dark hair and a heavy beard plastered over a deathly pale face. He wasn't sick; he just hadn't seen any sunshine in many years. He was dressed in a bright orange jumpsuit, and his hands were cuffed behind his back. Once inside the cage, the guard locked the door from the outside. Tim turned his back to the officer, who reached through a small opening in the door and removed his cuffs.

Tim unzipped the front of his jumpsuit and pulled out a book. "I really like this book, and I wonder if you might be willing to autograph this for me?" he asked. It was my first book, *Scandalous Grace*.

"I'd be glad to," I said. "But I've gotta admit this is the last book I'd expect you to be reading."

A broad grin spread across his face for the first time. "I particularly liked the first chapter, the one about those three guys who tried to rob you when you first got here," he said. He peered at me closely as though looking for some kind of reaction.

"What was so special about that story?"

He leaned closer. "You don't recognize me, do you?"

"I don't think so," I admitted.

"Jeris, I was the guy with the knife!"

We talked for nearly two hours as he shared his life's story. But what he really wanted to tell me came at the end of our conversation. "I'm a Christian now," he said.

Quite understandably, security officials were deeply suspicious of Tim's profession of faith. When he asked to be baptized in the chapel, they refused to take him to the chapel for the rite, because they thought he was planning another spectacular escape.

Tim chuckled. "They were right to be suspicious; I was planning an escape. But it was the kind they didn't need to worry about."

In spite of security objections, Tim insisted that he had a right to be baptized. In order to avoid a lawsuit, a compromise was worked out: Guards brought a huge whirlpool tub to maximum security and placed it in a locked cell. The tub was filthy and so was the water. Tim didn't care. While several officers remained alert outside, a minister was allowed into the cell to baptize Tim in a tub.

"I've still got a lot of problems," he admitted after telling me the story of his baptism. "I know I'll probably never get out of here, but that's OK now because I know what you're talking about when you say the only real freedom is the kind that comes through Christian faith."

That was one of the most astonishing interviews I ever conducted in prison. Only two words describe it adequately.

Amazing grace!

15

Notes From the Pen

I FELT like a bouncing table tennis ball as I was forced to move from cell to cell during those first few weeks. The few people I knew already celled with friends, so I continued on the merry-go-round. Each time I moved, something of value inevitably disappeared: my University of Maryland class ring, a gold Cross pen, stamps, a jar of Tang powdered orange drink.

Meanwhile I was given a $25-a-month job working as a clerk for Harley Seimer, a veteran prison official who worked as the hospital administrator. I had no interest in working long-term in the hospital, but I knew that was the one place in the prison where I could get a good feel for what really went on behind the walls and who controlled the strings—whether staff or inmates.

Harley was a silver-haired, blustery kind of man in his 50s who constantly growled and complained about inmate help. He insisted that his clerk was supposed to fix him a cup of coffee first thing in the morning when he came to work and again right after lunch. I was just stubborn enough to refuse to do it until he finally asked for his coffee each day. Despite his complaints, Harley Seimer was an old-school prison official who genuinely cared about inmates. He didn't tolerate verbal abuse from prisoners, but he didn't tolerate staff members who mistreated prisoners either. Inmates liked him. Even though he had only an R.N. degree, stabbing victims preferred to have him work on them because he had more experience than most doctors when it came to dealing with trauma care.

Harley was particularly proud of his 120-bed hospital. He took me on a tour the first day I worked for him. Millions of tax dollars had recently been spent to turn it into a fully-equipped acute care medical facility, complete with the most modern operating and emergency rooms. The facility was designed to provide medical care for any inmate who required hospitalization throughout the state. But it was a white elephant. The state was moving rapidly to contracting medical care out to free-world hospitals.

Except for a couple of nurses and two physician assistants, the hospital had very few free-world staff members in 1980. Prisoners handled most nursing care for sick or injured inmates. A couple of dollars placed in the right hand got you first-rate medical care and the best food. An empty hand was rewarded with studied indifference.

◆ ◆ ◆

Finally, I made a cell change of my own and moved into Todd's cell. I'd met him at breakfast one morning. He was a "jail-house lawyer," one of those inmates who specialized in producing writs for other cons—for a price, of course. He was a few years older than I, but I'd had a bellyful of celling with younger men. Every time I came back to the cell at night, something was missing, my cellie was using our cell for a shooting gallery or tattoo parlor, or he kept the TV on half the night.

Everything went well between Todd and me the first evening. He showed me his law books and some of the briefs he'd written. But he turned sullen when I killed a cockroach.

"I don't kill cockroaches," he said emphatically. "Don't you be doing it in my cell. Just brush 'em out onto the walk."

I wondered if he might be a little nuts, but bizarre behavior is common with men in prison. I shrugged it off, climbed up on my bunk, and began reading.

An hour later Todd suddenly jumped up from his bunk. "You think you're smarter than everybody else, don't you, you big _____ !"

I glanced down and saw the foot-long, double-edged shank clasped in his right hand. The handle was crudely wrapped with sticky masking tape so his hand wouldn't slip on the steel. He backed away two steps until he blocked the door. The cellblock had been locked down for the night, so I knew the guard wouldn't hear me if I yelled for help. Before Todd did anything else, I swung off the bunk with a pillow clutched in my right hand, and landed four feet away from him. I'd seen men whose arms had been ripped to ribbons when they tried to ward off a stabbing, so I held the pillow in both hands to block any slashing attacks from him.

"What's wrong with you, Todd? Have you flipped out?"

"You think you're so _____ _____ smart," he snarled, dropping into a crouch. His arm was cocked. He held the weapon lightly in his hand. The blade waved back and forth in the air before me.

"Todd, you're making a big mis . . ."

He leaped at me, the knife held high over his hand. I stepped in close to him and thrust the pillow straight up to block his arm. Before he had time to move, I hooked my right heel behind his knee and shoved hard. He stumbled backward, slamming into the wall just as I seized his right wrist. I twisted it hard in a hammerlock, and swung him around. His knees hit the concrete floor hard as I shoved his face down on the bunk. The shank dropped out of his hand.

I stared at the weapon. Fueled by fear, I grabbed the shank without thinking and brought it back for a killing blow. I stopped just before I thrust the blade between his ribs. I realized my fear had almost driven me to murder. He was just lying there, not resisting. Instead, he giggled.

I stepped back, dragged him off the bunk, and braced him against the wall with my elbow. The adrenaline rush passed, and I shook like a leaf. "Are you nuts?" I shouted. "Are you out of your ever-loving freaking mind?"

He kept giggling. His eyes didn't seem to focus.

I threw him on the bunk like a rag doll and pointed my finger at him. "Don't you move from that bunk for the rest of the night," I warned.

His face took on a diabolical look. "But you've gotta sleep sometime," he cackled, "and I've got more where that came from," he added, pointing at the shank in my hand.

The floor was slippery under my sweating feet, so I pulled on my boots. Just as I finished zipping them up, he leaped off the bunk again. This time

188

he held what looked like a long, thin Phillips screwdriver with a T-shaped handle on the end. I kicked straight out, catching him squarely in the groin. He doubled over, retching, and the screwdriver clattered to the floor. I snatched it up, then backed away when he slumped on the edge of the bunk.

It suddenly hit me: He wasn't trying to kill me at all. He had two good chances and bungled both of them. He wanted me to kill him!

"Listen up, Todd," I said when he stopped gagging. "I'm going to sit here on this toilet and keep an eye on you all night. I'm not going to kill you. That isn't going to happen, no matter what you do. But I swear before God if you get off that bunk one more time tonight, I will put you in the hospital with enough broken bones to keep you wrapped up in plaster for six months! Am I getting through to you?"

He lay there panting, glaring at me through glittering hate-filled eyes. I felt something profoundly evil, demonic within him.

"Boy, I'm gonna kill you, sooner or later," he hissed. "Maybe not tonight. But the only way you're ever gonna leave this joint is with a toe-tag."

Vaguely, I wondered who—or what—was speaking to me.

I put the weapons in a bag and left before Todd woke up in the morning. After dropping the bag in the dumpster, I headed for the hospital. I knew I could tell Harley Seimer what had happened without having to worry about him disclosing my name to anybody else.

"I know Todd. He's a nut-case," Seimer said bluntly. "We'll lock him up here for a while."

Later in the day I talked to Chip, the man in charge of psychological services for the prison. He was a short, slender man with red hair and a perpetual squint. He was a depressing man to be around because he was totally cynical and burned out on everything connected with psychiatric care for prisoners.

"Todd is one of those characters who wants to commit suicide at somebody else's hand," Chip explained. "Frankly, you'd have done him and everybody else a favor if you'd just killed him and put him out of his misery."

I chose to ignore the obvious ethical implications of what he'd just said. "Right! That would look just great on my record."

Chip shrugged. "What difference does it make? You can walk out of here today and write a Pulitzer prize-winning novel or kill the first three people you meet. With a 99-year sentence, it doesn't matter what you do. Either way you're stuck here for the next 15 to 20 years. As a matter of fact, the parole board will only assume you're just another slick con-artist if you go before them with too good a record."

Although Chip's cynical comments probably weren't intended to encourage me—to put it mildly!—he unintentionally helped me to realize something critically important: He was right! Whatever I chose to do with my life from this day forward, for good or ill, it would have absolutely no impact on my ever getting out of prison. But that realization didn't have the demoralizing effect Chip may have intended. Instead, I felt incredibly liberated. For the first time I realized I was about as free as one can get in this life—to do or be whatever I chose—without any regard for external rewards or consequences. For me the 99-year sentence meant simply this: Go to prison for the rest of your life. There, without fear or ambition, you are free to do whatever you wish and be whatever you wish. I smiled as I thought about lines from Robert Frost's poetry:

> I shall be telling this with a sigh
> Somewhere ages and ages hence:
> Two roads diverged in a wood, and I—
> I took the one less traveled by,
> And that has made all the difference.

Years earlier I had chosen the road "less traveled" back at the jail. I didn't intend to change directions!

◆ ◆ ◆

James L. Vandever, the associate warden of security, called me to his office that afternoon. I'd heard about him, but this would be the first meeting between us. He was a tall, burly man in his mid-50s with thick, bushy hair, who during his 25-year career had worked his way up through the ranks from guard to associate warden. Most prisoners liked Jim because he was honest and fair. Twice a day he had office hours at a window that opened on the compound. Prisoners could come to the window with any problem.

"He'll tell you where the hogs ate the cabbage in a New York second," was the way one inmate described him. Roughly translated, that meant Jim wasn't given to a lot of small talk or double-talk. If he had something to say, he came right to the point. If you asked him a question, he didn't pussyfoot around with an answer. It was yes, no, quit bothering me with that foolishness, or I'll think about it. And I'll think about it meant Don't call me, I'll call you.

He came directly to the point with me: "Jarvis, I've heard that you're having some problems getting a cell, and I'm gonna fix that right now. I've got an empty cell over in Unit II that has your name on it. You take a few days and find yourself a cell partner, OK?"

"I appreciate that, Warden."

He grinned. "I'll bet you didn't think I'd know about problems a new man was having."

"From what I've heard so far about you, I doubt there's anything that goes on behind these walls without your knowing sooner or later."

"That's a fact," he admitted. He wasn't bragging. It was true. "You let me know directly if you have any more problems. Keep a low profile, and try to avoid problems if you can. I want to see you get out of here in one piece."

"By the way, Warden, my name is Jeris."

"OK, Jarvis."

190

His was a rough-hewn sort of kindness, but it touched me at that moment because I had no doubt he meant what he said. He was a man one could trust and count on. We had many conversations over the years. Always brief. Always to the point. Always helpful. And always he called me Jarvis! At that moment, however, I didn't care what he called me. I liked the man. I had no idea about the kind of radical impact he would have on my life a few years down the road.

Keeping a "low profile" and avoiding "conflict" was a neat trick in a prison that was out of control. The prison's classification system was little more than a paper mirage. The most dangerous and predatory criminal psychopaths were tossed willy-nilly into the crowded population with short-timers and men convicted for relatively minor offenses. Consequently, prison life was much like combat: long stretches of mind-numbing monotony, interrupted unexpectedly with moments of pure terror. Prisoners had to be on alert at all times. Stabbing victims were carried to the hospital with boring regularity. Nobody knew when or how the next attack would come, but you had to be ready for it every second—even in your sleep. The constant danger, plus the need to be prepared for it, turned some men into psychotic walking powder kegs ready to explode at the slightest provocation.

In early 1981 I heard a commotion outside my office at the hospital. I stepped out just as inmates carrying another prisoner on a stretcher rushed by. It was Ralph Janow. He'd been stabbed in Unit IV. His T-shirt slowly turned red as blood poured from several wounds. I followed them into the emergency room.

"Hey, Jerry! I might not get to testify for you at your new trial if they don't plug these holes up pretty quick," he joked as Harley Seimer cut away his shirt.

"Don't you worry," Seimer said firmly. "You're gonna live to be an old man in spite of yourself."

Later I heard other inmates talking about Ralph in the chow hall. "He ain't hurt," one said.

"What do you mean 'he ain't hurt'?" I demanded. "He's got half a dozen stab wounds in him."

The man shrugged. "If he ain't dead, he ain't hurt!"

❖ ❖ ❖

Prison is the only place I know of where almost everyone expects a suffering person to endure his pain both alone and in silence. Prisoners had too many problems of their own to endure listening to another's, or they were too self-involved to care one way or the other. Because of staff shortages, prison employees barely had enough time or energy to keep up with the paperwork. And free-world people, with few exceptions, didn't want to hear about what really went on behind the walls, either because they didn't believe it or because the reality of prison conditions left them feeling frustrated over their powerlessness to do anything about it.

Every two weeks was "draw night." Inmates could draw a maximum of $55 per month. They went to a designated area of the cellblock to pick up

191

envelopes containing their scrip—money. Cash was contraband, and the prison hadn't yet gone to computer-controlled accounts for prisoners, so inmates made purchases at the commissary (cigarettes, coffee, snacks, and soft drinks) with metal coins called scrip. Larger coins were stamped $5 or $1. Smaller coins were the equivalent of a penny, nickel, dime, quarter, or 50-cent piece. Because of feeble security precautions, robbery gangs were out in force, circling around the units like a flock of vultures in search of wounded prey. They tried to select victims they knew wouldn't fight back, but occasionally they misjudged the man and a bloody fight would break out.

One style of robbery was simple extortion, known as "robbery on credit." The thieves had a list of victims they would visit immediately after they picked up their scrip. In order to be left alone, some inmates paid the robber gangs a percentage of what they drew.

Getting one's scrip safely was only part of the problem. The next part was getting safely to the commissary and back. Only five men were allowed in the commissary at a time. The rest gave their I.D. cards to an officer posted at the ball field gate and then waited in two long lines for their turn. Most officers took their jobs seriously. They patrolled the line constantly to prevent robberies. But when the weather turned cold, very few officers ventured out of their heated guard shack. That's when the thieves usually struck.

I stood on the ball field in a long line one evening, waiting for my turn to enter the commissary. It was a particularly cold day. The area was poorly lighted, and the sun had gone down. Men stood in small groups, stamping their feet and trying to keep warm. I noticed a short, skinny youngster standing in front of me because he kept nervously jingling the scrip in his pocket. He couldn't have been more than 18 or 19. The number stenciled on the back of his jacket was recent, so I knew he'd just arrived at the prison.

I saw three men step up close to him. One pulled his jacket open. Even in the darkness I caught a glimpse of the shank handle sticking out of his belt. I didn't have to hear the words to know what was going on. The kid glanced around as though looking for help, backing up one step at a time until he bumped into me.

I put my hand on the kid's shoulder. His head jerked around. I could see the fear in his eyes. He thought I was one of them. I spoke to the robber, quietly and without thinking. "This kid is probably gonna let you rob him because he's new to the joint. But I don't think you ought to do that."

"Mind your own business," the thief growled.

Me and my big mouth! I thought. Inmates simply didn't interfere with the penitentiary predators, but I was sick and tired of watching those bullies terrorize old men and kids who couldn't protect themselves. *In for a penny, in for pound,* I thought. I unbuttoned my jacket. The thief backed away. He wasn't sure if I was armed or not.

"I'm minding my own business," I said. "That money in his pocket is mine, and I'm going to get very upset if you try to take it."

Two of the would-be robbers stepped back. The one with the knife spoke to the kid. "We'll stop by and see you at your cell later," he warned.

Suddenly, another man in the next row spoke up. "Don't you be bothering that boy. And you'd better know his TV belongs to me. I'll cut your head off if you mess with *my* TV!"

A second voice joined in. Then a third and fourth. "His stereo is mine." "His commissary supplies are mine." "His stamps are mine." "His *life* is mine!" somebody yelled far in the back.

The would-be thieves scurried off the hill to a chorus of laughter. Although confused and frightened, the kid had guts. "You'll have to kill me. I ain't givin' you or anybody else my stuff," he said stubbornly.

"Hey, we got ourselves a banty rooster!" one of the men said. Others roared with laughter. "Lookie here, Rooster. Nobody is gonna rob you, so you just relax."

That was one of the few times I saw prisoners display any sense of social consciousness.

◆ ◆ ◆

After working in the hospital for a few months, I changed jobs after making arrangements to work as a reader in the prison braille class. It was a "make work" position as far as the job classification board was concerned because they didn't provide books, tapes, or a tape recorder. I just had to be there. But I already had a plan to read books on tape for Gayle, an old friend from high school days who suffered from cerebral palsy. Gayle and her parents, Dr. Gene Hackleman, a plastic surgeon, and his wife, Irene, began writing to me when I was first imprisoned at the jail. Later, I struck up a lively correspondence with Gayle's sister, Kris, a gifted artist. Throughout my years of imprisonment their letters came every month, full of family news, discussions about books and ideas, and enough warmth to keep me energized for days.

Gayle had a first-raté intellect, but her disability prevented her from reading. At the time very few taped reading services offered anything more consequential than the latest fiction. But she wanted to explore theology in depth, so for nearly two years she sent me boxes of tapes and the books she wanted to "read." I'd read the books on tape and mail them back to her. Finally, we'd spend several weeks exchanging letters and tapes discussing the subject covered in a particular book.

Meanwhile, Conn Arnold and I had become close friends. He felt deeply committed to prison ministry, and I wanted to help him in any way I could. But one thing quickly became clear to us: the hard-core convicts who needed a pastor most wouldn't come near the chapel. Although most prisoners believe in God, they generally were unchurched before they came to prison. Worse, they tended to view God as a Cosmic Supercop with hell as His ultimate electric chair! A legalistic *quid pro quo* made sense to prisoners, but grace was a foreign concept.

Like Jesus, Conn decided to go where the prisoners congregated: not the "temple" but the inmate organizations. I arranged for him to speak at a 7th Step pre-release class one Monday night.

"We have a Seventh-day Adventist churchman as our guest speaker tonight," I said. "He should fit right in with this group because his first name is Conn!"

The audience roared with laughter. But what made Conn Arnold a big hit with the prison population wasn't his speech but something very personal he did the following year. He arranged for the Harvest Celebration Singers to put on a concert for a packed house in the chapel. The room was already crowded when Conn and his wife, Dot, walked in. Conn was carrying his 3-year-old granddaughter, Kelly Jackson. I saw prisoners glancing at one another in surprise. Not a single guard was in sight. Women rarely came into the prison without a heavy security escort. And people just didn't bring children into the penitentiary! But like her grandpa, Kelly felt perfectly safe. Moments later, to the delight of scores of convicts, she was scampering around the room, climbing from one convict lap to another, and having a great time with the prisoners. I saw tears in the eyes of several men when they picked Kelly up. Some of them hadn't seen a baby in many years.

"I wanted my convict family to meet my free-world family," Conn explained later.

Whatever his reason, prisoners saw his act as a display of trust in them and caring for them. From that day on Conn could count on a large crowd whenever he preached in the chapel.

I chose to take a behind-the-scenes role in Conn's ministry. Contrary to a lot of free-world beliefs about prison ministry, most convicts resented having other prisoners lead out in church services. But I was free to act as a facilitator in bringing prisoners and Christian free-world volunteers together, either in the chapel or the 7th Step chapter.

❖ ❖ ❖

My mother and stepfather came to visit me at the prison during the summer of 1981. Mother had visited me at the jail, but this was the first time I'd seen Fred since Christmas of 1976. Fred and I had never talked about anything personal before, so I was surprised when he initiated a conversation while my mother went to the ladies' room.

"Look, I know there have been hard feelings between us for years," he began hesitantly. "I just didn't know anything about raising children when your mum and I got married. I wish we could go back and do some things differently, because I realize now that I was too hard on you. But we can't. All I can tell you is that your mum and I have always wanted the best for you. And I want you to know that we're both proud of you."

For the first time I saw my stepfather as something other than an abusive tyrant. He was an otherwise good and decent man who had, with the best of intentions, gone too far with his discipline in trying to prepare me for a tough world—to "make a man" out of me. Years of resentment and bitterness dissolved within me when he reached across the table to shake hands. Nothing more needed to be said.

❖ ❖ ❖

The first rumblings of a coming riot could be heard when corrections officials announced that effective March 1, 1982, the picnic area would be closed from December to March 1 each year. Visitation during the week would be abolished altogether. Budget cuts were given as the reason.

Prisoners exploded! Many wanted to burn the joint down, but cooler heads prevailed. On Monday, March 1, approximately 500 inmates crowded into the chow hall and refused to return to their cells or go to work.

"We're not going back to work until you agree to keep the picnic area open," inmates told prison officials.

Expecting the worst, heavily armed Metro police and Highway Patrol officers surrounded the prison as they waited for orders to rush the chow hall and crush the rebellion. The more sophisticated inmate leaders knew that Commissioner Bradley wouldn't back down, regardless of what happened. But they also knew how important the picnic area was to the prisoners. If they weren't allowed to blow off steam with a work strike, something worse was inevitable.

I spent the day with Tony Larson, one of the hard-core convicts I'd come to know. We patrolled the dining room and lawn outside, talking to different groups and individuals as the day wore on. When some young inmates broke out a batch of homemade prison wine, Tony seized it and poured it down the sink.

"There ain't gonna be no violence," Tony told one of the hotheads. "If you get drunk and start any trouble, I'm gonna finish you. Do you understand me?"

Anger ebbed and flowed like the tide as the hours passed. Riot-equipped officers had moved inside the prison and surrounded the lower compound. Finally, Warden Vandever issued an ultimatum: "Return to your cells now, and you will not be hurt."

"Lord, help us break this thing up without any violence," I prayed.

"That's it!" Tony shouted.

"It's time to go home!" Rick Bettner announced.

Several officers told me later they had expected a tough fight before they regained control. Instead, the crowd of inmates suddenly dissolved into small groups heading for the cellblocks. I stood on the walk in front of my cell in Unit II. To my right I saw an automatic rifle sticking through the porthole from the other side. The muzzle was pointed straight at my chest.

Meanwhile, back in the lions' den! I thought.

I knew the prison would remain locked down for several weeks, but at least there wasn't going to be a body count.

The months slowly turned into years. Federal District Court Judge L. Clure Morton finally handed down a ruling on the prisoners' class-action suit against the state in 1982. It was a blistering, 168-page decision in which he described the prison as "a place where violence and terror reign." He declared the entire prison system to be unconstitutional and ordered sweeping changes. The Alexander administration's response was an ill-fated program entitled "The Prison Plan of the Eighties." Senior corrections officials gutted the few remaining educational and vocational programs, virtually closed down the school, and planned to put everybody to work with a hoe in some unknown garden! My job as a book reader was also abolished.

◆ ◆ ◆

My first five years behind the walls were drawing to a close when I moved up to Self-determination Center in 1982. I enjoyed the freedom of a semi-private room, but detested the inmate governing committee. Men who couldn't control their own lives in the free world suddenly had power over other men, and they routinely abused that power. I didn't expect to stay long, but I decided to enjoy the "vacation" from the violence and chaos of the cellblocks for as long as it lasted.

In spite of the improved conditions, depression closed in around me again. I felt like an alien dumped in a foreign land, indescribably lonely and unwilling to become a part of the environment. My first response was guilt: a Christian isn't supposed to be depressed! Since I was clearly depressed and required antidepressant medication, I began wondering just how honestly I practiced my faith. Was it just pretense? That guilt didn't pass until I began taking seriously some of the biblical stories about Jacob, Joseph, Moses, and Elijah. Even Jesus was clearly depressed at times, and so was Paul. Only then did I begin to realize that depression doesn't necessarily reflect a lack of faith in God.

But what *did* it mean?

I struggled with that question for several weeks before the answer came.

First, I realized that depression is a normal, healthy response to profoundly sinful conditions we can't change. There's nothing sinful about depression until we surrender to it and allow it to dominate our lives. It's sinful only when we allow it to become the most important thing in our lives—our God!

Second, but most important, I realized that secrets make people sick, and I had too many secrets in my life. God was speaking to me through my depression. Today I believe depression is one of God's ways of confronting people with the need to make some fundamental changes in the secret parts of our lives. That's often the hardest truth for Christians to deal with because it always means we have to make some hard choices. It means coming to terms with some of our most cherished illusions about ourselves. It means change at the core of our being, and change always requires a willingness to endure some discomfort and pain. "No pain, no gain" is something that every athlete knows. That's equally true of growth in our emotional and spiritual lives.

I knew what my choices were. They were painful choices, but I was more tired of the pain associated with the secrets than I was afraid of the discomfort that came with needed changes. Since feelings tend to follow behavior, I decided to act.

First, I decided to tell my friends the truth about what had really happened on November 22, 1976. I was sick and tired of all the lies and evasions that were connected with Darleen. I made a list of every friend I had misled, then either wrote them a letter or sent them a tape. After being so dishonest in the first place, I didn't expect them to believe me. I also knew it was possible that I'd never hear from some of them again. Regardless of the consequences, I wanted that garbage out of my life—once and for all!

A few chided me for not trusting them enough to tell them sooner. Others, like Ed Ley, weren't even surprised. "I always suspected that," he said. "I figured you'd tell me about it whenever you were ready."

I felt more than a little foolish for hanging on to that secret for so long.

Second, everybody but prison officials called me by my nickname, Jerry. I decided to drop the nickname I'd used all my life and use the name on my birth certificate, Jeris. It was a symbolic gesture: Jerry had been the man who married Darleen and got himself into this mess because of his fear-driven inaction. By God's grace Jerry was dead and gone! The name Jeris reminded me each day of my need of renewal by God's grace.

Third, it had become obvious to me that my lawyer didn't intend to file an appeal on my behalf in federal court. I considered preparing the writ myself, but I decided to drop my appeals altogether. Morally I couldn't justify pursuing costly appeals in court based upon half-truths. Regardless of what prosecutors had done in terms of suborning perjury or making secret deals with Torbett, that still didn't excuse my obstruction of justice or perjury at trial. Eventually, I'd lay out the facts for the parole board and seek a commutation of my sentence from the governor.

Fourth, I decided to risk being more open and vulnerable to other people, to communicate my feelings honestly to them. That decision was put to the test when Ed Ley introduced me to Valerie Dick in the spring of 1982. She was a student at Southern Missionary College who worked for WSMC-FM, and she wanted to interview me for a documentary she planned to produce. Something clicked between us. Even though I felt ambivalent about romantic relationships over prison walls, we were exchanging a blizzard of letters and tapes by Christmas. Something in her love for me lanced that boil of estrangement from other people that had built up just beneath the surface of my life during the previous five years. I felt reborn—gloriously free to *be* myself, to love poetry and music again, to laugh at silly jokes, to be vulnerable to another person—in spite of the risks.

But the time came to "step back," as she put it. I tried to withdraw from her completely in order to protect my own feelings—to escape from them, to be more accurate. Valerie came to visit me the first day the picnic area opened the following March. The air was bitterly cold. So was I! She sat down at the table. I felt sulky and sat across from her. She got up, came over to sit beside me—and waited. She made it clear that our friendship was precious to her and that she wasn't going to let me throw it away.

Suddenly, in the midst of the bitter wind sweeping across the picnic area, I realized that I was at another crossroads. It was time to make another one of those important choices: If I really loved and cared for her, then I was non-negotiably committed to her happiness, well-being, fulfillment, and welfare. That meant thinking of what was best for her—letting go! It was surprisingly easy to do once I put it in those terms. While I felt some temporary loss, it soon was replaced with a warm, loving, and rewarding friendship that endures to this very day.

As I reflected on my relationship with Valerie in the following months, I realized that every right choice, no matter what the issue or circumstance, is *always* a liberating experience—if one is willing to risk the temporary pain of growth that comes in making hard choices.

Finally, after reading and thinking for years, I made another choice: I decided it was time to pay attention to friends who kept urging me to publish my writing. I went to work for *The Interim* newspaper, first as the copy editor and then as associate editor. In 1983 I took over as editor. That position gave me a telephone and access to every part of the prison, all the programs, and most of the staff. Perhaps most importantly, I had a private office to work in while I wrote in a journal I'd entitled *Notes From the Pen*. It also gave other prisoners a place to come and talk when they needed a listening ear. While there were many things I couldn't do to help, I could listen, which more often than not was all the help needed.

Editing a prison newspaper, however, adds a whole new dimension to frontier journalism! Most editors don't last long—they either get run off or burned out within a few months. Inmates get angry if every story or editorial isn't a blasting diatribe against the administration. Prison officials complained if they felt a story wasn't "balanced" as they thought it should be. I gave up the job three times, but, like a bad penny, it always came bouncing back to me.

Meanwhile, the inmate governing committee had me evicted from SDC. I appealed their decision and was reinstated. But I had no wish to live in the Self-determination Center as long as it was run by inmates, so I returned to the cellblocks to live.

◆ ◆ ◆

I met Mike Dutton, the newly appointed warden for TSP, shortly after he arrived in 1983. He was a tall, muscular man, who wore a beard. He looked more like a college philosophy professor than a prison warden. In fact, he was a professor: He taught a graduate class in criminal justice part-time. More importantly for senior corrections officials, he knew how to run a maximum security prison—and he intended to do just that. Brushy Mountain State Prison, located in the mountains of east Tennessee and used for maximum security inmates, was scheduled to be closed. TSP would become "the end of the line prison."

I asked him during our first interview how he planned to stop the escalating level of violence at TSP.

"I don't know exactly how I'm going to stop it yet," he admitted. "But I'll tell you this—and you can quote me: I'm going to put an end to this endless flow of blood if it's the last thing I do!"

I liked Mike Dutton from the first time I met him. He was blunt and hard as nails when it came to enforcing policy. He organized a highly trained tactical unit to deal with riots and other serious disturbances. He formed another unit, known as the "shakedown crew," to work exclusively on seizing weapons, drugs, and other forms of contraband. He abolished the inmate governing committee at SDC.

During his tenure as warden at TSP, he faced three major hostage situations. He brought all three to a conclusion without injury to anybody. Some of Dutton's decisions made my life difficult: he had the phone removed from my office and restricted the newspaper staff's movements. I didn't take that personally because I knew other staff members were abusing these privileges.

Although I'd been publishing stories and essays in the prison newspaper for a couple of years, I decided it was time to think about writing for free-world publications. Despite many obstacles and interruptions, I began on several stories. I expected nothing but rejection, but I dropped my first two manuscripts in the mail with a sigh of relief. One went to Dan Fahrbach, editor of *Insight*, and one to Kenneth Holland, editor of *Signs of the Times*. At least nobody could say I hadn't tried.

But positive, life-affirming choices always have consequences that play out in terms of cause-and-effect relationships over a long period of time. That was a defining moment in my life, but I had no idea what forces I had put in motion when I dropped those manuscripts into the box.

PART FOUR

BEYOND
PRISON WALLS

16

Meanwhile, Back in the Lions' Den!

I FELT euphoric when Dan Fahrbach and Ken Holland accepted my first submissions for publication. In addition to a check, both wrote encouraging letters in which they invited me to submit more material. I didn't need to be asked twice! I was hooked. I set a goal of producing a minimum of one new article each month.

A few weeks later Dr. Amos Wilson, a Presbyterian churchman and chief of chaplaincy services for the Department of Corrections, arranged for Ron Patterson, a senior editor at Abingdon Press, to conduct a creative writing class at the prison.

I was the first one to sign up.

Ron was a bearded, soft-spoken Methodist clergyman and editor who instinctively knew how to connect with inmates. Some could barely write a coherent sentence, but I admired the way he always found something positive to say about what they had written. Although I learned a lot of editing techniques from Ron during the 10-week class, I can't say that he taught me how to write. He did something much more important: He urged me to think beyond prison walls in my writing, to probe the dark underside of penitentiary life in search of spiritual meaning. His encouragement gave me a fresh perspective on my own experience. It also gave me the needed confidence to take my writing seriously as a vocation.

My modest success at writing had an energizing effect on me. After years of playing Hamlet about divorcing Darleen and submitting an application for a commutation of sentence, I took a deep breath and started each process. I filled out the required forms and wrote a lengthy narrative about Torbett's perjured testimony and what had actually happened on November 22. In addition to Bill Williams' affidavit, which swore that Torbett had lied when he claimed I visited him at the jail, I also included another affidavit that Rick Sharp provided in which he described Darleen's confession to him. To all of that I attached letters of recommendation from free-world friends and prison officials.

I also filed for a divorce.

◆ ◆ ◆

Writing from prison was a bit like writing into a black hole in space: I had no idea who was reading my stuff or what, if anything, they thought about it. But I learned the name of one person when Conn Arnold sat down beside me in the chapel on May 7, 1984.

"A friend of yours wants your address," he said.

He reached into his pocked, pulled out a letter, and handed it to me. It was short, just one page. I scanned it quickly—until I came to the signature. Then I froze: EDIE! After reading an article I'd published about Conn's work as a volunteer chaplain, she wrote him to say she'd recognized my byline and wanted to find out if I was the same man ("the first great love of my life" was the way she described me!) whom she had dated as a young girl. If so, she wanted my address.

Having Edie contact me in prison was certainly not one of the things we'd planned on doing when we were teenagers years before! For the first time in many years I felt terribly defensive and vulnerable about that number on my back. I told Conn I needed a few days to think about it before he gave her my address. After a few days of mulling it over, however, I realized my feelings were not appropriate. Moreover, even though nearly a quarter century had passed, deep within me I knew she wouldn't think less of me because of what had happened in my life.

I wrote to Conn a few days later and shared some warm personal recollections about Edie with him. I told him he could send her my address.

He did.

He also sent her a copy of my letter to him!

Although I didn't hear from her for several months, a mutual friend brought me up to date on her life. She was separated from her second husband and living with her four teenage children in Fletcher, North Carolina. It hurt deeply to hear about the suffering she had endured for the past 22 years. I couldn't help wondering once again what might have been if things had been different for us.

It turned out to be a long, hot summer in 1984. A lot of different issues required my time and attention, so I didn't have much time to write or to wonder why Edie didn't respond for a while. For one thing, several family members died within a few months of one another—my grandfather Whary, uncle Don Harris, and then my stepfather, Fred. These were men who had shaped my life. I loved them, and their deaths came like one hammer blow after the other. Prison is an awful place to go through the grieving process after the death of a loved one. I couldn't attend any of their funerals, so I didn't have any feeling of closure after their deaths. Even worse, grieving is a very private and solitary thing in prison. The prison walls loomed higher, and I wondered if all my family would die off before I ever left prison walls behind.

❖ ❖ ❖

Then there was Darleen.

I was talking to one of the teachers at the school when a clerk told me I had a telephone call.

I recognized the voice instantly: it was Darleen.

Although there had been no direct contact between us since 1980, I'd heard through the prison grapevine about her involvement in a variety of heterosexual affairs and lesbian relationships. Two years after she began serving her sentence, prison officials had reclassified her to minimum security, which allowed her to leave the prison each day to work as a secretary in one of the state office buildings. While there she carried on an affair with a senior corrections official, and it ended in pregnancy. She escaped to have an abortion. The escape charge was later reduced to a technical absence without permission. Prison officials confined her to the prison, but their decision was overruled by their superior. She was returned to the annex.

None of this had surprised me. For one thing her behavior in prison was identical to her free-world lifestyle. Second, some corrections officials and prison staff members—both men and women—considered the women's prison to be their own private harem. In 1988 the sexual abuse of female prisoners would explode in the national headlines when several male guards were either fired or arrested and charged with rape. Senior officials, however, were too well insulated to be touched by the scandal.

"What do you want?" I asked.

"I was hoping we might have a chance to talk—it's been a long time."

"OK, what do you want to talk about?"

"I heard you'd filed for a divorce," she said nervously. "I know our marriage is over, and I can't blame you for that. But I want you to know I'm a born-again Christian now. I just called to say I'm sorry if I've done anything to hurt you. I'd like to have your forgiveness."

I almost choked on the bile in my throat.

"Born again! Darleen, you've been 'born again' so many times you're gonna get trapped in the birth canal and drown one of these days."

That "if" hit me like a slap in the face. She had done everything humanly possible to destroy my life, and now she was apologizing "if" she had done anything to hurt me. She was avoiding her responsibility by hiding behind religious jargon. I wanted to tell her in the most colorful and graphic terms where to go with her request. But I also knew there's one big problem with telling people where to go: *They'll take you there with them!*

Jesus put the issue quite simply: "In the same way you judge others, you will be judged" (Matthew 7:2, NIV).

Darleen hung up quickly when I told her she was forgiven. I don't know what good it did her, or why she bothered to ask in the first place, because she had never made any attempt to undo the damage she had done to me. But I felt wonderfully alive and free after talking to her. Perhaps she didn't deserve forgiveness, but I deserved to be free from the crushing weight of hostility I'd felt toward her for a long time.

A few weeks later, she cleared up any lingering uncertainty I had about her overtures when she called me again. She came right to the point without saying hello.

"I guess you heard I was having a parole hearing soon," she said coldly. "Maybe you figured you could screw up my chances of getting out early with what you wrote about me in your stupid clemency petition. But you can forget it."

"I didn't know you were having a parole hearing. But how did you hear about my petition?"

"I've got highly placed friends! They told me all about it."

That supercilious tone set my teeth on edge as I thought about her affair with the corrections official. "No, Darleen, from what I hear you've got friends in very low places," I snapped.

She lost control. "You're never gonna get out of there, you _____ ," she screamed. "Do you hear me? I'll make sure you're *buried* behind those walls. When I get done telling the Board that *you* killed George and dragged me into this mess, they won't even consider your petition. You remember me when it happens."

"Darleen, you've really got delusions of grandeur . . ."

" . . . And I'm gonna cross-file for a divorce. When I get done with you none of those _____ Christian rags will publish a word you write. What do you think about that?" she hissed.

"I really don't care what you have to say about anything."

"You're gonna care about this . . ."

"It sounds like your recent born-again experience is wearing off rapidly," I observed dryly.

She slammed down the phone. That, happily, was the last direct contact I had with her. But behind the scenes she was able to carry through on some of her threats. One of her lesbian lovers on the staff at the women's prison had been transferred to TSP because of her relationship with Darleen—to do psychological counseling no less! Other inmates had warned me to avoid contact with her. I followed their advice. Nevertheless, she contacted the parole board chairman and claimed to know me well. She described me as a manipulative sociopath who had destroyed Darleen's life. Fortunately, I didn't find out about that conversation for many years.

Despite her prison record, Darleen was successful in conning several Christian volunteers engaged in prison ministry into helping her obtain parole. Although the acting associate warden of treatment urged the volunteers to find a more worthy candidate, they refused to listen. Instead, they used their influence to make sure she was granted an early parole in late 1984.

Judge Muriel Robinson, a blonde woman who looked more like a movie actress than a jurist, convened a special court to hear my divorce petition in the prison's parole board room on February 1, 1985. At the end of the proceedings, she leaned back in her chair and smiled at me. "Mr. Bragan," she said, "insofar as it is in my power to do so, I now declare you a free man!"

I almost fell off my chair laughing.

◆ ◆ ◆

My daughter, Tracie, was the third issue that needed my time and attention. She wanted to visit me, so I made arrangements for her to stay with Conn and Dot Arnold.

I hadn't seen her since 1977. She was 7 then, now 15. Although I had tried to stay in touch with her through the years, her stepfather, for reasons best known to himself, frequently interfered in our communication. I wasn't sure what to expect during our visit, but at the very least I knew she faced some unique challenges as a teenager because of my imprisonment. That had become particularly problematic for her at Takoma Academy after I began publishing stories in *Insight*. Classmates, who made the connection between her name and mine, in her hearing made disparaging comments about me to the effect that I was a "jailbird" and a "killer" who probably belonged in the electric chair. Unable to cope with the emotional conflicts she felt, she transferred to public high school.

I paced back and forth under the blistering July sun while I waited to be processed through the Vehicle Gate onto the picnic area. What would she be like at 15? I wondered. I knew she felt angry and resentful because she thought I had abandoned her years earlier. Could we bridge the gap created by those feelings? I didn't know.

The heavy iron gate swung open.

In spite of the years that had passed, I recognized her instantly when I saw her sitting with Conn at a table a hundred yards away. Then she saw me. My apprehension about seeing her evaporated when she jumped up and raced toward me across the picnic area. I struggled to control my emotions as we stood there hugging one another.

We had some tough issues to confront and process that weekend, with very few hours to do so. But I was delighted to discover that my maturing daughter was as forgiving as she was direct in her probing questions: What had really happened to George? Why did I cover for Darleen after George's death? What had happened between her mother and me? I think divorced parents who bad-mouth one another to their children create a lot of unnecessary and painful conflicts. Consequently, the last question posed a delicate balancing act between a need for being truthful with Tracie without getting into an inappropriate "he said/she said" discussion about old wounds between her mother and me.

I thought we had carved out the beginnings of a new relationship between us by the end of the weekend. Everything wasn't resolved. That would take several more years. But we had taken the first steps. I would have to trust in God's grace to lead us through the rest.

I would need it!

Shortly after Darleen was released from prison, I received a fresh taste of her capacity for evil when I learned that she had written a particularly vicious letter to Tracie. She described me in the most draconian terms as a deceitful, psychotic murderer who had destroyed her life and didn't care anything about Tracie. "You'll be better off if you just forget him and get on with your life," she wrote in conclusion.

At Christmas Darleen flew to Maine to visit my grandmother Whary. While visiting there, she told my cousins the same story she had told Tracie. I was reminded of an old saying when I learned about her visit with my family and the letter she had written to Tracie: "If you lie down with dogs, you're gonna come up with fleas!"

✦ ✦ ✦

My fourth pressing problem that summer was the escalating level of violence at TSP.

Inmate leadership within the penitentiary came unglued in 1983 as corrections officials began transferring prisoners willy-nilly in and out of the prison in order to meet court orders to cut the population. By the time transfers were halted, the population remained essentially the same—

except there were a lot more paranoid strangers who didn't trust one another.

Escalating violence within the prison led to penitentiary-wide shake-downs during the last two weeks in June. Internal affairs officers turned up 63 shanks, two match bombs, a .38-caliber pistol, 28 packs of marijuana, and 184 gallons of julep—a potent wine made with fruit stolen from the dining room. Stabbings and killings continued unabated despite the shakedowns.

I stood at my cell door while talking with Ritchie, another inmate, as we waited for the noon count to clear one day. Suddenly, I heard the sound of scuffling on the Rock just below my cell. Two men were wrestling with a third man, Bruce Binford. At first I thought they were engaged in typical horseplay that's common among men in prison. But then I saw the shanks.

"Jeris, they're gonna kill that man!" Ritchie gasped.

"There's nothing you can do. Don't watch it!" I shouted. I'd seen many stabbings, but this was a first for Ritchie.

One grabbed Bruce from behind, holding him in a full nelson, while the other closed in for the kill.

"Oh, God! Please don't kill me!" Bruce screamed as the blade plunged into his chest. "Help me! Somebody, please help me!"

Dozens of men stood by, laughing and joking as the stabbing continued. "Cut his head off!" one man yelled. Another man watched while eating a cheese sandwich. He never missed a bite. Others cheered the killers on. "Kill 'im! Kill the _____ !"

The cheering onlookers had nothing personal against Binford. He could have been anybody. The murder was just another way of breaking up the tedium, an entertaining show in the cellblock.

Within seconds the victim's screams for help were cut off as blood filled his lungs. He gasped for breath, coughed, and sprayed his attackers with blood. But the killers weren't content to end his life. They kept stabbing and hacking at his chest, neck, and back until the attackers and their victim were bathed in blood. Bruce finally dropped to the floor, his head nearly cut off, his fingers twitching spastically as blood flowed from his body onto the concrete.

As tension mounted and tempers flared in the following days, Elder Conn Arnold met with the few convict leaders left at the prison to announce his plans for a month-long evangelistic crusade in the prison chapel during July.

"I need your support," he told them.

He got it.

After he left a dozen men met with me in the newspaper office to discuss his request. The vote was unanimous.

"Frankly, I think this is the best thing that could happen right now," said Johnny Greene, a lifer and the foundation secretary for 7th Step. After 15 years of incarceration, he understood better than most the deadly pressure that was building up behind the walls.

Nearly 100 prisoners and free-world guests filled the chapel for the first service on Saturday, July 7. Few of the men were professing Christians.

Most rarely attended chapel services. "I don't care nothing about this chapel," one man said bluntly, "but Conn Arnold went out of his way to visit my mama for me, and I want to hear what he's got to say."

Four days later, on Wednesday, July 11, the penitentiary exploded again when 75 maximum security prisoners broke out of their cells in Unit I and seized control of the cellblock. One officer was critically injured from multiple stab wounds. Another was held hostage, with a knife at his throat for nearly two hours, before Warden Mike Dutton and his tactical squad regained control.

When Pastor Arnold and other free-world guests arrived at 6:15 p.m., they saw heavily armed officers, dressed in full riot gear, racing toward the main entrance of the prison. The revival appeared to be over before it really began. Everyone assumed the prison would remain on lock-down status for days, possibly weeks. But Dutton ordered the rest of the penitentiary to continue with its normal routine. "I'm not going to punish everybody for the violent acts of a few," he said.

Fearful of what might happen in a crowd, many prisoners said they would avoid the chapel for a few days until things returned to normal. When it was time for the service to begin Thursday evening, only a handful of men were there. Several convicts poked their heads in the door, looked around, and then left. Minutes later the chapel began filling rapidly.

Puzzled, I asked a friend why such a crowd had suddenly appeared.

He laughed. "The guys didn't think even Conn would have the guts to bring women in here the night after such a disturbance. But the word got around that Conn had brought his wife, secretary, and several other women." The inmate shrugged. "If they ain't afraid of coming up here . . ."

"This is a good thing," another man said. "Guys have been talkin' all day about the good spirit up here the past few days. I don't know much about religion, but I do know we ain't gonna let nothin' happen to stop this."

At the end of the last service, Conn put it straight to the prisoners: "God is looking for a few good men behind these walls," he said. "If you're one of those men, I'd like you to come up here in front of this crowd and take your stand for Jesus Christ."

Silence. Nobody moved.

Seconds ticked off as men silently reflected on everything they'd seen and heard during the previous month. Then they were on their feet, 30 of them, some of the most solid and respected men in the penitentiary, moving toward the front of the chapel. Several of the men warmly embraced Elder Arnold, while others wiped their eyes, stubbornly refusing to surrender to their deeply felt emotions. All 30 signed their names into the Freedom Fellowship. Five of them were baptized on August 30.

✦ ✦ ✦

I heard from Edie for the first time on February 3, 1985. It was a cheerful "walk down memory lane" letter. In addition to saying she loved my published stories, she wondered if I still played the piano. "To this day I never hear the Warsaw Concerto without thinking about you," she wrote.

She concluded by saying everything was just "wonderful" in her life. I knew better, but I didn't think it was appropriate to say anything. We exchanged half a dozen letters before she suddenly stopped writing in June. I was disappointed, but not surprised. Even though many people wrote to me after reading something I'd published, most stopped writing after a few months. I wondered why she stopped writing, but I didn't have much time to worry about it: the prison was teetering on the brink of another riot.

In the wake of several headline-making escapes during 1984, Tennessee lawmakers exploded. Rhetoric reached a fevered pitch and hastily written legislation was passed ordering all inmates into striped uniforms, effective July 2. Up to that time inmates had been allowed to wear free-world blue jeans and jackets as long as their number was painted on the back of the jacket. Within weeks sloppy-looking, poorly constructed jeans were shipped to the prisons for distribution.

The Turney Center Prison, located 70 miles southeast of Nashville, blew up late Monday afternoon on July 1. Within hours prisoners had seized control of the entire prison. They broke into the locked segregation unit and dragged several prisoners out. In addition to the suspected snitches, younger men were beaten and gang-raped repeatedly. Anything that would burn, including the chapel, was set ablaze.

Everybody at TSP knew a riot was coming. Inmates banged on their cell doors throughout the night, taunting officers with jeers and threats.

Warden Mike Dutton worked throughout the night, coordinating security and food services for the Turney Center. Even though the main prison was short of staff, prison officials unlocked the units Tuesday morning just as they would any other day. Jim Vandever was on vacation. Dutton and Jack Morgan, the associate warden of treatment, patrolled the compound outside the trapgate, talking to inmates and trying to calm things down.

But security officers were out in force in front of the units, fueling growing hostility by ordering men back to their cells if they weren't dressed in the striped uniforms.

Many people breathed a collective sigh of relief as breakfast came and went without incident. Although several men roamed the chow hall as they asked other prisoners for support in "taking over the joint," the vast majority wanted no part of a riot.

"I told them to forget it, when they asked me for help," a prisoner with 12 years behind the walls told me as we walked toward my office at the chapel. "They aren't any more upset about conditions than I am, but every man who's done any real time behind the walls knows a riot isn't the way to go. It just makes bigger problems, and everybody with any sense knows that."

Even though the majority of the population flatly refused to support those promoting violence, a few men stuck to their resolve. They had two things going for them: the prison was short of security officers, and the larger population had little group cohesion. The riot leaders banked on mass confusion and suspicion as a means of getting all inmates involved—

whether they wanted to or not. Like Samson, the hoodlums decided to pull the roof down on everybody's head.

The first sparks of a riot jumped off the human flint of anger when a dozen men, using the striped jeans and prison-issued shirts for fuel, began a bonfire on the ball field. Nearly 100 men were milling around the area of the gate to the ball field, the chapel, commissary, and clothing room, watching the brewing conflict with apprehension. Nobody knew for sure who was involved and who wasn't, but most were afraid.

At 8:00 a.m. several prisoners on the ball field piled clothes up and set them on fire. A "Code-1 on the ball field" alarm barked over dozens of two-way radios. Operations ordered Officer Hardcastle to close the gate. She couldn't carry out the order because inmates blocked her attempts as a dozen men charged the clothing room. Staff members abandoned the area, and seconds later smoke poured out of the room where the hated uniforms were stored.

Suddenly, somebody shouted, "Let's get the commissary next!"

I stood on the steps in front of the chapel, watching as a dozen inmates crowded around the entrance, kicking and pounding on the steel door. Somebody unlocked the door from inside. The free-world staff fled through the rear exit and sought shelter in the prison hospital. Pandemonium reigned inside the commissary for 15 minutes as looters hurled cases of cigarettes, pastry, bread, and other items through the door and out into the compound.

Curiously, despite a gathering crowd of inmates, few joined the looting for several minutes. "I figure security will be swarming all over the place any second," one prisoner admitted. "I don't want to get caught inside."

A brief window of opportunity existed when the growing rage and panic could have been stopped. That window slammed shut when an officer picked up a carton of cigarettes and threw it at an inmate. "You might as well get it now," he shouted. "This place will be locked down for the rest of the summer!"

Inmates swarmed over the area like locusts in a cornfield and swept up everything in sight.

As prisoners slowly moved across the compound, carrying the stolen commissary supplies back to the cellblocks, a dozen officers moved quickly in the other direction toward the vehicle gate. The invisible line between officers and prisoners was drawn in the dirt, but they greeted one another cheerfully.

Nobody knew what to expect next. Most inmates hurried back to the cellblocks. Thinking that security forces would be moving in any minute, the looters hastily shared whatever they had with anybody who wanted it. "I ain't gonna get caught with all this stuff in *my* cell," one inmate laughed while tossing cartons of cigarettes to other men.

Chaplains Amos Wilson, Cleveland Houser, and Bill Hall had already locked up the chapel. They stood beside me on the steps across from the commissary entrance and watched the situation steadily deteriorate. I saw several officers talking to a group of 50 men. At first it looked like the crowd might disperse, but then a couple dozen rioters broke off from the main group and ran toward the hospital entrance. An equal number broke into the hospital through a rear door near the administrator's office. A few minutes later somebody inside opened the front door and a similar number of men rushed in.

As 53 free-world staff members retreated toward the back of the hospital, all the pent up fury and hostility inmates felt toward the medical personnel exploded in an orgy of violence. Inmates methodically demolished everything in sight. All windows were smashed. The steel gate in the waiting room was twisted out of shape like a soggy pretzel. The doors into the outpatient department were broken down. Cabinet doors in the emergency room were ripped open and the contents flung hither and yon like dust in the wind.

Other men stormed into the record room. They yanked patients' files out of the cabinets and dumped them in a huge pile. Somebody tossed a match onto the paper. As smoke billowed up from the blazing pile of charts, a few prisoners withdrew altogether. "I didn't come up here for any dope, and I'm not gonna hurt anybody," he said. "But I did want people in the hospital to know how we feel about the way the nurses and PACs [physician assistants-certified] treat us on sick call."

Unfortunately, other prisoners weren't finished. Some officers abandoned their posts and left keys behind. As staff members escaped from inside the hospital through a rear door, 20 inmates worked their way toward the second floor, where the drugs were stored. Using confiscated hammers and crowbars, they broke through the wall and carted away boxes of syringes and narcotics. The looters fled when the tactical squad moved in to secure the hospital.

Little hope remained for an early end to the violence when looters got other men involved by handing out pills, vials, and syringes to anybody who wanted them.

In spite of mounting danger, wardens Mike Dutton and Jack Morgan stayed on the compound, talking to inmates, watching, waiting. With the possible exception of the ringleaders, most inmates were in a jovial mood.

"It's party time!" was shouted back and forth.

I returned to the cellblock to find officers nervously going about the business of locking inmates in their cells. "I guess this is the end of it," one inmate said with obvious relief. "Security will be in here in force any minute, and I don't plan to get caught in the cross fire."

But security didn't close in.

"Everything was going just fine for a few minutes," Officer Dale Johnson told me later. "Men were going back to their cells without giving us any trouble. But then something snapped. I don't know what it was, but it was as though somebody had flipped a switch. I started to lock one man up, but he shoved the door back. 'You aren't gonna lock me up,' he said. It wasn't a question; it was a blunt statement of fact. And I knew better than to argue the point."

"Everyone got scared about being locked in his cell when it became obvious that the place was out of control," one inmate leader explained as we watched from the Rock. "Last winter a big rumor was going around about a planned riot in which all the known snitches would be killed in their cells, along with everyone else who refused to come out. I think everybody in the joint heard about the plans."

I'd heard about that one.

"You'd be smart to stay out here until we see which way the wind blows," he suggested. "Everybody in here makes enemies at one time or another, including you. When things get crazy, you can't be sure what might happen. A lot of old scores get settled under the cover of a riot. Even though most of the guys won't take part in this thing, few of them are willing to remain alone in their cells either!"

Despite his warning, I returned to my cell and let the guard lock me in.

While standing inside my door moments later, I saw one of the ringleaders grab an officer on the Rock from behind. He pressed a shank against the officer's back. He was the first one I saw taken hostage. Altogether, nine other officers were seized simultaneously by rampaging convicts in the cellblocks and held hostage. Prison officials listened in horror as inmate leaders of the revolt were heard screaming over captured two-way radios that the hostages would be murdered on the spot if any attempt was made at storming the prison.

In less than 90 minutes the furious prisoners had destroyed $2 million worth of property, leaving the institution looking like a bombed city.

Angry black clouds of billowing smoke boiled over the burning chow hall as scores of heavily armed, tight-lipped lawmen raced through the front gates and took up positions surrounding the perimeter of the maximum security, gothic-style fortress. The neatly trimmed grounds of the prison soon looked like a combat zone, complete with a hastily assembled M*A*S*H unit, organized to deal with the expected heavy casualties.

As newspersons arrived on the scene they saw a white sheet hanging out a window in Unit IV. Even though the sheet was hung out backward, reporters could still read the crudely drawn letters in spray paint, which spelled out an ominous warning for all: REMEMBER ATTICA.

Everyone, including the prisoners, expected the day to end in a massive loss of life on both sides.

I got out of my cell again when another inmate, using keys captured from the guards, unlocked my door. Sergeant Conrad, Corporal Watts, officers Johnson, Greenhill, and Dobson had been seized and locked up in Unit II. Officer Fred Gant, a well-liked Black man, stayed up on 10-walk for several minutes, surrounded by Black inmates who didn't want to see him get hurt. Later they escorted him to the Rock, where he was locked in a cell with Dale Johnson. Sergeant Ronnie Carroll and officers Hicks and Simpson were trapped in Unit III. Another Black officer was grabbed in Unit IV. His wallet was stolen, but other inmates recovered his wallet and money, gave them back to him, and urged him to leave quickly. He did!

Corporal Watts was a tough, courageous officer. He tossed his keys into a locked shower when riot leaders burst into his unit. Although his life was threatened by one inmate, he stubbornly refused to tell where he'd hidden the keys.

I knew the hostages were safe for the moment, so I went outside and walked north across the compound. Heavily armed troops had already set up perimeter security, cutting the lower compound off from the hospital and ball field. I turned around and looked up toward the wall over the administration building. It was lined with sharpshooters who had their ball caps turned around backward. I could feel a dozen sights zeroing in on my chest as I stood there alone, watching and wondering.

Fear and fury, a deadly set of twin snakes, stalked the prison compound, spreading panic and paranoia in every direction. A prison riot is a brainless monster that staggers this way and that, crushing everything and everybody it touches without regard to future consequences. It smashes without mercy or compassion. While it cannot be stopped abruptly, I knew it could be nudged, slowly defused, until it ran out of steam and collapsed under its own weight.

It's not hard to believe in demonic possession when you observe the monstrous and demented way in which men behave during a prison riot. In spite of the chaos and confusion, however, I suddenly felt calm and confident of the outcome. Mental pictures of familiar biblical stories drifted through my mind. I knew more than the demonic was present. I could feel the powerful, almost palpable presence of God sweeping out over the smoldering caldron of human rage.

"Lord, I will fear no evil, for Thou art with me," I prayed. "Give us the wisdom and courage to act, and then add Your grace to our action."

In the midst of a rapidly escalating level of violence, a small cadre of tough and fearless convicts slowly assembled in the prison yard. Only months earlier many of the same men had sat in the prison chapel to hear Elder Conn Arnold's preaching. Johnny Greene, 39, a respected inmate leader with 15 years of incarceration under his belt, was one of those men in the chapel. "We're gonna be hip-deep in blood before this day is out if *we* don't get this place under control fast," he said, looking over the group.

Every man there knew what he was proposing. We also knew the possible consequences—losing our lives in a thankless effort that had little chance of success.

"I didn't want to live forever anyway," drawled Ray Humphreys, once a member of the elite presidential honor guard. Arnold had baptized him a few weeks earlier.

"We have to make two nonnegotiable decisions," I interjected. "First, we will not permit any attack on those guards. Second, we will not permit any inmate to attack another. If people start settling old scores we'll have a repeat performance of the slaughter in New Mexico."

"The crazies aren't gonna give up without a fight, especially once they get tanked up on dope," Johnny said bluntly. "I know you're not afraid *not to fight*, but are you willing *to fight* if we have to?" My beliefs about nonviolence were well-known.

"We'll just have to pray as we go and hope it doesn't come to that," I said. "But we *will* take whatever steps are necessary to prevent bloodshed."

Johnny pursed this lips thoughtfully and then grinned. "Let's do it! I'll get our people organized while you get Conn on the phone. See if he'll come out and act as a mediator. Everybody trusts him. Tell him we can protect him if he'll come."

"I'm afraid we're on our own," I said. "The phones are out, and Conn is out of town at his church's general conference in New Orleans."

Disappointment flashed across several faces, but Greene shrugged philosophically. "Then I guess we'll just have to adopt his slogan ourselves: *Straight ahead!*"

I returned to Unit II. Corporal Watts was complaining of chest pains. "You know he's got heart trouble or high blood pressure. He looks real sick to me," Anderson said.

Another lifer, Danny "Fat Rat" Sharp pushed through the crowd of inmates. "You're going with me," Sharp told Watts. Before anybody could object, Sharp led Watts out of the unit to safety.

Other inmates freed Officer Matt Dobson a few minutes later when they learned he had health problems. That left seven hostages: four in Unit II and three in Unit III.

Rioting inmates had complete control of Units II, III, IV, and V. Once they lost control of the hostages, they went to work demolishing everything in sight. Phones were ripped off the walls. Desks and chairs were reduced to splinters. Two inmates in Unit III carried a heavy floor buffer up to 10-walk, where they heaved it over the side and watched it shatter the guards' desk below. "I just wanted to see how high it would bounce," one of the prisoners chuckled gleefully.

Despite the violence and confusion, the prison community slowly separated into three distinct groups by 10:00.

Initially, the most visible group consisted of the original half-dozen ringleaders of the revolt. While their following never amounted to more than 50 to 75 men, they looked more substantial because they were highly vocal in their objectives and were all over the prison.

Some men joined them because they were afraid not to. "I gotta live with these guys later," one inmate explained. "When this is all over and done with, we're *all* gonna pay the price, whether we were involved or not."

The second group, and by far the least visible collection of men throughout the day, was made up of lifers and long-timers—men with 10 to 20 years behind the walls. The majority in this group was either Christian or Muslim.

The third group of prisoners was frequently confused with the first. The majority of inmates were in this group—"caught between a rock and a hard place" was the way one man described it. "All I want to do is stay out of the way of flying bullets from either side," he added. Later, after the dust settled, many of these men stepped out and joined forces with the long-timers.

Mike Phillips, 39, was a savvy inmate who had served 20 years on a

318-year sentence. He had returned to his cell when looting began in the commissary. "I've been through two riots already," he said. "Nothing good has ever come from any of them, and I'm not interested in a third." But like many other lifers, Phillips, who is a devout Catholic, couldn't in good conscience remain in his cell while all hell was breaking loose around him. When other inmates swept through the cellblocks, unlocking all the cell doors, Phillips stepped out and quickly surveyed the chaos. Some of the young men who started the violence were high on drugs and in over their heads, unable to control the forces they had unleashed. He knew something would have to be done quickly. The riot was rapidly getting out of control.

Don Hancock, another lifer, teamed up with Phillips, and they got the hostages moved from the shower stall in Unit III into a larger cell. "There was no way we could get them through this mob scene," Phillips later said. "People were scared and mad. The best we could do was make sure the hostages were locked up and protected from attack until the anger died down."

Later a cynical newswoman would compare those who secured the hostages with the Amal Militia in Lebanon who held the 39 Americans hostage for 10 days. "If we were anything like the Amal, I have a whole new sympathy for them," Phillips said angrily. "We'd all have been killed if we tried forcing the release of those officers earlier in the day."

One Christian lifer risked the wrath of other inmates when he slipped Sergeant Carroll a shank under the cell door and explained how to knock the cell sprinkler off if anybody tried firebombing him in the cell. "It's the best I can do right now," he whispered. "Just be cool, and we'll all get out of this alive."

While Phillips pulled one team of lifers together, Johnny Greene and Ray Humphreys were organizing members of the 7th Step chapter and the Adventist Freedom Fellowship to help provide for security in the cellblocks. Some leadership was beginning to emerge.

But would it be enough or in time? Nobody knew for sure.

A rape attempt was foiled in Unit II, but several other inmates went to Unit V and snatched two young kids from their cells and took them to a cell on 10-walk in Unit III. There the victims were gang-raped. Later that night one of the youngsters tried to hang himself in his cell. Many convicts were bitter and angry over the attack.

Meanwhile inmates from different units collected several dozen pairs of striped jeans and prison-issued shirts and dumped them in a pile approximately 10 yards in front of the trapgate. Gas from one of the lawn mowers was thrown over the clothes, then a match was tossed. Two inmates peeled down to their shorts and T-shirts on the spot, tossing their clothes onto the fire.

A third man, known as "Crazy Pop," stripped down to nothing more than a smile. He roared with laughter as he gleefully tossed his clothes into the blaze. Startled, other prisoners gawked in disbelief as the old man jumped and yelled. Prison officials watching through the operations window tried to keep a straight face as they watched the spectacle, but they also began laughing.

Although other tense moments would flare up during the day, the ice of mounting tension was broken as the naked man danced around the fire. It never did get started again as before. As the laughter died down, a pressurized fire extinguisher was tossed onto the smoldering fire. Fearing an explosion, several men ducked for cover. But another man ran to the fire, grabbed the canister, and tossed it away from the crowd.

But a sudden crisis turned the mood ugly again.

The wind direction shifted at 9:55 a.m., and smoke from the burning mess hall poured into Unit IV. "Nearly 40 men are still locked in their cells because a man with the keys wandered off somewhere to shoot up," an inmate explained.

Scores of prisoners, screaming for an extra set of keys, descended on the trapgate. Adding to the confusion, a fire truck, surrounded by heavily armed tactical officers, moved in behind the mess hall. A shotgun blast was heard. Inmates thought they were being fired on.

"Cut off one of those pig's heads!" somebody yelled. "We'll trade it for keys!"

Greene and Humphreys raced into Unit II to head off trouble. After a tense "consultation" with two riot leaders, Phillips secured the release of Sergeant Conrad, who promised to do what he could to get the keys for Unit IV. Some of the rioters angrily protested Conrad's release, but 15 to 20 other prisoners surrounded him and escorted him safely to the trapgate.

Seconds later, coincidentally, the keys from operations were given to Malika Haki and Ray Humphreys, who then raced toward the smoke-filled cellblock with nothing more than a towel over their faces for protection. In spite of the heavy smoke and personal danger to themselves, neither man came out until all prisoners had been freed from their cells.

"You're just plain nuts!" a friend said while pounding on Humphrey's back. For once Ray was too busy coughing and gagging for a snappy comeback.

Meanwhile, Officer Greenhill, held hostage for nearly two hours, was suffering from an attack of high blood pressure. Inmates got him out of the cell, hoping he would be able to relax while sitting in a chair on the Rock. One man brought him something to drink, and several others tried to reassure him that he wouldn't be hurt.

But nothing worked, and he was returned to his cell.

"I don't blame him for being scared," Dale Johnson said. "Even though we aren't being threatened all the time, it gets pretty nerve-racking when we see some of the men shooting up dope. People get ugly and do things under the influence of drugs that they wouldn't otherwise do. Nobody has touched us yet, but we've heard a lot of threats."

Fred Tackas, a physician's assistant, brought a blood pressure cuff and stethoscope to the trapgate. Moments later, Frank Aylor, serving a 99-year sentence for murder, stepped into the cell and checked Greenhill's blood pressure.

"It's nearly 200/120!" he snapped. "This man has got to go now!"

Again some of the rioting inmates crowded around yelling and sneering. "There ain't nothing wrong with him," somebody shouted. "He's faking."

"Nuts to him!" shouted another. "Who cares? Let 'im die!"

Aylor, a totally fearless man, looked at the crowd for a few seconds with disgust.

"I'm not gonna let you take him anywhere," one man warned.

Greene and Humphreys moved in, lightly tapping their clubs against their palms. "You aren't going to do anything but get out of the way," Greene told the belligerent prisoner quietly.

"I'm taking him out. *Now!*" Aylor said as he unlocked the door and stepped inside.

Greenhill could barely stand up, so Aylor pulled his arm up around his shoulders and helped him stand. The crowd backed up as the lifers pushed their way to the front and took up positions around Aylor and the staggering officer. An unidentified Black prisoner grabbed Greenhill's left arm and helped him steady him on his feet. Later I asked the man why he'd helped the stricken officer.

"I didn't have any choice," he replied, clearly confused by his own answer. "I *had* to do it. It's like something grabbed me and shoved me out there." He looked sheepish. "I guess that sounds dumb, huh?"

It didn't sound dumb to me.

A solid wall of angry and nervous prisoners blocked the path to the door. "Fat Rat" also stepped in. A dozen other lifers joined him, and the crowd fell back, making a clear path for those moving the officer out.

Four of the hostages had been released by that time. Dale Johnson and Fred Gant were left in Unit II. Sergeant Carroll and officers Hicks and Simpson were left in Unit III.

"That's it," one of the riot leaders shouted. "We're not letting anybody else go—no matter what—until we finish negotiations with the warden."

"Negotiations!" one lifer snorted in disgust, spitting on the floor. "You'd better start thinking about how to wind this thing down before those cops outside come crashing in here and kill 40 or 50 of us."

By 11:30 the riot leaders were largely on their own. They still blocked release of the hostages, but their support was vanishing. "Now what do we do?" was the important question for most convicts.

While small groups of men paired off to discuss tactics for ending the crisis, Ray Humphreys and a few other men organized a food detail for Unit I and VI. The smoke had cleared from the mess hall, so they loaded carts with racks of bread, gallons of peanut butter, and piles of sliced meat, delivering the supplies to officers in the isolated cellblocks.

"It's hard to concentrate on a riot while eating a peanut butter sandwich," one lifer chuckled philosophically.

At 12:30 p.m. a group of inmate leaders returned to the yard after talking with Warden Dutton and Assistant Corrections Commissioner Tony

Young. They broke off into half a dozen groups to advise the population of what had been said.

"It's real simple," Head Williams told one Black group. "The commissioner has agreed to let us have a live news conference with the media *if* all hostages are released by 2:00 and everyone returns to his cell."

A chorus of catcalls greeted his announcement.

"That would be real smart," one man said sarcastically. "If we give up those hostages and go back to our cells, those cops out front are going to come in here and beat all of us half to death."

"Yeah, he's got that right," another man said tiredly. "Remember what happened in 1975? When it was all over, Metro came in here with their dogs and clubs and had their own riot on our heads."

The tension was building again. Clearly few men wanted to continue the disturbance. But they also believed a bloody payback was coming from the heavily armed officers who had surrounded the prison.

Williams met the paranoia with an impassioned plea for common sense. "The warden has promised that no guns or dogs or Metro police will be allowed behind the walls," he argued. "Use your heads. This place is swarming with national news media, with federal officials, and our own lawyer. Nothing is gonna happen if we bring this thing to a halt."

"What's gonna happen if we don't?"

Williams turned and looked at the questioner. "Young says either he gets his people back by 2:00 or they're coming in shooting! Personally, I believe he means what he says."

The debate raged back and forth for an hour. Most men were ready to take the warden and the assistant commissioner at their word. Others were skeptical. "We're back between a rock and a hard place again," one man said tiredly.

Phillips and others took the bull by the horns at 1:30, releasing Sergeant Carroll and officers Hicks and Simpson. Then they took Dale Johnson out of Unit II. But one of the riot leaders panicked when they came back to get Fred Gant.

"You tell Dutton we ain't gonna let Gant go until *after* the news conference!" he roared. "Listen to me now," he yelled at the crowd. "As soon as we give up our last pawn, that will be the end of the news conference. They ain't gonna keep their word with us."

Phillips and Williams were disgusted. They tried to explain the problem to prison officials, but Young was furious. "I want my people back, and I want them right now!" he snapped and walked away from the trapgate.

Most prisoners were confused about what had happened. Others glared at the riot leaders with smoldering hostility. The crowd slowly moved into Unit II, and the argument went on. "I'd rather die like a man than live like a dog!" one man screamed as he looked through the cell doors at Officer Gant.

Suddenly another one of those "switches" that Dale Johnson described earlier in the day flipped. Half the crowd was determined to hold Gant regardless of the cost. The rest decided he was leaving. One man snatched the keys and shoved his way through the crowd to where Gant was held. He unlocked the door. Gant stepped out and looked around nervously. Seconds ticked off in the deadly silence as 30 men moved in around the frightened officer, walking slowly and deliberately through the crowd toward the cellblock door.

"Y'all come back and visit us sometime," somebody yelled.

People laughed.

The riot was over.

Warden Dutton kept his word and refused to permit any armed officers or dogs to come behind the walls. A team of unarmed men entered each cellblock, backed up by chaplains who were there to make sure there was no more violence. Heavy boots tromping along the walks and clicking locks to cell doors were the only sounds heard in the eerie silence.

A Christian officer whom I knew well stopped by my cell door. "Praise God, it's over without anybody getting hurt," he said quietly. "But I still don't understand how it ended without dead bodies stacked up like cordwood."

I nodded and held up the Bible I was reading. "It's happened before," I chuckled. "Listen: 'My God sent his angel, and he shut the mouths of the lions' " (Dan. 6:22, NIV).

✦ ✦ ✦

Four weeks later I received an answer to my petition for a commutation of sentence: DENIED. The board refused even to consider my claims or the evidence. A brief note informed me that I could apply again when I had served 10 years.

"Meanwhile, back in the lions' den!" I muttered as I tossed the board's letter into the trash.

17

Together Again!

THE ENTIRE prison was locked down in the wake of the riot. Except for showers, no one was allowed out of his cell unless he worked on the clean-up crew or food preparation. Meals, consisting mostly of balogna or peanut butter sandwiches, were delivered individually in brown bags to the cells for weeks. Frazzled security officers worked 12- to 18-hour shifts, seven days a week.

Coincidentally—or perhaps not—senior corrections officials finally decided to comply with the federal court order to abolish double-celling of inmates in the sardine-can cells at Tennessee State Prison. You could almost hear the collective sigh of relief when welders with their acetylene torches showed up in the blocks and began cutting down the extra bunk. For the first time in many years I felt profoundly "safe" from danger in my cell.

In spite of the reduced population, security remained tight and movement around the compound was restricted. Many prisoners chafed in confinement as one boring day drifted into another. I wasn't immune to those feelings. In addition, I was still smarting from the abrupt dismissal of my clemency petition by the parole board. But I knew that nothing is more energizing than taking some action—doing something, no matter how small the action—when it felt as though events and circumstances had taken control of my life. Instead of surrendering to normal feelings of frustration during the long weeks of lock down, I spent my time reading and corresponding with a growing list of friends who wrote in response to various stories I'd published.

I particularly enjoyed a lively taped dialogue that developed between me and some teenagers at several junior and senior academies where old friends of mine taught. They used my "story theology" as part of their religious education classes and encouraged the students to communicate with me. We talked about everything from sex and drugs to guilt and grace. It was an eye-opening experience for me. I was startled to discover that the kids had a poorly defined understanding of God's loving grace. Most were firmly convinced that their salvation was exclusively contingent on their behavior. This legalistic form of perfectionism was a deeply rooted belief that stoutly resisted any other perspective. Perhaps worst of all, they believed that their behavior was never going to be "quite good enough to make it into heaven."

Not surprisingly, the teens manifested a vexing degree of ambivalence toward God. On the one hand they loved God and wanted to be "good enough" to earn their place in heaven, but on the other, because they believed they never would be quite "good enough," they manifested a thinly disguised resentment and hostility toward God, as well as the religious tradition that placed them in the midst of such a frustrating catch-22.

It was this dilemma that gave me the idea of putting a book together which contained a collection of short stories about people who either mediated God's grace to others or who encountered the delightful comedy of God's grace during difficult circumstances. The stories were about ordinary people I knew—prisoners, a probation officer, a housewife, a prison chaplain, a man on death row, a free-world volunteer, and an Adventist churchman. It was story theology, entitled *Scandalous Grace*. I submitted the manuscript to the Review and Herald Publishing Association. I didn't think they would publish the manuscript, but I'd already learned that real happiness is the by-product of having people to love, something to do, and something to hope for in the future. I already had more friends to love than any one man deserves in a lifetime, so working each day on the project also gave me something meaningful to do and something to hope for. Perhaps most importantly, writing the book gave me something to think about besides all the years that were passing me by.

I felt an indescribable sense of accomplishment when Richard Coffen, vice president for editorial services at the publishing house, wrote to tell me he not only liked the book but wanted to publish it. Setting aside theological beliefs about the state of the dead, I thought I'd died and gone to heaven!

✦ ✦ ✦

Meanwhile, Edie and I began corresponding again. I loved the sound of her voice, so she talked to me on cassette tape. Even though she kept up a cheerful front, I could tell from listening between the lines that she was struggling with discouragement and depression associated with feelings of guilt about her failed marriage. I recognized those symptoms instantly!

At Christmas she sent me a framed piece of her cross-stitching of a rainbow over a tree. Beneath the pattern were some words that struck close to home: "We weren't promised an easy life. We were promised help to live it." Included in the package were some of my favorite books by Robert Schuller, a dozen photographs of Edie and me when we were kids, plus a note. "I'd like to visit you. I need a friend—if you've got room for another one," she said.

I wrestled with a collage of conflicting feelings as I studied the pictures, remembering our relationship from years earlier. I did want to see her, because I remembered her with such great warmth and affection. But I wasn't doing very well at fighting off my own feelings of discouragement. It was my ninth Christmas behind the walls. I didn't think I would ever get out of prison. Despite my success in writing, the prison walls seemed to get higher with each passing year. It got harder and harder to connect emotionally with "normal" people in the free world, but at the same time I was acutely aware of my loneliness. Consequently, I knew there was a downside to seeing Edie: I was afraid that old feelings would get stirred up by seeing her again in person.

I worked out what I thought was a clever compromise. Instead of a personal visit between us in the prison visiting gallery, I made arrangements for her to attend a 7th Step Remotivation class on Saturday afternoon, February 8. It would give us time to talk, plus she could meet some of my free-world friends who worked as volunteers at the prison, but the environment would ensure some emotional distance.

God must have been very amused by my cautious plans!

I turned 40 on January 11, 1986. Ten years had passed since this living nightmare had begun. On balance, in spite of the stress and difficulty of surviving in prison, I felt pretty good about turning 40. I knew the years ahead wouldn't get any easier, and I had no idea of what would happen next. But I had a strong sense of God's abiding presence in my life. That realization didn't make the hard times enjoyable, but it did put those times in perspective and that made them bearable.

Seeing Edie so close to my birthday was an unexpected present. But Saturday was a long, anxious day as I paced back and forth in my cell while waiting for her arrival. I had some real fear about losing my composure when I saw her, so I had purchased a hankerchief earlier in the week to keep with me. It was hard for me to grasp the fact that an old friend wanted to see me so badly that she would drive 1,400 miles to do so.

My mouth went dry when she walked into the room. I noticed a faint haunted look in her eyes, but she was even more beautiful than I remembered. Although I still recognized the teenage girl I'd known years earlier, hers was the rich, enchanting beauty of a mature woman. I thought about one of George Bernard Shaw's quips: "A woman of 40 deserves the face she has." Clearly she was coping well with whatever pain had overtaken her in midlife.

"It's so good to see you," she whispered when I hugged her.

I was incredibly profound in my greeting. "Yeah!" I mumbled, not trusting my voice with anything more complicated.

The class was unusually crowded that day. The chairs were jammed close together to accommodate as many people as possible. We sat side by side, with our shoulders and arms pressed together. I think she knew I couldn't take my eyes off her, but she just smiled whenever our eyes met. Later I discovered that she was remembering, as I did, our days at academy when we sat as close together as possible in chapel because we couldn't hold hands in public.

The three-hour class passed in a blur. It was time for Edie to leave.

"I can walk with you to the trapgate," I said, "but I can't hug you when you leave. It's against the rules for inmates to display any affection with free-world guests on the compound."

She nodded, but she wasn't any happier about it than I. She turned to say goodbye as the trapgate slowly opened. Tears glistened in her eyes. Given the distance she had to travel, I realized I probably wouldn't see her again for a long time.

"Nuts to the rules!" I said, hugging her.

She pulled my face down and kissed me on the cheek. I remembered that first kiss in 1959, 27 years earlier. I'd been branded for life then. I still was! "I'm coming to see you again," she said fiercely as she stepped into the trap. "I don't know how or when, but I'm coming back."

I turned to walk away. My feelings were too muddled to be around other people, so dinner in the chow hall held little appeal. I turned toward my cellblock, but a yard officer stepped in front of me. I thought he was going to remind me of the rule about displays of affection. Instead, he grinned. "It looks like you got a late birthday present," he said.

I mumbled something but kept going. Once in the cell, I pulled a curtain over my door, turned out the lights, and stretched out on my bunk. That's when the tears came. I wept as I hadn't since I was a child. I grieved for all the losses I had experienced, for the long and empty years, for the suffering Edie had endured, and for all the "what might have beens" with her had other people left us alone.

◆ ◆ ◆

Except for the emotional upheaval of seeing Edie, however, I thought February 8 was just another ordinary day. I didn't realize that her visit would mark a turning point in my life, that God had already set forces in motion to turn my world upside down in ways I didn't even begin to imagine. But then again almost none of us recognizes a miracle of grace until long after the event has passed and we can see from a distance how God has led our steps through the ruin and rubble of life.

She came to visit me again in March, then in May and June. We talked for hours as we walked around and around the picnic area, sharing as only old and trusted friends can the details of all the bleak and painful years that had passed since we had last met in 1961.

Curiously, after the first two visits, the intervening years seemed to melt away. It felt as though we'd never been apart, and our conversations were a time of poignant discovery. I thought she had broken up with me in 1961 in great anger for reasons I didn't understand, and she thought I didn't care about her anymore because I never responded to her letters and phone calls. We learned that others had intercepted our letters and failed to deliver telephone messages. We talked about the times we had been in the same place but missed making connections. I learned that she had stopped writing during the summer of 1984 because she was acutely depressed and didn't want to inflict those feelings on me in prison. And I discovered that during tough times we both sang "When You Walk Through a Storm" to help recapture shredded hope and courage. But there never was enough time, so we talked with each other more on tape—hundreds of hours!

As our love grew and I felt the emotional walls crumbling all around me, I remembered how fond the late Protestant theologian Paul Tillich was of quoting an old English translation of Genesis 2:18 during marriage ceremonies: "It is not good for man to be alone; let us make for him *one who answers.*"

Edie was the "one who answers" for me. But therein lay the problem: How, given my current predicament, was I supposed to "answer" her? I loved her beyond words, yet because of that, I could not invite her into all the pain and suffering I knew would come with a romantic relationship over prison walls. I thought at times that God was playing a rather cruel, mean-spirited trick on us!

I turned to Dr. Barbara Wallston for advice. We had become close friends during the past six years. Although she wasn't precisely clear about what she believed theologically, she claimed that her friendship with me had in some way renewed her faith in Judaism. During the most recent Yom Kippur she had even gone to the synagogue and participated in the ritual of fasting and reflection on the past year of her life. Clearly the process had been a deeply moving spiritual experience. Given her years of radical feminism, fierce agnosticism, and commitments to scientific objectivity, however, she still was a little embarrassed by her emerging faith. "It's enough to make me believe in miracles," she said dryly.

She skipped over my rationalizations and came directly to the point: "Do you love Edie?"

"Yes."

"Does she love you?"

"Yes."

"Then please tell me what the 'big problem' is as you see it?" she demanded.

"Because I love her and care about her, how can I even think of being so selfish as to get her life entangled with mine when there's virtually nothing of value I have to offer her. I should be thinking about what's best for her, instead of how I feel."

Barbara scowled at me through her thick glasses "Oink, oink, oink!" she said.

"What's that supposed to mean?"

"It means you're thinking like a sexist pig!" she chuckled. "For a man who claims to have strong commitments to equality for women, you're talking like a typically patronizing male."

"How can you say . . ."

She shook her finger at me. "No, this is where I talk and you listen. I've met Edie. She's a highly intelligent, mature woman who has the right to make up her own mind about what she does or doesn't want. And *you* don't have the right to be making decisions about 'what's best' for her. I've heard you define love as an 'unqualified commitment to another person's growth, fulfillment, welfare, and happiness.' What you owe her is honesty in that kind of love. The rest is up to her."

◆ ◆ ◆

I thought about Barbara's counsel for several weeks. During our June 15 visit in the picnic area, I told Edie that I loved her but my prospects for getting out of prison anytime soon were very poor. "You fill up my life to the brim with more joy, warmth, and happiness than I ever dreamed was possible. But you need to know that prison life can be harder on the wives and girlfriends than on a man in prison. Visits and telephone calls are both short and infrequent. There will be times when I won't be able to be with you or even talk to you when you need it most.

"There's little I can do to help you with the financial or emotional strains you'll have to face with your four children. A lot of free-world people will think you're an idiot for getting involved with a 'convicted killer.' You're new here and the guards are pleasant and courteous now. But that won't last. Once they get used to your coming regularly, some of them will treat you just like they do every other family member of a prisoner—like human garbage. They'll make you feel small and powerless in ways you can't even imagine now. You won't like it, and there's nothing you'll be able to do about it—unless you want them to make your life even more miserable!"

I stopped and looked at Edie. "That's all the good stuff you can expect. Do you want to hear about the bad?"

"I know what you say is true," she admitted. "But I don't care. I'll deal with it as it comes. I love you, and you love me. I believe that God has brought us back together again after all these years. Like the disciples, I don't believe He invited us out into the middle of this stormy 'lake' to drown. Nothing else matters."

I looked at her for a long time. "Then do you want to marry me when this movie is over?" I asked.

"Yes, I do!"

◆ ◆ ◆

Edie purchased a small condominium near Madison, Tennessee. On July 14, after a grueling 18-hour drive from North Carolina, she and her four children moved into their new home. During the first year she worked at several different jobs until she found one she really liked as the assistant to the personnel director, Marcy Jones, at Tennessee Christian Medical Center.

Except for her mother and one of her brothers, Edie didn't have any friends living nearby whom she could talk to about our relationship. Consequently, I had warned her to be discreet with fellow employees about her relationship with me in order to avoid a lot of discriminatory treatment. She told everybody! Instead of criticism, which is precisely what most girlfriends of prisoners receive from their employers, the staff at Tennessee Christian Medical Center promptly made a liar out of me. I was astonished! Everybody—from the president, Don Jernigan, and vice presidents Terry Owen, Brent Snyder, Larry Crissup, and Jim Culpepper to the ladies in housekeeping—offered her warmth, encouragement, and emotional support during the next several years.

Our second biggest concern was how Edie's children would react to me. After all, they were teenagers, and I wondered what they would think of their mother's decision to commit her life to a prisoner serving a 99-year sentence for murder. But after a few visits things clicked between us. I thought they were a great bunch of youngsters, and they seemed to enjoy visiting and talking with me. Then our problem was having enough quality time alone for Edie and me. Given other possibilities, however, Edie and I thought that was a nice problem to have.

There were difficult times as well. In addition to all the normal family conflicts that emerge as teenagers begin the breaking away process, Edie faced enormous financial strains as a single mother trying to support herself and four children—two of whom were in church schools. Bitter words, anger, and resentment percolated just beneath the surface because they were pulling in five different directions at once. The solution proved to be surprisingly easy. Except for the youngest son, the three older children all

226

had part-time jobs. Once they agreed to pool their resources, the financial strain eased and so did flaring tempers.

I felt a profound sense of emotional and spiritual renewal as a result of my relationship with Edie. She looked 10 years younger, and friends said I'd lost the "haunted look" on my face. After what we had been through, each in our own kind of prison, we both thrived on loving each other and being loved, and that seemed to generate an enormous amount of generalized joy, hope, and optimism about the future.

◆ ◆ ◆

By early 1987 I was cranking out a prolific amount of writing for a couple dozen different Christian magazines. Edie loved reading my manuscripts in rough draft. Moreover, she proved to be a superb editor. It felt good working together on projects and to see my ideas in print. The letters and cards I received from hundreds of readers were an unexpected bonus. "You're gonna have to get your own post office box if this keeps up!" one guard grumbled as he shoved 20 letters through my cell bars one day.

Letters from friends, both old and new, affected me like a shot of B_{12}. During difficult times, when life seemed so meaningless and purpose-less, letters from people who said that something I'd written had made a difference in their lives pumped me up with courage and resolve. The response of readers to *Scandalous Grace* was so encouraging that I submitted *Detective in Search of Grace*, another collection of short stories, to Pacific Press Publishing Association. It was published early in 1988.

Edie was surprised when she discovered that I'd dedicated the book to her with a poem. Although I modified the poem for the book, I'd actually written it in the late 1960s when my grandparents told me about the problems she was facing at the time:

> Edie
> A woman remembered
> For 25 years,
> Though unseen.
> Your memory remained in the backwoods of my mind
> Like the haunting cry of a distant eagle.
> Now my cup runneth over
> From the sweet gift of God's grace—
> Your love for me.

I didn't earn a lot of money writing—perhaps $200 or $300 a month on average—but it gave me a great deal of personal satisfaction to send that money to Edie to help with bills, to purchase something extra for the kids at Christmas, and to pay for the food she brought to the picnic area.

We lived for the weekends, when we could be together again in the picnic area. She always arrived at 8:00, bringing a picnic lunch. Most of the officers who searched visitors were pleasant, professional men and women who went out of their way to make people feel as comfortable as possible when entering the prison. The few who weren't could make life miserable for everybody—especially a couple of the lesbian guards who didn't seem to know the difference between frisking and fondling women visitors while searching them for contraband. Knowing when to complain to prison officials and when to simply endure the abuse was a dicy task because retaliation could be severe.

Once Edie was processed in, I'd be notified in the cellblock of her arrival. Usually she had the table all set up and something hot to drink before I got out there. It was brutally hot in the summer, and cold air blowing in off the river in winter would chill us to the bone. Edie didn't handle the heat well, so I got a chance to pamper her with ice packs when it got too hot, and we huddled around the fire in winter for warmth. In either case, we never left early. Those four to six hours were too precious.

✦ ✦ ✦

Although I had some real misgivings about the probability of success (I had served 10 years in 1987), I decided to take the parole board up on its suggestion that I submit another application. My skepticism wasn't motivated by general pessimism; it was practical. I knew that two of the five board members had flagrant conflicts of interest where I was concerned. One was a man who'd had a personal relationship with my ex-wife. The other, Ed Hoover, had worked as a special investigator at the time of my trial for the district attorney who railroaded me into prison with perjured testimony. Because he had been involved in our trial, he had voluntarily recused himself from participating in Darleen's parole hearing. But I knew the board had no policy governing conflict of interest. I doubted that he would recuse himself in my case, and there was no way I could force the issue. Despite the problems, I had to try something to gain my freedom.

I cautioned Edie about getting too optimistic. "The entire clemency process is riddled with corrupt political overtones," I explained. "The facts in my case are politically messy. General Gerbitz and his cronies back in Chattanooga are powerful Republicans, and it's most unlikely that the current board, which is still dominated by Republicans appointed by Governor Lamar Alexander, won't touch my case with a 10-foot pole."

"If you think it's so hopeless, then what's the point?" she asked.

"I choose to live with hope," I replied, "but my hope isn't contingent on any particular outcome. I hope things go well, of course, but my hopefulness is rooted in something more important than outcomes of any particular kind—it's a hopeful spiritual conviction that life is meaningful, that it has purpose—no matter what our circumstances—and that struggling by God's grace to persevere against evil is worthwhile in and of itself."

Edie went on a campaign to get as many letters from friends as she could to support my petition. More than 100 responded. Meanwhile I retained Steve Carr, formerly the general counsel for the parole board, as my attorney. He listened politely when I told him about the conflicts of interest with two board members. But he knew these people and didn't seem to take what I said seriously.

"You should never have been convicted in the first place," Steve said. "Besides, I've never seen a more strongly documented case for wrongful

228

conviction. Plus you've got the best institutional record in prison that the board has ever seen. I don't understand what you're so worried about."

Christian friends were even more emphatic. "I have this conviction that God is going to change things when you least expect it, and you'll be on your way home soon," one insisted.

Maybe, I thought. But I still felt as though I had the sword of Damocles hanging over my head. From personal experience I knew prison is one place where Murphy's law is usually the dominant principle: Whatever can go wrong, will! In any event, after witnessing 10 years of the most grotesque savagery imaginable in this human zoo, including 29 stabbing murders, I wasn't persuaded that God was in the business of arbitrarily interfering with the abuse people inflict on one another just for their personal convenience.

Yet I still hoped that God would answer our prayers for release.

On Wednesday, December 23, 1987, the parole board held a preliminary review at their office in downtown Nashville to decide whether or not my case merited a formal hearing. To get that I needed three of the five votes. I wasn't allowed to attend, but Edie and several of my friends were present. The chairman allowed Steve to speak briefly on my behalf before the members announced their decision. He didn't submit any evidence on my behalf of wrongful conviction. Instead, he proffered what still seems to me to have been a flabby argument to the effect that I was really a nice guy and they ought to let me go.

Ed Hoover pounced. He claimed that he knew little about my case except for what he had read in the newspapers at the time. But then he proceeded to present the state's "open-and-shut" case against me, describing me in the most horrific terms as a cold-blooded killer who had murdered a man for money. "I'm not saying he should do the entire 99-years," Hoover said, "but he just hasn't done enough time yet." (Hoover left the parole board one week later to work for District Attorney Gary Gerbitz again.)

Another board member, Donna Blackburn, who had never met me and wouldn't know me from Adam's housecat if she bumped into me, added fuel to the flames. "I've got family members out here in the free world, and I don't want murderers like Jeris Bragan around them," she announced.

Two board members weren't persuaded by the heated rhetoric.

Edie called me at the prison school to give me the results. "I'm afraid it's bad news," she said.

"Well, that won't be an entirely new experience," I replied. "What's the verdict?"

"We lost. The vote was three to two," she said. Her voice trembled. I knew she was on the verge of tears, and I suddenly felt very tired, alone, and betrayed—again.

To add insult to injury the board sent me a one-line letter explaining the reason for their denial: "Doesn't rise to a level to be considered."

A familiar biblical passage kept ricocheting around like a spent bullet in the back of my mind as I walked through the prison yard toward my cellblock: "We know that all that happens to us is working for our good if we love God and are fitting into his plans" (Rom. 8:28, TLB).

I shivered uncomfortably in the winter chill. More than once I'd shared that promise with friends when they struggled through hard times. But now the words tasted bitter in my mouth. The promise sounded like an empty cliché. I manifestly did *not know* and could *not see* how in all things God was working for *my* good.

I looked up at the slate-gray sky. "Thanks a lot, Lord. And Merry Christmas to You too!" I muttered angrily.

In spite of my feelings, I walked up to the prison chapel later that night to celebrate Christmas Mass. Bishop James, Father Ralph, the sisters, and Catholic laypeople who volunteered their time at the prison had become very special friends over the years. Although I am Seventh-day Adventist, I believe that God has His people in every church, so I'd come to appreciate the rather large and rambunctious body of Christ in all Christian traditions that ministered behind the walls. Moreover, Christian brothers from different traditions tend to support one another's faith in prison. We shared open communion, regardless of which faith community a prisoner is connected with.

The congregation was standing for prayer as I stepped into the back of the chapel. "I pray for those who were denied clemency this morning," I heard one of the men say. And the congregation responded in unison: "We pray to the Lord."

Later, tears stung my eyes as Father Ralph handed me the wafer. "The Body of Christ," he said quietly.

He knew I wasn't Catholic and that our religious traditions viewed the sacramental symbols quite differently. But none of that mattered. He knew of my discouragement, and in that moment we were just two fellow pilgrims, Christian brothers, each in need of the saving, rescuing, resurrecting grace that can be experienced most profoundly during Communion.

Dr. John Mallette, an ordained deacon and a professor at Tennessee State University, presented the cup. "Be of good cheer, my friend. The Lord bless you," he said.

As I walked through the prison compound that night, I stopped and looked up at the star-studded sky. Nearly 2,000 years ago Christ had put aside His divine power and glory to join us in the crucible of human uncertainty, unfairness, and suffering. I wondered if He had always been certain of God's abiding presence during rough times in His life. But then I remembered His cry of utter despair from the cross: "My God, my God, why have you forsaken me?" (Matt. 27:46). Those weren't His last words, however. Faith burst forth as His life slipped away: "Jesus called out with a loud voice, 'Father, into your hands I commit my spirit' " (Luke 23:46).

I understood how He felt.

It was a deeply spiritual moment as I stood alone in the middle of the prison compound, surrounded on all sides by walls, barbed wire, and gun towers. There was something about the Christmas season and Communion at the end of that difficult day that provoked a truly energizing moment of epiphany for me. During a day of great pain and restlessness, I suddenly felt a deep-rooted spiritual awareness of Christ's abiding presence in my anguish. The same problems remained. I had no idea what the future held. But in that moment I felt mysteriously resurrected, more confident about whatever came next in my life. I felt a renewal of hope and courage, even though both seemed either silly or pointless under the circumstances.

The experience was something beyond words or logic. I could accept or reject the offer of grace, but I could not analyze it. Like Job, I didn't have an intellectual answer to my questions. Instead I had something far more transcending—God's presence. That was good enough for the moment.

Then a humorous thought struck me. I remembered a line from a Christian saint who faced great adversity, but she argued that God never allows us to bear more than He can trust us to handle. "I just wish He didn't trust me so much!" she complained good-naturedly.

I laughed as I thought about her words. Humor is so incredibly redemptive when all looks grim and lost.

"Thank You, Lord, for trusting me with this," I chuckled as I headed toward my cell.

◆ ◆ ◆

A few weeks later I moved from the cell blocks up to SDC. Warden Dutton had abolished the inmate governing committee, so I was glad to be back on the hill again, mostly because I could talk to Edie on the phone for as long as we wanted each day. Eventually, she purchased a speaker phone so she could talk to me and still avoid getting a permanent crick in her neck! A friend gave her a 50-foot cord so she could take it with her outside or to any other part of the house. At night, when she was ready to sleep, she would set the speaker phone on a pillow next to her head, and I'd read to myself for several hours while listening to her sleep.

Although we were separated by walls and many miles, I think we were emotionally closer than many couples we knew who lived in the same house together.

◆ ◆ ◆

The day after my 42nd birthday I called Edie and found her in tears. Her 74-year-old mother, Elsie, had committed suicide that morning. She had been depressed for years because of guilt. Although she knew her husband had sexually abused her daughter, she did nothing to stop it. Despite what Edie said to convince her that she was forgiven, Elsie clung to her guilt as though it were a life raft rather than the death trap it actually was. She was so determined to die that she had crawled into the back of her Volvo station wagon and pressed her face down against the floor near a hole so she could inhale the carbon monoxide most efficiently.

It was her third attempt in two years.

Edie was devastated. But I captured a glimpse into a profound theological truth about the human journey from desolation to consolation as she went through a terrible time of loneliness and despair after her mother's death. There was nothing I could do to change things. All I could do was hold her when she wept, listen to her as she talked through her feelings, and assure her that I loved her and cared deeply about what she was going through.

231

I didn't think that was worth much at the time.

"You don't understand," she said. "I can cope with *anything* as long as I know you love me, care about my feelings, and stick with me while I work through them."

Staggered by that thought, I realized that what she said was true of my own experience. Invariably it had been in the midst of the worst personal desolation that I'd experienced most intimately the redemptive and revitalizing consolation of Christ's presence. Moreover, that grace almost always had been mediated directly through friends who cared about me.

✦ ✦ ✦

In May of 1988, Edie and I were in the prison picnic area, attending a picnic sponsored by the 7th Step Foundation. I glanced up and saw Fred Steltemeier, a wealthy Nashville attorney and businessman, walking toward us. He was a tall, slender, distinguished-looking man in his late-50s. His hair was thinning and turning white, but he was built like a marathon runner, which he was.

I'd seen Fred and his wife, B.J., once before a couple of weeks earlier when he spoke at a 7th Step pre-release class. He had a powerful, booming bass voice. I thought at the time that he could have had a great career as a radio announcer—or a drill sergeant. He and his brother, Bill, also an attorney, had been active as prison volunteers in the 1960s and 1970s before they had burned out under the stress of dealing with prisoners.

B.J. stood out in the midst of other free-world women because she looked so elegant—and nervous. She had never been inside the prison before. Her apprehension went through the roof when an alarm went off on one of the walls shortly after the program began. Guards thought somebody had escaped over the wall. They rushed in to count heads, then locked everyone in the room until the count was clear. Inmates had mobbed them after the program. B.J. looked like she wanted to "escape" herself, so I'd left without introducing myself.

Fred stuck out his hand as he approached us. "Jeris, my name is Fred Steltemeier."

I shook hands with him and introduced him to Edie.

"We don't have too much time to talk right now, but I'd like to hear about what brought you to prison," he said.

"Why?" I asked. His blunt question surprised me. I didn't intend to sound rude, but I knew it came across that way.

Fred laughed. "Why? What difference does it make? I've heard some rumors about what happened at your trial. And people I know have told me you don't belong in prison. If everything I've heard about you and your case is true, well, I think the subject might be interesting to explore."

Briefly, I told him first about my own responsibility for providing Darleen with an alibi. Then I told him about Torbett's perjury, the secret deal he had made with the district attorney's office, and his subsequent escape from the county workhouse.

"Since 1977 I've been through three courts, nine judges, and two parole boards without getting anybody to review the trial record or the evidence,"

I said. "If you want a real loser of a case to work on, mine is a good place to start. And I don't have any money to pay a lawyer."

Fred laughed again. "The good Lord loves lost causes, and so do I. And I don't need your money. I've got more than I can spend. But let me tell you one thing up front about me: If I decide to take on your case, I'll do everything I can to help you—if you're telling me the truth. But I'll drop you in a heartbeat if you ever lie to me about anything."

"Fair enough."

"Good. When you get back to your cell, I want you to write up a brief narrative about what happened. Send that and all your trial records to me at this address," he said, handing me a card. "I'm not gonna promise you anything until I've reviewed all the facts. I learned a long time ago to never promise a prisoner something unless I know I can deliver."

We joined Fred and B.J. later at their table to eat. Edie and B.J. hit it off like old friends as they discovered mutual interests in country decorating and antiques. B.J. and Fred owned a historic home in Franklin, so Edie was delighted when they invited her to visit. "At our age we'd better be glad these women love antiques," Fred chuckled.

Edie and I just looked at each other after they left.

"Is that man for real?" she asked.

"Who knows?" I replied. "Maybe the comedy of God's grace strikes in the form of this German Catholic lawyer!"

◆ ◆ ◆

It took me two weeks to prepare the documentation Fred required and get it off to him in the mail.

Meanwhile, I called Ed Ley. I'd met him for the first time in 1979 when he first began working as a volunteer in the Adventist jail ministry. A former Florida police officer, he had gone back to school after his conversion to earn a degree in theology at Southern Missionary College. He had wanted to be a pastor, but divorce killed those plans. He married Bonnie, a nurse and a delightful Christian woman, in 1982. Both of them wrote and visited me regularly, and our friendship had grown stronger with each passing year.

In 1988 Ed worked as an adult parole officer for the State of Tennessee. I figured he could track Torbett down—if he was still alive.

"I'll never get out of here if we don't find him," I told Ed.

He didn't hesitate. "I'll do everything I can."

I knew I could consider it done.

Only one thing was problematic for us: Edie and I wanted to get married, but I winced at the thought of putting her through a wedding ceremony in prison. She deserved better than that. "You're going to feel awfully lonely after we get married out here and you have to go home alone," I reminded her.

"I don't care!" she said stubbornly.

"Well, let's wait a few more months and see what develops," I suggested.

She agreed.

Several weeks passed without a word from Fred. I had begun to think he'd lost interest until I called Edie at home one night. "Fred wants you to call him right away," she said.

"What's up?"

"He didn't say exactly. He just said he'd talked to Gerbitz, Lanzo, and Bevil today, and now he wants to talk to you."

I took a deep breath. "Well, hook us up on a three-way and let's get this over with. I hope you realize they probably scared him off."

"Maybe, but I don't think that's what happened."

The conviction in her voice surprised me. "Don't get your hopes up, Edie," I warned.

Fred answered the phone. I could tell from his voice that he was furious about something. He plunged in without preamble. "You know, Jeris, I really wasn't sure you were telling me the truth about all the stuff that went on down in Chattanooga. I wasn't sure even after reading the file. But after meeting with those three prosecutors today, I'm sure now!"

"What happened?"

He chuckled gleefully.

"Fred, you're enjoying the suspense too much. What happened?" I asked again.

"Well, first of all I caught them in half a dozen lies when they told me about different things that had supposedly been testified to at your trial. Since I had just finished reading the transcript, I knew they were lying through their teeth and I just had to wonder why. When that line didn't work with me, they started calling you everything but a White man and talking to me like I was some hick out of the hills. When I stood up to leave, Stan Lanzo said, 'Don't you have anything better to do with your money than help that no-good _____ ?' I told him I was semi-retired, had plenty of time and money, and spent it any way I pleased. I told him I had decided for sure that I was going to give your case my undivided attention."

He paused for a moment. In the background I could hear Edie crying softly.

"I went to see several other people after I talked to those characters," he continued. "I'll bet you won't be surprised to hear I got a lot of doors slammed in my face. That just makes me wonder all the more about what they're hiding."

"What does this mean in terms of your taking my case?"

"This means I'm with you all the way, no matter how long it takes or what kind of roadblocks we run into," he said. "First, we're gonna get you out of there. Then I'm going to do everything in my power to see that those people are disbarred. I'm as strong a supporter of law enforcement as you're ever gonna find, but people like them are just a bunch of crooks hiding out behind badges. They're a disgrace to the law profession and more dangerous than the people they prosecute."

I told him that Ed was looking for Torbett.

"That's a good idea," he mused. "You stay on top of that while I start some real digging into the files. You never know what kind of critter will come scrambling out once you start turning over the rocks."

✦ ✦ ✦

Fred spent months turning over the rocks, sifting through old records, and interviewing witnesses. Our biggest break came when he discovered that no warrant had ever been issued for Torbett's arrest when he escaped from the county workhouse. Leon Haily, the criminal court clerk, called Fred's attention to an original copy of the October 18, 1978 "Agreed Order" that had led to the dismissal of the habitual criminal indictment against Torbett. It had been signed by the judge and all the lawyers.

"You aren't gonna believe what these rascals actually put in writing," Fred told me when he handed me the document during a visit at the prison.

I read through it quickly. At the bottom of the page, the district attorney had given as a reason for dismissing the indictment the fact that they knew in 1975—two years before I was ever indicted or tried—that one of the charges against Torbett was flawed "because of a faulty search warrant." In the first place, we couldn't find any evidence in Torbett's records that a search warrant had ever been issued. More importantly, however, the D.A. admitted six weeks after my trial that a deal had been struck with Torbett a month before I was arrested.

"These people are so bold they don't even worry about what they put in writing!" Fred said, shaking his head in disgust. "It may take a while longer, but things that will lead to your freedom are slowly coming into focus."

✦ ✦ ✦

Meanwhile, I kept writing and waiting.

I met Steve Womack, a successful novelist and former newspaper reporter, when he began teaching a creative writing class at the prison in August of 1988. He was a slender man in his mid-30s. He had thick brown hair and frequently wore aviator glasses and a flight jacket. He was a pilot, who also taught a class in screenwriting at Tennessee State University. Although he'd never been behind prison walls, his warm and easy style earned the trust of the two dozen convicts who signed up for his class. That quickly dwindled to three—Bill Elliot, Woody Eargle, and me—when the rest discovered his class meant real work.

In addition to attending his classes, I also interviewed him for a feature story I published in the prison newspaper. "Why do you spend every Monday night behind these walls?" I asked. "Surely you have better things to do with your time."

"Actually, it's quite simple," he said. "I've been blessed in my life, and this is my way of giving something back."

During the next four years, he gave all three of us a great deal in terms of his time, critique, and—most importantly—his friendship.

✦ ✦ ✦

In October Fred and Ed finally located Torbett in Atlanta, Georgia. When confronted, he admitted that his testimony at my trial was totally false, given in exchange for the state's promise to drop the habitual criminal indictment. He admitted that District Attorney General Gary Gerbitz and his assistant, Stan Lanzo, were the ones who made the deal with him. The most shocking revelation came when the escaped fugitive admitted that he had been in and out of state prison in both Texas and Alabama since he had "escaped" from Tennessee. But his status as an escaped convict was never detected because Chattanooga authorities had suppressed the warrant charging him with escape. That was part of the state's deal with him, Torbett said.

In spite of his admissions, Torbett refused to testify publicly without federal protection. He claimed that Chattanooga authorities would kill him before he ever got to testify if they got him in their custody again.

When the U.S. attorney in Atlanta refused to investigate, Fred went directly to the Tennessee attorney general's office in Nashville and laid out the facts of the case. Deputy Attorney General Jerry Smith expressed interest in the case but said his office lacked the investigative staff to do anything about it. But he did write a letter in early 1989 to the U.S. attorney in Knoxville, requesting a federal investigation of the facts to determine whether or not county prosecutors had engaged in a criminal conspiracy to violate my civil rights.

Three weeks later Fred was interviewed in Chattanooga by an assistant U.S. attorney and F.B.I. special agent Bill Curtis. They promised a thorough investigation.

"We'll have you out of there before Christmas!" Fred said.

I was ready to pack for departure.

✦ ✦ ✦

The proverbial second shoe dropped just before Easter of 1989. Special Agent Curtis called Fred on the telephone to say it was the opinion of the U.S. attorney that the statute of limitations had expired on any crimes that might have been committed by officials at my trial. "There's nothing we can do," Curtis said. "Bragan will have to go back to court again if he ever wants to get out of prison."

I felt numb. Despair closed in around me. Like the disciples who had participated in Jesus' triumphal march into Jerusalem, only to see Him arrested, beaten, and executed like a common criminal a week later, my burning hope for release from prison was demolished. I knew it would probably take *years* to pursue further appeals in the courts.

At the same time I learned Torbett had disappeared again.

It had been a long time since I had felt so unequivocally defeated. "I don't know what to do now," I told Edie.

She was stubbornly determined. "I don't have any ideas either," she admitted. "But I do know this: *God didn't call us out into the lake to drown!*"

After Edie went to sleep that night I began browsing through the book of Job. My eyes suddenly focused on a familiar passage. After a series of catastrophic events in which his children were murdered and the loss of everything he owned had flung the wealthy man into instant poverty, Job spoke: "The Lord gave, and the Lord hath taken away; blessed be the name of the Lord" (Job 1:21, KJV).

TOGETHER AGAIN!

The impact of those vexing words from Job had first disturbed me when I studied theology at Columbia Union College in the 1960s. I wondered what would possess a man to say such a thing after such senseless tragedy? Were his words a manifestation of pious passivity? "Hey, God! Hit me again! I love it!" Didn't he have the guts to get angry over such an injustice? Frustrated because I could not understand him, I wanted to reach into the book, grab Job, and shake him until he answered my question: "What do you mean, 'blessed be the name of the Lord'? Were you just babbling incoherently, unaware of what you were saying because of your pain, or did you know something that I don't?"

Then it hit me like a heavy fist wrapped in concrete: Job's words did *not* reflect pious passivity. On the contrary, his was a defiant faith rooted in the kind of raw human courage that stubbornly refuses to accept bitter suffering as the final word. Those defiant words were a faith-filled judgment for God when all the available evidence seemed to suggest that random chaos and meaninglessness had taken over his existence.

Job bellowed a fierce challenge to the dark underside of life: "This is how I choose to respond. Evil is *not* the defining truth. God's loving grace, even when shrouded in suffering and mystery, *is* the defining truth! So *'blessed be the name of the Lord'*—no matter what happens to me, no matter what my circumstances, no matter how badly I hurt."

I thought about Buggy Torbett, the prosecutors, the police, and Darleen; the courts that had refused to honestly review my trial record, the parole board officials who didn't even make a pretense of reviewing my petition, and officials with the United States Justice Department who simply ignored the criminal practices of a Republican prosecutor.

But I realized that nothing they had done mattered to me anymore. Like Joseph's experience, God had transformed into my good all the evil they planned. I knew I would never have gotten around to writing for publication in the free world. I never would have met some of the scores of friends whose love had so richly blessed my life if I hadn't come to prison. And most of all, my path probably would never have crossed Edie's again except through the prison gates.

"Yes!" I muttered. *"Blessed be the name of the Lord!"*

"Did you say something?" Edie mumbled sleepily.

I laughed. "Yes. I said, Do you still want to get married in prison?"

She was instantly awake. "Are you serious?"

"I'm serious as a heart attack! As long as you know that my future is clouded and uncertain, I'm ready to get married—even in prison. Is that what you want to do?"

"*Yes!*" she shouted.

"Do you want to marry me when this movie is over?"

That's what I had asked Edie three years earlier when we first committed ourselves to one another. At the time I thought the "movie" was nearing an end, but Murphy's law continued to prevail! In terms of my freedom, the only light I saw at the end of the tunnel was the light of an oncoming train.

Clearly, this movie was, to mix a terrible batch of metaphors, a play with no concluding act!

I had never had any doubt about wanting to marry Edie. The only issue was when and where. I felt considerable ambivalence about prison marriages in general because of the suffering it invariably put a woman through. A good marriage in today's world is difficult to achieve under the best of circumstances. Creating a meaningful marriage over prison walls presented some special challenges. As long as I remained in prison, for example, there would be no honeymoon and we never would have any time alone together.

Admittedly, the prison picnic area on the weekends frequently resembled a Roman orgy in progress as couples engaged in blatant displays of sexual activity. I understood what drove people to seek intimacy in that environment, and I didn't feel judgmental about it. But that kind of behavior simply wasn't acceptable for us. Aside from moral issues, I thought engaging in intimate sexual contact in public was the last human surrender to the insidious evil that characterized every aspect of prison life.

It really troubled me that Edie would have to go home alone when the wedding ceremony was over. I knew her well, so I had a good idea about how she would feel, and I didn't want to put her through that. But she made it clear that she she loved me and wanted to share my life—no matter where I was or what our circumstances. I didn't understand that kind of love any more than I understood God's grace. I decided to accept it, without analysis!

Planning a wedding anywhere presents a variety of interesting problems, but getting a prison wedding organized offers some unique challenges for even the most creative imagination. The required memos and paperwork would bring joy to a well entrenched government bureaucrat. A memo, signed by two wardens, was required for every detail. Even the bride and groom for the top of the wedding cake had to be described in detail before it could be approved and allowed in. But a traditional wedding cake was prohibited. Edie got around that dilemma by inviting our guests to bring frozen Sara Lee cakes.

First, we had to fill out a marriage request form. Usually, a one-year waiting period was required. Fortunately, Dr. Amos Wilson, the senior chaplain, knew both Edie and me, so he waived that requirement. I wanted nothing to do with a marriage in the prison chapel. While it's a lovely chapel, the idea of marrying Edie behind the walls, surrounded by barbed wire and gun towers, held little appeal for me. I wanted the ceremony to be outside on the picnic area, as far away from the walls and bars as possible. Happily, Amos understood my feelings and gave his approval.

I had asked Edie to go steady with me on December 8, 1959, and we saw each other again for the first time in 25 years on February 8. Consequently, the eighth was an important date for us. We had to get married on the weekend, so we chose April 8, 1989, for the wedding date. Next we had to find a minister who was available to perform the ceremony on that day. We particularly wanted Elder Conn Arnold because he was a close personal friend and the one who had brought us back together again. Since he had to be out of town, we asked Dr. Cleveland Houser, an Adventist chaplain at

TOGETHER AGAIN!

Tennessee State Prison who had become a good friend during the five years he had served at the prison. He agreed.

Our biggest problem, however, was the guest list. We had many free-world friends who wanted to be with us in person to celebrate that day. But prison policy regarding guests for a wedding allowed only eight people, including family members. Edie and her four children took up five slots, which left just three more. We got around that problem when a dozen other inmates offered us the use of their visitation list. We scrambled for several weeks getting visitor application forms filled out, photographs attached, and signatures from the prison counselors and wardens approving the visitation.

Malika Haki, a Black ex-Marine who was my best friend behind the walls, stopped by my cell the day before the wedding. He'd scrounged some cornstarch from the chow hall and mixed it with water. He waved the bottle at me. "I've got some great starch here," he said. "Give me your clothes, and I'll show you how an ex-Marine can make the shabby prison blues you've gotta wear tomorrow look like a Marine dress uniform!"

He returned two hours later.

"This is all I've got to give you and Edie for a wedding present," he explained. "It ain't much, but at least you won't have to be embarrassed about how you look around all those free-world people."

I couldn't believe what he'd done. He'd starched and ironed the striped jeans and blue denim shirt until they were stiff enough to stand alone. There wasn't a wrinkle left anywhere. It was one of the best wedding gifts we received.

We chose April, instead of another month, because we expected a balmy spring day. Instead, an Arctic blast swept in over Tennessee on April 8, 1989. It was bitterly cold. The misery index was completed by a steadily drizzling rain and a hard-driving, penetrating wind blowing in off the river.

As I walked out onto the picnic area, I discovered Murphy's law was wreaking havoc in the form of one of the guards. He loved giving orders to free-world people and generally throwing his weight around. He was a grossly obese man, so he had plenty to throw. Other guards joked that he'd been hired by the pound. He looked like a stereotypical fat Southern sheriff, and he had an abrasive, authoritarian personality to match his appearance. He had allowed half the wedding party to enter the grounds before arbitrarily stopping the other half, which included Edie, for an additional 20 minutes.

Rather than fume over the pointless delay, I walked up the hill to meet some of our guests who were trying to keep warm as they huddled around several charcoal fires burning in the grills under the large cabana in the center of the picnic area. Actually, it was just an eight-sided roofed shelter without walls, which covered six picnic tables and measured approximately 35 feet in diameter, but everybody called it a "cabana" because the word sounded so civilized.

Steve Womack introduced me to his fiancée, Dr. Cathy Yarborough, a Vanderbilt-trained clinical psychologist. She was warm and gracious, so I resisted the temptation to suggest we all needed our heads examined for standing around in the cold.

Then I heard somebody yell my name. I turned around just in time to catch Ed Ley's wife, Bonnie, as she jumped into my arms. In addition to his other skills Ed was a talented photographer. I wanted him to shoot our wedding pictures, so he shook hands quickly and went right to work.

"Are you really gonna get married?" Bonnie asked.

"Sure am!"

"Why did you have to pick such a cold day?" she complained good-naturedly.

Edie arrived moments later, followed by her four children; her brother, Melvin; and several other friends: Randy, Pam, and Kara Dickman from Savannah, Tennessee; Grace Wormhood from New Hampshire; Ruth and Daryl Gallant from Maine; Naomi Skelton from Georgia; Dick Snyder, Barbara Frazier, Steve and Robin Smith, friends from the hospital; Donna and Dave Montague, friends from church; and Michelle Tishauer from Connecticut.

Edie carried a single pink rose and wore a red coat over a simple white silk blouse and skirt. I knew she was dressing down in order to avoid making me feel shabby in my prison clothes. She could have worn burlap and still would have been the most beautiful woman in the world that morning! Her warm smile was strong enough to banish the clouds because the sun kept breaking through, if only momentarily.

"Edie is the only one here who doesn't seem to know it's cold," Steve joked.

Edie is a naturally gregarious and extroverted woman who feels comfortable with people under any circumstances. But after so many years of social isolation in the prison, it took me a while before I could relax with so many people around us at one time. By the time Dr. Houser arrived at 10:30, however, I was beginning to thoroughly enjoy our cheerful and exhuberant group of friends.

We began the ceremony at 11:00, surrounded by family and scores of friends—both from the free world and from behind the walls. The biting wind dissipated, and the sun burst through gloomy clouds when Donna Montague sang a cappella our favorite song, "The Rose." It was a poignant moment. Behind us I could hear people crying softly. Perhaps it was because the song lyrics packed a particularly powerful emotional punch under the circumstances. Or maybe it was because Edie and I had to keep passing my handkerchief back and forth between us as we struggled to maintain our composures.

At the end of Dr. Houser's homily, I turned to speak to our friends. "Contrary to what Dr. Houser said a moment ago, I didn't ask Edie to go steady with me 29 years ago," I said. "Actually, it was 29 years, 4 months, and . . ." I stopped and checked my watch. ". . . 17 hours ago!"

Everybody laughed.

"It's a bitterly cold day," I continued. "But it's so much warmer because you're all here with us. I just wish we'd done this many years ago. For me, Edie is a sweet gift of God's grace."

Overcome with emotion, I had to stop for a moment. "What can I tell you? I'm Irish."

After exchanging our vows, Edie and I placed a wedding band on each other's finger. These weren't just ordinary rings. They had been designed and manufactured by a friend in the prison metal shop. Each ring was made from two tightly entwined stainless steel welding rods that had been hammered into a circle and polished until they glistened. Given the circumstances, I thought the symbolism of entwined steel welding rods had great appeal.

"I now pronounce you man and wife," Dr. Houser said. "You may now kiss your bride."

I did so with great relish and to the sound of applause!

"OK, that's enough!" Cleveland joked. People roared with laughter as we turned and faced them.

"I'm very happy to be the first to introduce Mr. and Mrs. Jeris Bragan," Houser said.

We shared a lot of hugs and tears with friends, and then it was time to celebrate with food and wedding cake before they left. Fortunately, most of them got a piece of the cake before the storm returned with a vengence. A strong gust of wind swept through the cabana and blew the cake into the dirt.

Edie and I went on our honeymoon—a long walk alone around the picnic area. "I want to tell you something, Edie," I said. "These years in prison have been tough, but I would do every minute of it again if that's what it took to find you after all these years."

She hugged me tight.

"Are you going to be all right?" I asked her.

"I've never been happier in my life."

The freezing weather drove away most of our friends, but some stayed with us. We pulled several trays out of the grills, piled charcoal in them, and placed them on the ground in a circle. Soon we had roaring fires for warmth as we huddled together and talked until the picnic area was closed.

It was hard saying goodbye to Edie that night.

"At least we're finally together again," she whispered.

I could tell she was crying as she walked away.

18

An Easter Miracle

EDIE WASN'T alone on our wedding night—our home was packed with friends. Dick Snyder knew that Edie was feeling a little blue, so he offered to take everybody out to dinner at the Old Spaghetti Factory in Nashville. Later we talked on the telephone while she opened our wedding gifts.

"I'm going to wrap everything back up so we can open them together when you come home," she said.

I winced. "Edie, that may be a *very* long time."

"No it won't!" she replied. "I don't know when you're coming home, but I *know* it's going to be soon. The only real question is this: What do we do now to expedite the process?"

I hesitated. "Actually, I do have an idea. I don't want you to get your hopes up again, but I've been doing some digging around in the prison law library. It's clear that the state courts are never going to give my appeals a fair hearing, so I think it's time to file a writ of habeas corpus in federal court."

"What's that?"

"It's a special kind of appeal, which I can write and file myself. Unlike other forms of legal appeal, which can get you booted right out of court because of procedural technicalities, federal judges have a great deal of discretion in reviewing a prisoner's habeas corpus' claims. He has the power to consider the validity of my claims, not whether I dotted every technical *i* or crossed every *t* exactly right."

"Do you think it would do any good?" Edie asked. I could hear the hopeful sound bubbling up in her voice.

"I don't have any idea. But we're down to one irreducible fact: There's absolutely nothing else left for me to do in the courts."

"Then let's do it."

It took me a month to write it—a 73-page document. It was my last realistic shot at freedom through the courts, so I quoted directly from the trial record as I described in minute detail how the state had used secret deals and perjured testimony to secure a jury verdict against me. I thought of David's words as I dropped the petition into the prison mailbox in May: "I waited patiently for the Lord; he turned to me and heard my cry. He lifted me out of the slimy pit, out of the mud and mire; he set my feet on a rock and gave me a firm place to stand. . . . Blessed is the man who makes the Lord his trust" (Ps. 40:1, 2, 4).

I understood what he meant!

There was no reason to be optimistic. I'd already been before nine other judges in three different courts. But unlike elected state judges, whose decisions are often heavily influenced by their personal relationships with prosecutors, I knew that federal judges are appointed for life. They tend to be fiercely independent and take their role as protectors of the constitution very seriously. I felt confident about the outcome of my appeal *if* the judge actually read the trial record itself, not just the briefs filed by lawyers. If he didn't—then it was back to square one again.

✦ ✦ ✦

While waiting for the court's response, I turned my attention to another book project. Most of my published magazine articles focused on some aspect of spiritual faith in the midst of concrete suffering. Initially I received a trickle of response from readers, but that turned into a small flood of thousands of letters as the years passed. (Contrary to popular opinion about the American postal system, some letters reached me with addresses as simple as "Jeris Bragan, Tennessee Prison in Nashville.") In reading these letters, I discovered that people were struggling with all kinds of "prisons" in their own lives. Caught in the vortex of destructive marriages, careers, financial crises, and health problems, they faced tougher prisons than one made of concrete and steel.

In addition to sharing their own struggles with me, however, writers invariably asked me the same question at some point: How do you manage to keep your own faith in God intact after all these years in prison?

Ironically, I had been intrigued with the religious problem connected with human suffering in a world created by a perfect, all-powerful, loving God ever since I read the book of Job for the first time when I was a boy. Since then I'd read scores of books on the subject, including Dr. Jerry Gladson's doctoral dissertation! But I'd never thought seriously about the subject within the context of my own life. Like most people, I took my own faith pretty much for granted and rarely gave it much more than passing thought. Also, I'd been too busy trying to survive—to stay alive—to spend any serious time or energy in reflecting on my experience.

My third book, *When You Walk Through a Storm*, emerged as I studied the Scriptures and reflected on my years of incarceration. I wrote from a personal perspective—one ordinary man trapped in a modern-day lions' den—as I struggled with questions that have plagued Christian believers for centuries: Is it possible to make sense out of suffering? Why does God allow suffering? How can we understand God's will? What does the promise in Romans 8:28 really mean? Where can we hear God's voice speaking to us today? How do we build character from the modern-day lions' den we face? How do we forgive the unforgivable? What is real happiness?

It was Tuesday, September 25, 1989, and I was working on the final draft of my book. Four anxious months had passed since I filed the writ of habeas corpus. My initial optimism, admittedly qualified at best, had evaporated entirely. I was surviving more on Edie's hope than any real belief that the court would reverse my conviction. When I talked to her that night, I tried to warn her about what to expect.

"This thing is going to drag on forever, but in the end nothing will change," I grumbled.

She hesitated a moment before replying. "I don't know if I should tell you this or not, but I've got . . . I don't know quite how to describe it, but

I've had this incredible feeling all day long that *something* really good is happening on your case behind the scenes."

Women's intuition, I thought irritably. I knew Edie well enough to know she was telling me the truth about what she "felt," so I stifled the temptation to dismiss her feelings. But I didn't have any confidence in vague, subjective feelings. Nevertheless, partly to humor her but mostly to bolster my own sagging morale, I checked with her several times over the next few days to see if she still had that same "feeling."

She did.

The following Monday, October 2, Edie was practically euphoric with optimism when I talked to her on the phone in the morning before she went to work. I felt a lot of apprehension because her hopeful feelings appeared to be out of control.

"Edie, please be careful," I warned. "Don't set yourself up for a big letdown like you did when we went to the parole board." I didn't want to burst her bubble, but I knew how it felt to hope for something so badly, just to have it all come crashing down.

She recognized my concern for her, but she laughed gaily. "Jeris Bragan, I'm telling you that God didn't call us out into the middle of this lake to drown. Something really good is about to happen. I don't know what exactly, but we're going to be very happy before this week is out. I'm absolutely certain of that!"

I kept my mouth shut.

Later that day, I was editing the last few pages of my book when a guard knocked on my door. "You've gotta go to the post office to sign for a certified letter," he said.

I took a deep breath. This was it: I knew the federal court always sends responses to prisoners via certified mail. I walked down the hill with all the enthusiasm of a condemned man marching to his own execution. I wondered how Edie would take this latest setback as I signed the receipt, and the clerk handed me a slender envelope. *It doesn't take much paper to say no,* I thought as I opened it with shaking fingers.

I scanned the document until I came to these words: "ORDER: The Court finds that the petitioner [Jeris Bragan] has presented a prima facie [unless refuted] claim of a conviction in violation of his constitutional rights. Accordingly, respondent [the state] is hereby ORDERED to file an answer to the petition within 30 days from the entry of this Order. This case is hereby referred to the Magistrate for further proceedings."

The order was signed by Federal District Court Judge John T. Nixon.

Tears stung my eyes when I saw the date he had signed it: Tuesday, September 25, 1989!

I couldn't believe what I was seeing, so I read the document again and again.

On that lovely afternoon in the fall, dressed in a drab prison uniform and surrounded by walls, gun towers, and barbed wire, I felt once again the reality of God's promise for those who wait. I leaned against the stone wall and began laughing. I laughed with pure joy until the tears ran down my face, even though I knew that other prisoners walking by must have wondered if I'd finally gone over the edge.

I looked up and whispered a quiet prayer of thanks. It was then that I saw a lone eagle soaring high over the prison, and I remembered a passage from the Old Testament: "They that wait on the Lord shall renew their strength; they shall mount up with wings as eagles; they shall run, and not be weary; and they shall walk, and not faint" (Isa. 40:31, KJV).

Edie burst into tears when I called her with the news. Fred and B.J., who had become close friends by this time, were ecstatic. "We'll have you out of there by Christmas for sure!" Fred said.

"That's the second time you've said that. I hope you're right this time," I said.

❖ ❖ ❖

I finished *When You Walk Through a Storm* with this sentence: "I knew other difficult days probably lay ahead, but for me the storm was over!"

I didn't know then that the "storm" was going to get even more intense before it collapsed.

Judge Nixon turned the proceedings over to Federal Magistrate Kent Sandidge, who functioned essentially as an assistant judge. His job would be to conduct hearings, review the evidence, and then provide Judge Nixon with a final report and recommendation about what to do with my petition. First, however, he ordered the federal public defender's office on October 10 to represent me in all future proceedings. After reviewing my petition, however, Henry Martin, the director of the public defender's office, decided the case would take too much time for one of his lawyers. He retained Tom Bloom, a Nashville lawyer in private practice, to perfect my appeal.

I contacted a Nashville lawyer to find out what he knew about either Tom Bloom or Magistrate Sandidge. He didn't know Tom. "It's hard to predict what Sandidge might do with the facts in your case," the lawyer told me. "Among lawyers he has a reputation for being a 'loose cannon.' By that I mean he's liable to do almost anything or nothing, depending on how he feels at the time."

Tom Bloom came out to the prison to see me and to collect my box of trial records a few days before Thanksgiving.

He wasn't what I expected.

Tom was an imposing man of six foot three inches. Dressed in a plaid shirt, blue jeans, and cowboy boots, he looked like a political refugee from the '60s. He had sparkling blue eyes, and his long black, curly hair was pulled back from his face into a neat ponytail. I thought he looked more like a prisoner than I did! He read the expression on my face perfectly.

"Don't worry!" he laughed. "I always wear a pin-striped suit when I appear in court."

At least he had a sense of humor.

Tom was brutally honest. "You won't be out by Christmas," he said. "This will take many months to process. I'm sure you know that very few appeals are ever successful, so there's no guarantee about the outcome. And there's one more thing you should know: Although I've handled a lot of

246

post-conviction appeals in state courts, I've never done a habeas corpus before. I'll do the best I can, but I'll be learning the procedures as we go along."

"I can't be any worse off than I am now," I said.

I liked Tom from the beginning. Behind the cultivated facade of a faintly cynical lawyer, he was a genuinely committed man who cared about his clients.

◆ ◆ ◆

Two months later Andy Sher, a reporter for the Chattanooga *Times*, came to the prison to talk to me about my appeal. He was a tall, handsome, sophisticated man who covered Capitol Hill for the paper. Most recently he'd published an investigative series on political corruption that continually plagued state politics. Despite his credentials, however, I felt a lot of ambivalence about talking to any Chattanooga reporter, especially when he either couldn't—or wouldn't—tell me why his newspaper was interested in my case in the first place.

If Andy sensed my distrust, he didn't say anything about it. Instead, he laid out what he had learned as a result of his investigation up that point. "You can talk to me on or off the record," he said. "It's up to you."

Once I talked to him, I knew he could write anything about me that he wanted. I knew from personal experience that some reporters had no qualms about slanting quotes from a prisoner so he looked like a fool—or, for that matter, misquoting him. But I decided to take a chance and tell him everything he wanted to know—the good, the bad, and the ugly. What he did with the information was up to him.

My decision to trust Sher's integrity turned out to be a good one. After an extensive investigation, he published a four-part series on the front page of the paper from July 30 to August 2, 1990. It was entitled "Justice on Trial—A Case of Conflict and Doubt." Friends of mine thought he could have written a stronger story, but I thought it was a fair, well-balanced piece of writing. I particularly liked the timing of the story. District Attorney General Gary Gerbitz was running unopposed for reelection, and the last part of the series was published on election day.

Two years passed before I discovered that it was an old friend, John Odom, who had originally briefed senior editors at the newspaper on the facts of the case. I'd first met John in 1975 when I set up my detective agency in Chattanooga. At the time he was a private consultant who specialized in arson and explosive investigations. After I was convicted and sent to prison, John and his wife, Myrna, wrote to me each month. Their letters always included a batch of 50 stamps—every month for the next 15 years.

◆ ◆ ◆

During the summer of 1989, Edie's and my path crossed two other old friends from our days at South Lancaster Academy: the limey kid, Al Trace, who still spoke with a faint British accent, and Myron Mills, the preacher's kid. Although years and distance had sent each of us in different directions, I think we were a little surprised—and delighted—that we still shared many experiences that were common to our baby-boom generation: problems in careers, marriages, teenage children, and theological conflicts. Al now worked in marketing for Pacific Press Publishing Association in Boise, Idaho, so he helped shepherd my new book through the publishing process. He also encouraged me to begin thinking about a future book, *Beyond Prison Walls*. Although he didn't live nearby, we still talked frequently on the telephone, and he came out to the prison to visit every time he was in Nashville.

Myron was closer to home. He had become a professor of emergency medicine at Vanderbilt University's medical school. No matter what the weather, Myron always spent one day of the weekend at the prison with us when he wasn't working, plus we usually talked on the telephone several times a week. Although he had spent 20 years of his life polishing his skills as a physician, he had wide-ranging interests in everything from theology and psychology to ham radio and flying. Exploring ideas with him was like a shot of intellectual vitamin B_{12}!

I got an extra bonus from Myron's friendship—getting to know his father, Pastor Merle L. Mills, a Seventh-day Adventist churchman who had done everything from pastoring small churches to serving as president of the Trans-Africa Division. Although retired, Merle, like his son, retained a keen interest in everything from the churning politics in Burma to a variety of blowing theological winds. I never had a conversation with him that I didn't enjoy, so I respectfully dubbed him "The Bishop."

In October Al came to Nashville with a film crew from Dan Matthews' television program, *Christian Lifestyle Magazine*, to shoot some video of Edie and me and of several friends for a program they wanted to broadcast about my experience. The video ended with me saying that I planned to continue doing the same thing in the free world that I did in prison: write, teach, and do some counseling. The only thing that would change, I said, would be my address.

◆ ◆ ◆

Meanwhile, Tom had filed his first brief with the court on my behalf, and an assistant state attorney general had fired back her first response. Briefly, she argued that even if the evidence we submitted about Torbett's secret deal and perjured testimony was true, the federal court should still dismiss my petition because the evidence hadn't first been heard in the state courts. At the same time, she admitted that I had no remedy in state courts because the statute of limitations had expired on my right to appeal and that precluded my going into state court. In effect, she reasoned that I was barred from appealing to any court, regardless of the merits of my claim.

It was clear that the same state attorney general's office that had requested a federal criminal investigation of those men who prosecuted me was now going to do everything in its power to block my appeal.

Tom filed a motion, requesting a formal hearing before the federal magistrate. A date for the hearing was set for November 9, 1990.

Although Tennessee State Prison was in the process of closing down—as a result of the 1982 federal court decision—and the level of violence dwindled with each passing month as the population slowly decreased, rumors of another riot circulated constantly in the unstable prison environment. But three years had passed without a killing, so people began to relax—insofar as that was possible in this human powder keg—for the first time in decades.

But terror, like a shark waiting to attack, always lurked just beneath the deceptively calm surface.

I was coming in from the picnic area one Sunday afternoon after spending the day with Edie. Another inmate had just called Steve Drake, a young friend of mine, out of SDC to talk to him on the ball field. Steve was standing in the middle of the road, looking around for the man who had called for him. The man crept up from behind, shoved a pistol against the back of Steve's head, and pulled the trigger. Steve fell to the ground. His attacker calmly stepped over the body, shot him once more between the eyes, then walked away.

The killer was three months short of parole!

Once again I was reminded of just how abruptly life could end behind those savage walls.

♦ ♦ ♦

I wasn't allowed to attend the hearing on my petition before the federal magistrate, but I called Edie at Fred and B.J.'s home shortly after it was concluded. I wanted to talk to Edie first, not because of her legal expertise but because of her intuitive judgment.

"It went very well," she said. "The judge sat there and grinned through the entire proceedings, and he seemed to be leaning in our favor. Personally, I think he's already made up his mind."

And Fred agreed. "Tom is one of the most brilliant young lawyers I've ever met. He did a great job."

"What happens next?" I asked.

"I thought the magistrate was going to rule in our favor from the bench, but he took everything under advisement. I think we'll have you out of there by Christmas yet!"

I didn't remind him this was the third time he'd said that. But I did sing a different song for Edie on the phone that night: "I'll Be Home for Christmas."

But Christmas came and went without a word from the Court.

♦ ♦ ♦

Edie and I had just celebrated our first wedding anniversary when the magistrate handed down his report and recommendation on April 22, 1991. I learned about it the following Saturday afternoon when a copy was delivered to me in the mail moments after I'd come in from visiting with Edie in the picnic area. I flipped to the last page. My heart sank as I read his stinging words: "I recommend that the petitioner's motion for summary judgment be denied. I also recommend that the Court, upon its review of this record and the proceedings in the State courts, determine that an evidentiary hearing is not required to determine the issues presented; and, further, the Court determine that justice requires the dismissal of this petition for the writ of habeas corpus."

Tom was shocked. Fred was furious. I was depressed. Edie stubbornly refused to lose hope.

"We're not out of court altogether," Tom said. "Admittedly, we would be in a better position if the magistrate had found in our favor, but Judge Nixon is the one who signs on the dotted line. I'm going to file objections to the magistrate's report and ask Judge Nixon for a full evidentiary hearing."

"What do you think our chances are?" I asked.

Tom hesitated. "Not good," he replied. "But let's proceed and see what happens."

I had turned 45 in January. Even though I tried to live philosophically and spiritually beyond prison walls, I realized that I'd now spent one third of my entire life behind those walls. That was difficult enough to grasp. What was even worse was the realization that somewhere, sometime, I'd lost the ability to visualize living in the free world again. I didn't even daydream about it anymore, and I couldn't recall when I'd last dreamed about anything that projected me into the free world. The world I'd been born into now seemed as foreign and disconnected from me as the reality of prison had once been.

Several weeks passed before Judge Nixon ruled on our objections to the magistrate's recommendation. Without commenting on the merit of Tom's objections, he ordered an evidentiary hearing to be held on Monday, November 18, 1991. I knew I should feel happy and hopeful again, but I didn't. "I feel like the winter of discontent is about to set in," I told Edie the night before the hearing.

She refused to adopt my gloomy assessment.

"Let me suggest another possibility," she said. " 'For, lo, the winter is past, the rain is over and gone; the flowers appear on the earth; the time of the singing of birds has come' " (S. of Sol. 2:11, 12, KJV).

"You've always said I'd come home in the spring," I said, trying to humor her.

"That's right, and it's going to be *this* spring."

Fat chance, I thought. But I kept my skepticism to myself. My apprehension didn't reflect a lack of faith in God; I knew God could do anything He pleased. But I'd seen too many people suffering unjustly, and my faith simply wasn't contingent on God's performing any particular miracle on my behalf.

Monday, November 18, was a beautiful day. Transport officers summoned me to the transportation building at 7:30 a.m. There a surly corporal put me through a degrading strip search before wrapping the bellychains around me and snapping the cuffs on as tight as he could. He was one of those few psychotic guards who loved the power he had over prisoners. He glared at me throughout the process, challenging me to object. I just stared at him, directly and without blinking. He snapped the handcuffs tighter. I knew my hands would be purple by the time we got to court.

Just outside the vehicle gate, the officers stopped the car and picked up Ralph Janow. Because he was about to be paroled, Ralph was living in a minimum security dorm outside the walls and didn't have to be handcuffed. He was shaking with anger.

"Jeris, they told me I've gotta go to court because a federal judge said so, but I'm telling you right now I ain't gonna testify," he snapped as he got into the car.

"That's up to you," I replied.

"Look, I ain't mad at you. I know what they did to you, and I wish I could do something to help. But if I say anything now, those prosecutors down in Chattanooga will either block my parole or make my life miserable once I do get out."

I didn't resent or blame Ralph for feeling the way he did. "You do whatever is best for you," I said.

The transport officers parked a couple of blocks away from the courthouse, so I had to walk through heavy pedestrian traffic in my prison uniform and cuffs. People stared at me curiously. One elderly woman smiled at me. I heard Ridge Beck shout my name from a car just as we approached the courthouse entrance. I knew the guards were jumpy, and I didn't want them to grab their guns, so I just nodded and kept walking.

An hour later I was escorted in chains to Judge Nixon's courtroom. Just outside the door the cuffs were removed. Once inside, I noticed that several marshalls were strategically placed near exits to block any escape attempt. While I understood the need for security in general terms, it had never occurred to me to think in terms of escape and their preparations always jolted me.

I glanced through the courtroom. Edie sat surrounded by our friends. Dot and Conn Arnold were present. Conn was just recovering from open-heart surgery, and should have been in bed. Fred and B.J. waved to me. I noticed Shannon—Edie's son—Dick Snyder, Steve Womack, Myron Mills, Joyce Moore, and Ed Ley. Father John Keunneth, an Episcopal priest, and Grover Hastings, a Church of Christ pastor, were there, and so was Ridge Beck, who had driven down from Washington, D.C., to attend the hearing. Ridge had used informed sources within the United States Justice Department to locate William Torbett again. Tom Bloom was in chambers with Judge Nixon and the assistant state attorney general, informing them of Torbett's present location.

I barely had time to catch my breath when Judge Nixon ascended the bench and the hearing began. Tom Bloom and Anthony Daughtry made their opening statements, and then Tom filed several sworn affadavits and other documents with the court before he called me as his first witness. Under direct examination, I recounted what had happened concerning Torbett's testimony at the 1977 trial.

Things went well until Tom asked me a question I wasn't prepared for: "Why have you waited so many years to file this writ of habeas corpus?" he asked.

Tears of frustration stung my eyes as I looked out at Edie and thought about all the years that had passed, the bitter and relentless struggle to carve out some meaning in my life behind the walls, the hope for release that had been smashed again and again, and the galling hopelessness I felt at that moment.

I started to speak: "For many . . . years . . . I . . ."

Surging emotions cut off my words.

"That's all right. I'll withdraw the question," Tom said.

"No," I whispered. "Give me just a moment, and I'll answer."

A marshall brought me a glass of water. I drank it while trying to regain my composure.

"I got very depressed for many years," I finally choked out.

"No further questions," Tom said.

Daughtry seemed distracted, complaining to Judge Nixon that he didn't have time to digest the contents of what Tom had filed with the court. But Nixon overruled each objection. After a break for lunch, Fred Steltemeier and Ed Ley testified about their search for Torbett and what he had told them when confronted in Atlanta. Delo Brock, another prisoner, testified that Torbett had bragged to him about getting away with perjury at my trial.

But Ralph Janow was the one witness who surprised me. Before being sworn in, he told Nixon that he didn't want to testify out of fear of what Chattanooga authorities would do to him if he did. Nixon denied his request to be excused and ordered him to answer Tom's questions. At that point I expected Ralph to claim he couldn't remember anything. Instead, he sighed with exasperation and proceeded to answer every question, fully and truthfully, just as he had 15 years earlier.

As miracles go, I thought, parting the Red Sea was small potatoes compared to giving Ralph a change of heart!

About 3:30 p.m. the hearing suddenly ended. Nixon told both lawyers that he didn't need anything further and abruptly left the bench. Tom was sweating profusely as he gathered up his papers.

"What was your impression of the proceedings?" Tom asked me.

"It seemed to go so well it's scary," I admitted. "Judge Nixon overruled every state objection; he accepted every piece of evidence you submitted, including the sworn affidavits; and allowed each witness to answer all your questions. But, as a practical matter, what does that mean?"

Tom thought for a moment. "It means one of two things. Either Judge Nixon has decided to rule in our favor, so it doesn't matter what we submit; or it means he's decided to rule against us, so it doesn't matter what we submit."

"You lawyers are such a comfort!" I grumbled.

Edie winked at me from the front row of the courtroom, since the marshalls were making sure there was no contact, and mouthed the words "Are you ready to come home?" Everybody who attended the hearing was elated, including Fred. "You're gonna be home by Christmas!" he insisted.

"That's the fourth time you've said that," I joked. "I believe you're right, but I wonder if it's going to be a Christmas in this century!"

✦ ✦ ✦

Christmas came and went again without comment from Judge Nixon. On January 11, 1992, I turned 46. I woke up that morning with an unsettling and burning conviction in my mind. It was clear, unambiguous, uncompromising: *God is going to perform a miracle for you and Edie at Easter!* Not sometime *around* Easter but *at* Easter. The conviction was unsettling because I felt hope lunging forward in my heart like a puppy straining on a tight leash. Was God trying to tell me something? Or was I grasping at straws, doing wishful thinking?

I didn't know what to make of it, so I didn't say anything to Edie. Her hopes had been shattered enough during the past seven years without my setting her up for more of the same. I didn't have much time to think about it anyway, because Tennessee State Prison was closing down rapidly. The Self-determination Center was closed, and I was moved down to Unit II. Two weeks later, after having spent 12 years under the looming shadow of the "castle," I was shipped two miles down the road to Riverbend Maximum Security Institution, a new prison where Mike Dutton now served as warden. I had a dishwashing job waiting for me. I didn't like the idea of living in a maximum security prison, but that was the only way I could remain in Nashville. That was important to both Edie and me.

April 17—Good Friday—passed quickly. My small candle of flickering hope burned out when the day ended. As I walked slowly up the hill to the visiting room that night to see Edie, I felt both discouraged and foolish for even seriously entertaining the possibility that God was going to do something extraordinary for us at Easter.

Edie noticed my gloomy disposition immediately. "What's wrong?" she asked.

I told her about my conviction.

"Why didn't you tell me about this before?" she asked. "You never keep secrets from me."

"I realized I was probably grasping at straws."

While we talked I reminded myself, as I had many other times over the years, that God doesn't ask us to *feel* faithful when the roaring lions of discouragement close in, just to *be* faithful.

Edie reminded me again of the saying that had become our motto: "Do not mourn what cannot be. Celebrate, rather, what is!"

In spite of my disappointment, I knew we did have a lot to celebrate. Instead of concentrating on the gloom and doom, Edie and I started talking about all the different ways in which God had blessed our lives during the past seven years. We focused mostly on the hundreds of friends—Baptists, Methodists, Episcopalians, Presbyterians, Mormons, Catholics, Seventh-day Adventists, and others—who had contacted us during the past three years to tell us that total strangers had organized prayer bands to pray for us.

We were particularly touched by a retired Catholic religious, Sister Theresa Voorn, who wrote frequently from Holland to tell us that she and her sisters in the convent prayed for us every day. She had contacted me for the first time several years earlier after reading some of my articles in *New Covenant*, a Catholic magazine. In March she sent Edie and me a copy of a letter she had sent to President George Bush, in which she demanded my immediate release. Some White House staffer is probably still trying to figure out that one!

It may be a cliché, but there is great spiritual wisdom in the old song lyrics about counting blessings instead of sheep. There is nothing in life—*absolutely nothing!*—that can more quickly transform sagging morale into cheerful optimism than practicing the spiritual strategy of counting blessings instead of blisters.

I wasn't ready to dance an Irish jig when it was time for Edie to leave, but I did feel surprisingly energized.

That weekend proved to be one of the most meaningful Easters of my life. Although keenly disappointed that nothing had happened in terms of my release from prison, I felt a special closeness to the first disciples, who lost hope on that terrible Friday of their lives. I felt a mystical sense of Christ's Easter presence in my disappointment. Maybe our prayers weren't going to be answered at Easter, but at the end of the day, still smarting and hurting, we both could say with Job: "Blessed be the name of the Lord."

Monday morning, April 20, I had just arrived at work when I received a call from an officer in the administration building. "You've got a lawyer here to see you," he said. That wasn't unusual—Tom and Fred frequently came by to see me when I didn't expect them.

It was Tom. I saw him through the glass door as I approached. Unsmiling, he stood there, holding a thick document in his hand. I knew it was Judge Nixon's decision. Dread, like a sharp pain, cut through me. You'd think, as many times as I'd been through one disappointment after another, that I'd be getting used to it.

Tom shook hands and passed the document to me. "Read it and smile!" he said softly.

I didn't get it. I started reading Judge Nixon's order, one word at a time: "The Court is in receipt of the Magistrate's Report and Recommendation in the above style action to which objections have been filed. For the reasons stated in the contemporaneously filed Memorandum, the Court hereby REJECTS the Magistrate's Report and Recommendation."

What! My eye snapped back to the key word: "REJECTS." A typo? Somebody's idea of a sick joke?

My knees buckled, and I staggered backward, falling abruptly into a chair as I struggled to focus on the words in the next paragraph: "The petition for habeas corpus filed pursuant to 18 U.S.C. 2254 is hereby GRANTED. Accordingly, the respondent is ORDERED to release petitioner from custody unless petitioner is afforded a new trial within sixty (60) days from the entry of this Order."

Tears made it hard for me to focus as I glanced down to the bottom of the page to see when the order had been entered on the official court docket. It was April 17, 1992—*Good Friday!*

Nixon's 38-page decision, attached to the order I'd just read, was a bluntly worded document in which he sustained each point I'd argued for 15 years: the prosecutors had intentionally solicited perjured testimony from Torbett; they did have a secret deal with him for his testimony; they did intentionally mislead the court, jury, and defense counsel about their quid pro quo deal; they intentionally used his perjured testimony in closing arguments to obtain a tainted conviction; and, had the jury known the true facts, Nixon wrote, the outcome of my trial might very well have been different.

"BLESSED BE THE NAME OF THE LORD!"

I don't have any idea what else Tom and I talked about that morning. I doubt anything I might have said would have been very coherent. I tried to call Edie with the news, but she was out of her office. When I finally got to talk with her, two hours later, I found out that she was still shaking with excitement—someone had told her I sounded ecstatic when I'd called. "I probably look normal, and I'm walking and talking normal," I said, "but I'm still in shock!"

I picked up the phone to call my mother later that afternoon. As the phone rang, I thought of all the years she had endured the pain of my imprisonment. (Every month, for 15 years, she sent me a box of my favorite books and news magazines.) During the past year she had fought a stubborn battle with cancer and chemotherapy. I'd never once heard her complain.

I heard her voice on the phone. "Can you handle some good news for a change?" I asked.

"I suppose I could try," she laughed.

Four hours had passed since I received the news, but I still had trouble maintaining my composure as I read Judge Nixon's order and gave her a brief synopsis of his findings.

Later that night Edie set up a three-way telephone call with Tom Bloom. "What happens now in terms of my getting out of here?" I asked.

"I've talked to several other lawyers since we met this morning, but nobody seems to know," he laughed. "Nobody has ever won one of these in court, so your guess is as good as mine."

"So give me your best educated guess," I replied.

"I think it goes like this: Nixon has given the state 60 days to either cut you loose or re-try you. The state also has an option to appeal his decision within 30, so there's nothing more for us to do until they decide which way they're going."

◆ ◆ ◆

The next 30 days felt more like 30 years! If the state appealed, I knew the process could take another two or three years to resolve—with me in prison. I had the option to petition for release through an appeal bond, but I didn't think Judge Nixon would grant one. Even if he did, Tom said he would probably set it so high that I couldn't make it anyway.

"I don't care what it is," Fred growled. "You get Tom to petition the judge for bond. I'll put up the money."

On May 17 the clouds rolled in again when the state attorney general's office announced its intention to appeal Nixon's decision. On May 21 Tom filed a motion with the court to have me released on bond. When he returned to his office, he found a message from Judge Nixon's secretary, informing him that Nixon had ordered an emergency bond hearing for the following day, Friday, May 22, at 3:30 p.m.

Edie was ecstatic. May 22 was her birthday.

"I don't want to get your hopes up," Tom cautioned Edie and me during a three-way call that night. "As I understand it our hearing will be the last order of business for the week before the judge goes to Washington, D.C., for a judicial conference. He'll probably take our request under advisement and rule on the matter at some point later on."

"I've got to go do a little housework," Edie said when we finished our conversation with Tom.

She left the phone for a while, but it wasn't housework she wanted to do. I would have had a stroke if I'd known her real intentions: She went outside and wrapped a dozen yellow ribbons, with enormous yellow bows she'd bought months earlier, around each tree in our front yard.

Brette Lea, a reporter for WTVF, channel 5, came out to interview me on Friday morning. I'd met Brette when she covered other stories at the prison for her station. Besides being a consumate professional, Brette also was a warm and generous young woman who had let me turn the tables and interview her several months earlier for a feature story I'd published in *Listen*, a teen magazine. Al Trace had called her from Boise to tell her about the bond hearing, so she wanted to interview me in case I was suddenly released that day. I wasn't feeling particularly optimistic about the outcome, but I tried to be positive for the camera.

I wasn't allowed to attend the hearing, so I called Edie at noon Friday. "Happy birthday, Baby!" I said.

"I hope you don't mind, but I just went to the shopping center and bought my own birthday present," she replied.

"Of course I don't mind. What did you get?"

She hesitated. "Actually, what I got won't fit me. I know you don't want to come home in prison clothes, so I bought you a navy blue blazer, dress shirt, gray slacks, belt, shoes, and socks to wear home tonight."

It felt like a block of lead had settled in my stomach. *Dear God, this is going to be one very depressed lady tonight,* I thought.

"You aren't mad at me, are you?" Edie asked.

"No, of course not. It's your birthday, but I don't want you to set yourself up for a lot of heartache tonight."

She laughed gaily. "Yes, this is my birthday, and God is going to give me a special present today—*you!*"

◆ ◆ ◆

I left work early that day and went back to my cell. I didn't want to be around anyone else, so I put on my pajamas, fixed a cup of hot chocolate, and tried to unwind by watching TV. I knew I could handle the disappointment, but what really stung each time something went awry was my realization that Edie hurt as badly as I did.

At 4:03 p.m. I heard several inmates shouting outside my cell. Then I heard the guard inserting his key into the heavy steel door. He pulled the door open and looked at me with a baffled expression on his face. "Bragan, you're outta here!" he said, jerking his thumb over his shoulder.

Stunned, I just looked at him stupidly. "You've gotta be kidding," I said.

"I'm not kidding," he insisted. "Pack up your stuff. You don't live here anymore!"

It was count time, so the unit was locked down. I didn't have time to say goodbye to any of the men I'd known for years, but the officers did let one old friend, John Brown, stay out of his cell to help me pack up my belongings.

I felt as though I was walking in a strange dream world as I pushed the laundry cart containing my property through the prison compound toward the administration building at 4:45 p.m. Other prisoners were crossing the compound toward the dining room for dinner. Word of my release had raced through the prison. I heard old friends shouting at me from far away.

"Don't forget us!"

"Give Edie a hug from me!"

"Good luck!"

"Man, I'm happy for you!"

"I knew God would answer your prayers!"

Security officers handed me the clothes Edie had delivered. "Go try these things on while we check your property out," one man said.

I got out of the hated prison uniform. The dress shoes and soft fabric of the shirt and slacks felt strange against my skin. I noticed I was sweating profusely, even though it was cold in the room. Vaguely I realized I was in deep shock, so I forced myself to slow down, to do some deliberate, steady, deep-breathing exercises.

Dressed, I stood in front of a mirror and stared at the familiar stranger looking back at me. Short phrases zipped around in my mind like minature race cars on a track:

"Blessed be the name of the Lord!"

"Holy, holy, holy—Lord God, almighty!"

"Blessed is he who waits upon the Lord!"

"He shall rise up on wings of eagles!"

"Praise God from whom all blessings flow!"

A guard interrupted my thoughts: "The official order just came through," he said. "It's time for you to go."

At 5:10 p.m. I stepped through the metal detector and into the waiting room crowded with family members who had come to see their fathers, husbands, brothers, sons, boyfriends. These were old friends whom Edie and I had come to love over the years. I realized this was where Edie had waited with the others to see me so many times and that she would never have to go through that again. Suddenly I realized they were standing up, applauding as Edie rushed toward me.

I remembered the way I always began our visits and telephone calls. I looked at Edie, the woman I had loved for so many years, and grinned. "Well, are you having a nice day?" I asked as I swept her up in my arms.

I noticed Tom Bloom and Fred Steltemeier standing nearby. Those two men, each in his own way, were living mediators of God's grace for Edie and me. I knew I wouldn't be standing there except for the hundreds and hundreds of unpaid hours they had spent in securing my liberty. But more than their legal and investigative skills, they had blessed us with their friendship. I thought about all the time we had spent on the phone with Fred and B.J. during the years—praying together, laughing together, fighting back tears of frustration together. I thought about the nights when Tom had let us call him at home when things were going bad and we just needed to know he wasn't ready to quit. I had to struggle to hold back the tears as I hugged both men.

Then I noticed Cheyenne, Edie's 19-year-old son, standing several feet away, shooting pictures with his camera. "Let's get out of here before they change their minds," I whispered as we hugged each other.

Shock rolled in again as we walked through the prison gates at 5:15 p.m. Brette had to rush to the station with part of the story, so she sent another reporter and camera crew to shoot film as we left. I felt like a man out of place and time as I climbed into Edie's Ford Escort on the passenger side. "It's not my car; it's *our* car!" she reminded me again.

"OK," I laughed. "But I haven't owned a car for a long time, so I'll have to get used to the idea again."

On the drive home Edie told me what had happened at the bond hearing. "Judge Nixon was so wonderful!" she said. "He sat and listened while Mr. Daughtry argued that you were a danger to society and shouldn't be released. Tom said that was crazy—of course he didn't use that word, but he was so angry everybody knew what he meant. As proof, he introduced copies of all those letters people wrote on your behalf in 1987 for the parole board. Anyway, when it was all over Judge Nixon ordered you released immediately on your own signature bond. We don't have to put up any money. I guess the judge isn't worried about you, because you don't even have to go to the clerk's office until Monday to sign the papers."

"It sounds like you enjoyed the hearing."

"I sure did, but you haven't heard the best part. When Tom reminded the judge of all the state's delaying tactics in the past, the judge came back and made the attorney general call the prison from his chambers to personally order your release."

"That was a nice touch!"

Edie giggled. "There's something funny that happened later. Do you remember all the times you told me I'd probably run into Judge Nixon somewhere in the courthouse and I should be careful to avoid saying anything to him that might sound like I was trying to influence him?"

"Actually, since you kept saying he looked just like Santa Claus, I was afraid you might just hug him!"

"Well, anyway, I was standing outside the courtroom with Brette Lea waiting for Tom to get the written order, when I saw Judge Nixon coming down the hall. I couldn't let him walk by without saying something to him."

I looked at her when she giggled again. "What did you say?"

"I said, 'Good evening, Judge Nixon. I hope you have a nice weekend.'

He had this big smile on his face, and he said: 'Thank you, I will, and I hope you have a nice weekend yourself!' "

I roared with laughter. Who said federal judges don't have a great sense of humor!

I glanced at the speedometer and smiled: 40 miles an hour in a 55 miles per hour zone. I realized that Edie was driving slowly because she had remembered what speed felt like to a person who hadn't been in a car for a long time. She kept her distance from the traffic rushing past us.

◆ ◆ ◆

Thirty minutes later she turned left onto Larkin Springs Road. From a block away I recognized our home. The front yard was ablaze with yellow ribbons! Shannon, Edie's 21-year-old son, was waiting for us, sitting on the front steps. Tears stung my eyes again when I realized he had been crying.

"Welcome home!" he said, hugging us both.

It was a poignant moment when I stepped through the front door of Edie's home—yes, *our* home! I got it!—for the first time. Like her eyes, the house practically sparkled. It was full of wonderfully normal smells I had long since forgotten: hardwood, potpourri, food. Fascinated, I wandered slowly from room to room, enjoying the incredible collage of colors and shapes of everything: the Dorothy ruffled curtains on the windows, the antiques she had collected through the years, the shelves stuffed with books.

She followed me into the last room. The walls were covered with knotty pine. A large desk stood by the window. "This is your office for writing, if you want to use it," she said.

I wanted it!

I noticed a huge Boston rocker by the large picture window in our living room. Instantly, I knew that was my spot. I sat down in the chair, rocking slowly back and forth as I looked through a window that wasn't framed by prison bars and tried to collect my scattered thoughts.

"I've got a present for you," Edie said, handing me a large, gift-wrapped package.

As I fumbled with the unfamiliar process of opening the box, I realized I hadn't opened a gift package in 15 years. Edie had to help me. I lost my composure completely when I finally saw what it was: a framed piece of Edie's cross-stitch.

"I told you that God was going to bring you home this spring," she said as she read from memory the lines she had stitched: "For, lo, the winter is past, the rain is over and gone. The flowers appear on the earth, the time of the singing of birds has come" (S. of Sol. 2:11, 12, KJV).

I glanced at my watch. It was 6:15 p.m. I realized that we had missed Brette Lea's broadcast about us on TV. For years I'd eaten dinner at 4:30, so hunger pangs got my attention. I looked in the refrigerator. It was empty. I glanced up and saw a shocked look on Edie's face. I burst out laughing. "You went out and bought me a suit of clothes because you had enough faith in God to believe I was coming home tonight, but you forgot to get groceries!"

259

We hugged and laughed until the tears ran down our faces.

"So I'll take you out to dinner your first night home," she said.

The phone rang, and I picked it up.

It was my mother. "Jerry?" she asked in a shocked voice.

"Hi, Mom. It's me. Don't worry. I just got tired of all the waiting and decided to escape from prison tonight," I laughed.

We went to Major Wallaby's. I realized that some of the diners had already seen the evening news because several people smiled and waved at us as we followed the waitress to our table. We were seated in the center of the room on a slightly elevated platform. From there we could see everybody else in the restaurant. I picked up the metal knife and fork. Metal utensils weren't allowed in prison, so for years I'd eaten my food with disposable plastic. I held the china cup in my hand, turning it slowly back and forth as I enjoyed the feel of glass against my skin.

Edie reached across the table and took my hand. "Are you all right?" she asked softly.

I glanced around at all the normal-looking people. My senses were assaulted with wonderfully foreign colors, smells, feelings. I laughed and leaned toward Edie. "I know we look just as normal as the rest of these people," I said, "but I wonder if they realize they have an alien sitting among them?"

She directed my attention to a man across the room who had raised his glass to us in a toast. "I don't think he believes you're an alien," she reminded me.

◆ ◆ ◆

WTVF ran the same story about us several times that weekend, and both Nashville newspapers carried the news of my release on the front page the following morning. Everywhere we went that weekend total strangers stopped us to talk. Several had tears in their eyes when they hugged Edie and pumped my hand in congratulation. I was quite befuddled by the intense emotional response of strangers to our experience.

Saturday morning I called my mother to assure her again I was actually a free man.

"Has Edie decided to send you back yet?" she teased.

Later that morning we went to the Boulevard Seventh-day Adventist Church in Madison, where Edie had been a member for several years. I knew she felt some ambivalence about returning there because the church board had refused her request in 1987 when she asked them for support with my clemency petition.

"How do we know he's innocent?" one woman had snapped.

Their denial had been blunt and hurtful to her. Nevertheless, we had many close friends in the congregation: Bill Snider—the new pastor, Dick Snyder, Allen Craig, Joe Chandler, Patsy Flanigan, Terry and Susan Owen, Joyce Phelps, Dr. Lloyd Walwyn, Donna and Dave Montague, and many others. They had given both of us a great deal of emotional support with their prayers and friendship during the intervening five years, and we wanted to worship with them.

I looked around at the huge congregation in the church as we stood with them to sing the opening song. It was hard for me to believe that I'd been sitting in a prison cell only 18 hours earlier. For years, whenever people asked me how the legal battles were going, I had joked: "The score is still Lions 10, Christians nothing!"

Tears streamed down my face as I tried to sing the triumphant song "The Lord in Zion Reigneth." I remembered that day so many years earlier when my father took me out to drive for the first time. *His hand never left the wheel.* Somewhere, far away, I thought I could hear the sound of God's merry laughter.

Indeed, the Lord in Zion reigns!

EPILOGUE

Blessed Be the Name of the Lord!

Edie had arranged to take two weeks off from work so we could have a real honeymoon together. But the phone started ringing Friday night and didn't stop for weeks. Dwight Lewis, a reporter for *The Tennessean*, called us at midnight the night I came home to get some quotes for his story. Edie was indignant. Being a writer myself, however, I appreciated his need to get the facts straight. When it became obvious that some reporters were genuinely interested in the spiritual dimensions of our story, we decided we might as well delay our honeymoon to a later time and accepted their invitation for interviews. "Ours is a story about God's goodness," Edie said. "Media interest is fickle, so we should take the time to share our story with people while the media is interested."

I particularly liked the story Carrie Ferguson published on the front page of *The Tennessean* four days later with these headlines: "Wronged Man Refuses to Be Bitter: In Prison 15 Years, He's Cleared of Killing." She described my feelings perfectly in the first paragraph: "There is little harshness in the manner of Jeris Bragan, who, despite serving 15 years for a murder he has been cleared of, says he's been 'more blessed than blistered.' "

The second weekend we went to Portland, Tennessee, on Sabbath to attend the Kentucky/Tennessee camp meeting. I saw Elder Conn Arnold, my friend and pastor for so many years behind prison walls, walking toward us just as the congregation sang the Doxology. Tears stung my eyes again as he hugged both of us and we sang: "Praise God from whom all blessings flow!"

◆ ◆ ◆

I realized that my freedom might be temporary when the state attorney general's office filed notice of appeal with the Sixth Circuit Court of Appeals in Cincinnati. Only a few weeks later, however, they abruptly changed their minds, agreed that Judge Nixon's findings of fact were irrefutable, and filed a petition with the Court, in which they requested that their appeal be dismissed.

Relieved that the long ordeal was over, I began exploring the possibility of attending either St. Paul's Seminary, which is sponsored by the Methodist Church, or the Seventh-day Adventist Seminary at Andrews University to work on a master of divinity degree. I was so happy to be free that I had no interest in taking legal action against Chattanooga prosecutors or pursuing a civil suit against the state for my wrongful imprisonment.

"I realize you don't want to appear vindictive, but these people need to be held accountable for what they've done," Fred argued.

"There's an old rule," I replied. "If you get into a spraying contest with a skunk, you're gonna smell like a skunk yourself when it's all over. I really don't want to spend several more years of my life wrestling with those skunks."

✦ ✦ ✦

But the prosecutors wouldn't leave me alone.

Before I had time to apply for admission to the seminary, Stan Lanzo, the executive assistant district attorney general in Chattanooga, announced that the county prosecutor's office was going to re-try me. He issued a legal document demanding my presence in court for an arraignment and "further proceedings."

Tom Bloom filed a motion with Judge Nixon, requesting that he quash the subpoena temporarily until a hearing could be held to determine whether or not the state could retry me. Nixon granted the motion.

At that point I asked Fred Steltemeier to file a formal complaint against Gerbitz and Lanzo with the Board of Professional Responsibility, the agency that handles disciplinary action against lawyers in Tennessee, in order to have them disbarred. I didn't feel vindictive toward the prosecutors, but for years I had heard rumors about similar incidents involving other defendants. Those rumors were confirmed to my satisfaction when Fred and I went to Chattanooga one day to talk to a former detective on the major crimes squad.

"There's no reason for you to feel like you were singled out for special treatment," the ex-detective said. "That's the way they get a lot of convictions. They're still doing the same thing today, and they're gonna keep right on doing it until you or somebody else takes them into court and forces them to testify under oath."

I wasn't optimistic about the outcome of our complaint when I discovered that lawyers are the only professional group in Tennessee whose disciplinary proceedings are conducted entirely in secret, as mandated by state law. The complaint process against every other licensed professional, whether physicians or plumbers, is conducted under Tennessee's "sunshine laws," meaning in public.

"Our investigations are confidential to protect the client," Lance Bracy, the chief disciplinary counsel, insisted. "If you reveal to anybody that you've filed a complaint against Mr. Gerbitz or Mr. Lanzo, that disclosure alone is grounds for dismissing the complaint," he continued.

"That's pure rubbish!" I told Fred. "Everything is done in secret to protect the lawyers."

Next I asked Tom Bloom to explore the possibility of filing a civil suit against Gerbitz and Lanzo in federal court.

Despite our apprehension about facing another trial in Chattanooga, Edie and I decided to get on with our life together. We began speaking and conducting "Faith Under Fire" seminars on weekends for various churches and civic organizations. Frankly, I was stunned by the hundreds of people who turned out for our programs in Savannah, Tennessee; Fletcher, North Carolina; Spokane, Washington; and other places.

✦ ✦ ✦

Ralph Janow, who had been paroled in June, telephoned me in August from Chattanooga. He sounded tense and nervous.

"Do you think Fred might help me find a job in Nashville and get my parole transferred up there?" he asked.

"I'm sure he would," I replied. "But I thought you wanted to stay in Chattanooga."

"I do," he admitted, "but they're gonna kill me if I stay around here."

"What are you talking about?"

"I've heard some rumors on the streets that Gerbitz and Lanzo are gonna nail me to the wall because of my involvement in your appeal," he said. "I dunno if it's true or if somebody is just trying to scare me, but I can't afford to take the chance of finding out."

I knew he felt a great deal of paranoia about what the police and/or prosecutors in Chattanooga might do to him when he was released, but I really didn't take his fears seriously. Nevertheless, I gave him Fred's telephone number.

He called Fred as soon as he hung up from talking with me. Fred was as skeptical as I was, but he promised to help him.

Three weeks later Fred received a call from Ralph's girlfriend, who said that Ralph had been shot to death in Redbank, a suburb of Chattanooga. His body, which had been covered in acid to conceal his identity, was found on the side of a mountain in Soddy Daisy, Tennessee. Gary Lord, a career criminal who had once told Ralph's girlfriend that he was doing undercover work for the Chattanooga district attorney's office, was charged with the murder.

After the shock wore off, Fred wrote a letter to the civil rights division of the United States Justice Department in Washington, D.C., requesting a federal investigation of Ralph's murder.

It took them five months to respond.

✦ ✦ ✦

Meanwhile, we had run into a brick wall with Lance Bracy and the Board of Professional Responsibility. Gerbitz and Lanzo simply denied our allegations. After a private meeting between Bracy and the two prosecutors, Bracy announced his decision.

"Mr. Gerbitz and Mr. Lanzo tell me they're going to re-try your client," Bracy told Fred in late November. "Therefore, we're going to hold your complaint in abeyance until after the trial is concluded."

Fred was furious. "What you're telling me is that you're giving those crooks a vested personal interest in the outcome of the trial!"

"If you don't like our decision, you always have the option of taking the issue to chancery court," Bracy said mildly.

Regardless of the merits of our complaint, the board demonstrated little interest in pursuing the disbarment of a powerful prosecutor.

Tom wasn't optimistic about the success of a civil suit either. After researching the law, he concluded that prosecutors have a blank check to engage in almost any kind of criminal behavior while prosecuting a case, and they are immune from any civil suit.

"It looks like we can't penetrate that closed fraternity of corrupt prosecutors," I told Fred in exasperation.

As usual Fred refused to be intimidated by the obstacles. "We can still take them to court and hold their feet to the fire," he growled. "We may not prevail, but they'll know they've been in a fight when I get done with them."

◆ ◆ ◆

There have been many high points since my release from prison. One of the sweetest was the day my 23-year-old daughter, Tracie, met me at the airport in Baltimore. She was 7 in 1977 when we last spent time together in the free world. Now she is a nursing student and is engaged to Chad, a warm and good-natured Irishman, who plans a career in law enforcement. We spent a delightful weekend looking at photo albums and talking into the early hours about everything from politics to religion.

While were talking together one evening, she brought out a small country-style porcelain house she used for burning incense. As I watched the smoke slowly curling upward from the chimney, I said, "Edie would love that."

Tracie sent me a package the next day. Inside was an identical incense house for Edie.

◆ ◆ ◆

In August Edie and I boarded a U.S. Air jetliner for Maine. In addition to visiting my family, I'd been invited to speak at the old church we had attended as teenagers. My mother and my sister Glenice picked us up at the airport in Portland. On the way home to Norridgewock we stopped by Glenice's summer home on Great Pond, which she had recently purchased from our parents.

Edie and I walked down to the edge of the lake. The moon shone brightly down on us as we remembered the times, so many years earlier, when as teenagers in love we had, on this very spot, dreamed together about the future.

Edie leaned back against me, and I encircled her with my arms. "We made it, Baby," I whispered.

She looked up at me and smiled, pointing at the lake. "I told you God didn't bring us out into the middle of the lake to drown."

"Yes, you did," I admitted.

Everything was still up in the air. It looked like Gerbitz and Lanzo were going to get away with what they had done. And, like the sword of

Damocles, the threat of another trial still hung over my head. But none of that mattered as we stood together again on the shore of Great Pond. By God's grace we had safely "crossed over to the other side," and I was confident of God's protection in the future.

"Do you know what I'm thinking?" I asked Edie.

"Yes, I think I do," she replied.

We both said it together: "Blessed be the name of the Lord!"